BEST of the BEST
from
KENTUCKY

Selected Recipes from Kentucky's
FAVORITE COOKBOOKS

BEST
of the BEST
from
KENTUCKY

Selected Recipes from Kentucky's
FAVORITE COOKBOOKS

EDITED BY
Gwen McKee
AND
Barbara Moseley

Illustrated by Tupper England

QUAIL RIDGE PRESS

Recipe Collection© 1988 Quail Ridge Press, Inc.

Bluegrass Winners© 1985 The Garden Club of Lexington; *Cabbage Patch: Famous Kentucky Recipes©* 1952 Cabbage Patch Circle; *Campbellsville College Women's Club Cookbook©* 1987 Circulation Services; *Capital Eating in Kentucky©* 1987 American Cancer Society, Kentucky Division; *The Cookie Connection©* 1981 Lottye Gray Van Ness; *The Cooking Book©* 1978 The Junior League of Louisville, Inc.; *Cooking with Curtis Grace©* 1985 Curtis Grace; *CordonBluegrass©* 1988 The Junior League of Louisville, Inc.; *Country Cookbook©* 1977 Fundcraft Publishing, Inc.; *The Courier-Journal Kentucky Cookbook©* 1985 The Courier-Journal and Louisville Times Co.; *The Crowning Recipes of Kentucky©* 1986 Madonna Smith Echols; *Dining in Historic Kentucky©* 1985 Marty Godbey; *Entertaining the Louisville Way©* 1983 The Queens Daughters Inc. of Louisville; *The Farmington Cookbook©* 1986 Farmington Historic House Museum; *Fillies Flavours©* 1984 The Fillies Inc.; *The Heritage of Southern Cooking©* 1986 Camille Glenn; *Kentucky Derby Museum Cookbook©* 1986 Kentucky Derby Museum Corp.; *Kentucky Kitchens©* 1985 Telephone Pioneers of America, Kentucky Chapter #32; *Lake Reflections©* 1968–87 Circulation Services; *The Monterey Cookbook©* 1986 The Monterey Cookbook; *More Than Moonshine: Appalachian Recipes and Recollections©* 1983 University of Pittsburgh Press; *Mountain Laurel Encore©* 1984 Bell County Extension Homemakers; *Mountain Recipe Collection©* 1981 Ison Collectibles, Inc.; *Sample West Kentucky©* 1985 Paula Cunningham; *Seasons of Thyme©* 1979 Charity League of Paducah, Inc.; *Somethin's Cookin' at LG&E©* 1986 LG&E Employees Association, Inc.; *Southern Food©* 1987 John Egerton; *A Taste from Back Home©* 1983 Barbara Wortham; *A Tasting Tour Through Washington County Kentucky©* 1987 Springfield Woman's Club; *To Market, To Market©* 1984 The Junior League of Owensboro, Inc.; *What's Cooking for the Holidays©* 1984 Irene Hayes; *What's Cooking in Kentucky©* 1982 Irene Hayes.

ISBN 0-937552-27-5
Library of Congress Catalog Card Number: 88-90826
Manufactured in the United States of America
Chapter opening photos and cover photo courtesy of
Kentucky Department of Tourism
First printing, October 1988 • Second printing, February 1990
Third printing, June 1991 • Fourth printing, October 1993
Fifth printing, January 1996 • Sixth printing, August 1998
Seventh printing, January 2000

Library of Congress Cataloging-in-Publication Data

Best of the best from Kentucky.

Includes index.
    1. Cookery—Kentucky. 2. Cookery, American.   641
I. McKee, Gwen. II. Moseley, Barbara.   .59769
TX715.B4856374 1988   641.59769   88-18266   Best
ISBN 0-937552-27-5

QUAIL RIDGE PRESS
P.O. Box 123 • Brandon, MS 39043 • 1-800-343-1583
Email: info@quailridge.com • Website: www.quailridge.com

CONTENTS

Lincoln's boyhood home in Hodgenville.

PREFACE

It has been said that you'll never meet a Kentuckian who isn't going home. And of all the words and phrases used to describe Kentucky, the most fitting one is indeed "home" . . . a place that is comfortable and inviting . . . a place you want to return to.

Ah, Kentucky . . . the soothing sound of its name brings a vision of gentle bluegrass countryside with thoroughbred horses grazing behind miles of painted wooden fences. We invite you to swing the big gate open, rumble over the cattleguard, and take the narrow winding road all the way back to the house. When you're most-nearly there, you can smell the stew simmering on the stove and the cornbread baking in the oven. Peep in the door and you will see a freshly made raspberry jam cake sitting on the big wooden table in the middle of the friendly kitchen. A smile and a warm hug greets you . . . welcome to a Kentucky home.

Kentucky's cooking heritage goes back to simple mountain-folk food beginning when Daniel Boone crossed the Cumberland Gap in 1775. Kentuckians have been blazing new trails in cooking ever since.

In *Best of the Best from Kentucky*, forty-five of the leading cookbooks within the state lend some of their favorite recipes to help tell the tale of the wonderful food heritage that exists in this state today. Many of the favorite recipes are directly attributable to the Kentucky Derby, which has been elegantly celebrated for decades with traditional dishes such as Derby Pie, Mint Juleps, and the extravagant Derby Day Burgoo. The hospitality of the state is renowned in its historic taverns and hotels, with the famous Hot Brown Sandwich originating from the Brown Hotel, a Kentucky institution.

We are extremely grateful to the 45 contributing cookbook authors, editors, and publishers who helped make this book possible. Their cooperation and assistance and kindness are very much appreciated and will be remembered. Each contributing cookbook has its own unique features and flavor, and we have attempted to retain this flavor by reproducing the recipes as they appear in each book, changing only typeset style for uniformity. A complete catalog of these contributing cookbooks begins on page 269. We do beg forgiveness for any books that might have been included that we inadvertently overlooked.

Our sincere thanks go out to all the food editors from newspapers across the state who recommended cookbooks for inclusion; the book and gift store managers who thoughtfully lent their knowledge of popular books in their area; and a big special thanks to the lovely Kentuckians we met along the way who shared their knowledge of cooking and traditions of their beautiful state.

We are also grateful to the Kentucky Department of Tourism—especially Mary Ellen Isham—for their assistance, photos and information. And to our talented illustrator, Tupper Davidson, whose creative drawings add so much Kentucky flavor to the book, we give our highest praise.

Kentucky does not have to be a vision or a dream. We have been all over the state and it is real and interesting and historical and beautiful . . . and delicious. We are very pleased to share these Kentucky recipes from prized Kentucky cookbooks, prepared by proud Kentucky people.

Gwen McKee and Barbara Moseley

CONTRIBUTING COOKBOOKS

Bell Ringing Recipes
Best Made Better Recipes, Volume II
Bluegrass Winners
Cabbage Patch: Famous Kentucky Recipes
Campbellsville College Women's Club Cookbook
Capital Eating in Kentucky
The Cookie Connection
The Cooking Book
Cooking With Curtis Grace
CordonBluegrass
The Corn Island Cookbook
Country Cookbook
The Courier-Journal Kentucky Cookbook
The Crowning Recipes of Kentucky
Dining in Historic Kentucky
Entertaining the Louisville Way, Volume II
The Farmington Cookbook
Favorite Fare II
Favorite Recipes
Fillies Flavours
The Heritage of Southern Cooking
Historic Kentucky Recipes
Holy Chow
*The Junior Welfare League 50th Anniversary
Cookbook*
The Kentucky Derby Museum Cookbook
Kentucky Kitchens

CONTRIBUTING COOKBOOKS

Lake Reflections
Larue County Kitchens
Let Them Eat Ice Cream
The Monterey Cookbook
More Than Moonshine: Appalachian Recipes and Recollections
Mountain Laurel Encore
Mountain Recipe Collection
My Old Kentucky Homes Cookbook
Sample West Kentucky
Seasons of Thyme
Somethin' s Cookin' at LG&E
Southern Food
Stephensburg Homecoming Recipes
A Taste from Back Home
A Tasting Tour Through Washington County, Kentucky
To Market, To Market
What's Cooking for the Holidays
What's Cooking in Kentucky
The Wyman Sisters Cookbook

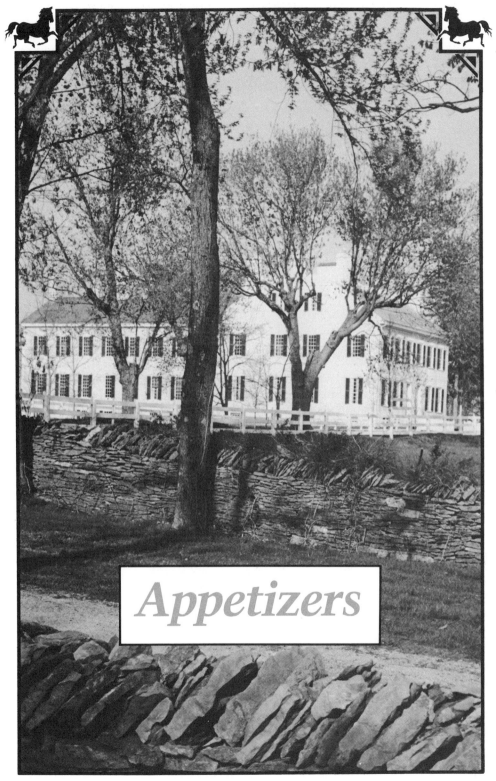

Appetizers

Shaker Village of Pleasant Hill.

Welcoming Wine
A wonderful way to say hello.

1 (6-ounce) can frozen orange
  juice concentrate
1 (6-ounce) can frozen lemonade
  concentrate
2 cups cold water
1 (750 milligrams) fifth white
  wine

1 cup orange liqueur
1 (28-ounce) bottle carbonated
  water
Ice
Orange slices

Place frozen concentrates in punch bowl or large pitcher. Stir in 2 cups of cold water. Mix until smooth. Stir in wine and orange liqueur. Add carbonated water and ice. Stir gently. Top with orange slices. Yield: 22 servings.

To Market, To Market

Derbynog

3 eggs, separated
¾ cup strawberry liqueur
1½ cups whipping cream

¼ cup sugar
Strawberries, sliced
Mint sprigs

Beat together egg yolks, strawberry cream liqueur and cream until fluffy. In another bowl beat the egg whites. Gradually add sugar. Continue beating until stiff peaks form. Fold whites into cream mixture. Chill. Serve in cut glass punch cups garnished with strawberry slices and mint sprigs. Makes 1 quart.

Fillies Flavours

Wine Sherbet Cooler

1 quart lemon sherbet (may use
  lime, orange or pineapple)
12 ounces Chablis

1 (12-ounce) can diet lemon-
  lime soda

Mix half the sherbet, wine and soda in blender. Blend on high speed 15 seconds. Pour into glasses and repeat. Serves 8 (6-ounce) old-fashioned glasses. This is just as good without wine. Just double the amount of soda.

Holy Chow

Kentucky Mint Julep

100 proof Kentucky bourbon	Mint leaves
Simple syrup	Crushed ice

SIMPLE SYRUP:

Mix 1 part boiling water to 2 parts sugar. Stir until dissolved.

Place 3 to 4 mint leaves in julep glass. Add crushed ice. Press down with spoon to bruise leaves. Add 1 ounce bourbon and ½ ounce simple syrup; stir well. Pack glass with crushed ice and fill with bourbon. Garnish with mint leaves.

Hint: Traditionally, this is served in a frosted silver mint julep cup.

To Market, To Market

Mr. Closson's Mint Julep

This recipe comes from Burton Closson of Cincinnati. The technique of steeping mint leaves in Bourbon caught the attention of cookbook committee members.

SIMPLE SYRUP:
Boil equal amounts of sugar and water. Cool and refrigerate.

MINT-FLAVORED BOURBON:

1 quart Bourbon—Old Rip Van Winkle	Fresh mint leaves (enough to stuff the bottle)

Wash and dry mint leaves. Add to Bourbon and let steep in the bottle for 3 days. Remove leaves and discard them. To serve fill julep glass with crushed ice. Pour 1 to 1½ tablespoons of simple syrup over ice. Fill glass with mint-flavored Bourbon. Stir. Garnish with sprig of mint.

The Kentucky Derby Museum Cookbook

Bourbon Slush

2½ cups tea (2½ cups water and 2 small tea bags)
1 (12-ounce) can frozen lemonade, thawed
1 (6-ounce) can frozen orange juice

2 cups Maker's Mark Bourbon
1 cup sugar
6 cups water

Let tea cool, then mix all together and freeze in a plastic container. When ready to serve, scoop into a glass. Garnish with pineapple chunks or a cherry on a toothpick, or mint. Yield: 3 quarts.

The Kentucky Derby Museum Cookbook

Kentucky's unique bourbon industry produces 85% of the U.S. output, producing 1 million barrels a year.

McChord Place Strawberry Slush

2 small boxes strawberry Jello
3 cups hot water
3 cups sugar (less is better)
3 cups cold water
2 small cans frozen lemonade
2 large cans unsweetened pineapple juice

1 large can unsweetened orange juice
2 packages frozen strawberries or 1 quart fresh
1 cup bourbon or vodka (optional)

Mix Jello and boiling water till thoroughly dissolved, then add sugar. Mix well; add the cold water and the juices. Stir in the strawberries. Freeze this mixture in plastic containers.

About three hours before serving time, remove from freezer to semi-thaw. When ready to serve, put in punch bowl; add frozen or fresh strawberries and stir until slushy. Yield: About 20 servings.

A Tasting Tour Through Washington County

Spiced Lemonade

SPICED SYRUP:

4 cups sugar
2 cups water
6 cinnamon sticks

3 cups lemon juice
6 lemons, sliced
Whole cloves as needed

In a saucepan, combine sugar, 2 cups water and cinnamon. Bring to boiling point. Reduce heat and simmer for 10 minutes. Cool. In a large container, combine spiced syrup with 2 gallons cold water and lemon juice. Chill thoroughly. Serve with sliced lemons studded with cloves. Makes 2½ gallons.

Cooking With Curtis Grace

Fresh Mint Stinger

1 ounce white crème de menthe
1 ounce crème de cacao
1 ounce green crème de menthe

1 ounce brandy
1 scoop vanilla ice cream
2 sprigs of fresh mint

Combine all except mint in a blender or food processor. Garnish with mint sprigs. Serves 2.

Let Them Eat Ice Cream

Sodom and Gomorrah Punch

1 fifth (100 proof) Kentucky
  bourbon
1 fifth champagne

2 (12-ounce) cans of grape juice
  concentrate
1 (28-ounce) bottle of ginger ale

Pour above ingredients (in same order as listed) into a large bowl or pitcher. Stir 69 times to the left with a silver fork or for those of us who are poor writers, we are allowed to use a wooden spoon. Then after this is finished, place container into freezer for at the very least an hour and a half. This drink is great for parties of six or so, and it works equally well for two thirsty friends.

    This recipe is the one and same (updated a little) recipe that brought God's wrath upon the two cities that bear its name. Lot's oldest daughter carried this same recipe from Sodom as she ran into the mountains for safety with her father and other sister. This lone recipe is the main reason that the devastated land became repopulated again.

The Corn Island Cookbook

Hot Buttered Cranberry Punch

½ teaspoon whole allspice
3 (2-inch) sticks cinnamon
1 tablespoon whole cloves
⅓ cup brown sugar

1 pint cranberry juice cocktail
1 (#2) can unsweetened
  pineapple juice
1 tablespoon butter

Combine allspice, cinnamon, cloves and brown sugar. Place in percolator basket. Pour cranberry juice cocktail and pineapple juice into bottom of percolator. Perk 5 to 10 minutes. Remove basket. Add butter. Serve hot.

What's Cooking in Kentucky

Bourbon Punch

1 large can pink lemonade,
  undiluted
1 (64-ounce) bottle 7-Up

1 jar maraschino cherries
1 cup (80 proof) bourbon

Mix all ingredients in large bowl. Freeze. Serve slushy.

Somethin's Cookin' at LG&E

Golden Anniversary Punch

1 (6-ounce) can orange juice
  frozen concentrate
1 (6-ounce) can lemonade frozen
  concentrate
1 (6-ounce) can frozen pineapple
  juice

1 (12-ounce) can apricot nectar,
  chilled
½ cup lemon juice
1 quart orange sherbet
2 large bottles ginger ale, chilled

Add water to frozen concentrates according to directions on cans. If frozen pineapple juice is unavailable, use 1 large can of pineapple juice. Add chilled apricot nectar and lemon juice. Just before serving, spoon in sherbet; to keep carbonation, carefully pour ginger ale down the side of the bowl. Makes 20–25 servings.

Lake Reflections

Boiled Coffee

Back when Joel Cheek's empire was still just a gleam in a country drummer's eye, all coffee was boiled, there being no other way to extract the brew from the beans until fancy percolators and drip pots came along. All the old cookbooks, South and North, offered one or more versions of boiled coffee. No one makes it like that much anymore, but it's still a superior method. If you have ever tasted an expertly made brew from an enamel pot that has been suspended over a campfire, you have known the essence, the highest form of this marvelous liquid. The pleasure can be approximated on a kitchen stove in the following manner.

½ cup ground coffee   ½ cup cold water
1 egg   6 cups boiling water
Pinch of salt

Scrub an old-fashioned enamel coffeepot and rinse it with boiling water. Drop into the pot 8 tablespoons (½ cup) of freshly ground coffee (coarse grind). Break an egg over the grounds, crush the eggshell and add it with a pinch of salt and ½ cup of cold water, then stir everything together well. Set the pot over medium heat, pour in 6 measuring cups of boiling water, stuff the pot spout with a paper towel to trap the fragrant aroma inside, and bring the coffee to a boil. When it reaches that point, reduce the heat and simmer for about 3 minutes; then take the pot off the stove and wait 3 minutes more for the coffee to steep and clear. The egg, the shell, and the coffee grounds will coagulate in a lump in the bottom of the pot, leaving 8 serving cups of aromatic, crystal clear, intensely flavorful coffee that should pour without straining. To keep the remainder hot after you've poured a round, set the pot in a pan of very hot water. Do not boil again.

Some people call this egg coffee. By whatever name, I share Mrs. W. T. Hayes' enthusiasm for the brew. In her *Kentucky Cook Book*, published in 1912, she said that her egg coffee would "make any man glad he has left his mother."

Southern Food

Kentucky Coffee

1 pint bourbon
1 pint cold espresso or strong
regular coffee

1 pint coffee ice cream
Freeze dried coffee crystals

Combine all but crystals in blender or food processor. Garnish each cup with coffee crystals. Serves 6.

Let Them Eat Ice Cream

Liptauer Cheese

2 large packages cream cheese,
softened
2 sticks butter, softened
½ cup sour cream
4 anchovies, chopped
1½ tablespoons capers
1½ tablespoons caraway seed

¼ cup chives
1 clove garlic, crushed
1 teaspoon salt
¾ teaspoon dry mustard
½ teaspoon freshly ground
pepper

Use mixer to combine thoroughly the cheese, butter and sour cream. Add other ingredients and pack mixture in a smooth mold. Chill, unmold and dust thickly with paprika. Serve with thin slices of pumpernickel. Serves 30.

The Farmington Cookbook

When Kentucky joined the Union in 1792, the terms "commonwealth" and "state" were synonymous. Back then, the British Parliament declared that government by a king was "unnecessary, burdensome, and dangerous," and that thenceforeward the British nation was a commonwealth, or free state. There are only four states designated as commonwealths—Kentucky, Massachusetts, Pennsylvania, and Virginia.

Please With Cheese

1 (16-ounce) box cheese
  crackers, crushed
1 (8-ounce) package cream
  cheese, softened
1 cup sour cream
½ cup stuffed green olives,
  chopped

½ cup celery, chopped
½ cup green peppers, chopped
¼ cup onions, chopped
2 tablespoons lemon juice
1 teaspoon Worcestershire sauce
1 teaspoon salt
Dash of Tabasco

Grease a 9-inch springform pan. Cover the bottom of pan with half the crushed crackers. Mix cream cheese and sour cream; blend in olives, celery, green pepper, onion and seasonings. Spread cheese mixture over cracker crumbs. Top with remaining cracker crumbs. Cover and refrigerate overnight. To serve, remove sides of pan. Garnish with a border of sliced stuffed olives, cut into wedges and serve with fresh fruit.

Fillies Flavours

Beer Cheese

1 pound sharp Cheddar, finely
  ground
1 pound mild Cheddar
1 clove garlic, minced
1 teaspoon salt
1 teaspoon dry mustard

4–5 drops hot pepper sauce, to
  taste
3 tablespoons Worcestershire
  sauce
1 (12-ounce) can beer

Combine all ingredients, except beer, and beat with electric mixer. Pour in beer slowly and beat until cheese is very smooth. Store in covered jar. Remove from refrigerator at least 30 minutes before serving. Beat once more. Serves 12–16.

The Kentucky Derby Museum Cookbook

The Kentucky Horse Park in Lexington is the only park of its kind in the world dedicated to the horse.

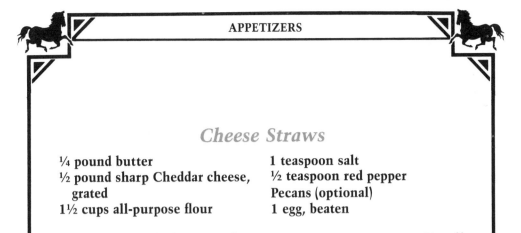

Cheese Straws

¼ pound butter
½ pound sharp Cheddar cheese,
  grated
1½ cups all-purpose flour

1 teaspoon salt
½ teaspoon red pepper
Pecans (optional)
1 egg, beaten

Let butter and cheese soften to room temperature. Mix all ingredients except pecans and egg well and roll into 1½-inch roll, about the size of a half-dollar. Refrigerate. Slice in ¼-inch sections. Brush each slice with beaten egg and place pecan half on top. Also, may be shaped over a stuffed olive and rolled into balls. Bake at 350° and serve warm. Yield: 3 dozen.

Senator and Mrs. Wendell Ford of Kentucky
Seasons of Thyme

Savage Sausage

2 pounds sausage
1 clove garlic, pressed
3 tablespoons flour
2 cups milk
2 cups onions, chopped
½ pound fresh mushrooms,
  sliced

¼ cup butter
2 teaspoons soy sauce
2 tablespoons Worcestershire
  sauce
2 cups sour cream
Salt to taste

Brown sausage and garlic. Drain. Sprinkle with flour. Add milk, simmer until thick. Sauté onions and mushrooms in butter until tender. Add to sausage mixture. Add seasonings and fold in sour cream. Keep hot in chafing dish. Serve with melba toast. Serves 10–12.

Fillies Flavours

Brokers Tip

2 pounds Velveeta cheese,
  melted
2 pounds sausage, cooked and
  drained

1 (13-ounce) can evaporated
  milk
1 (1.75-ounce) package dry
  garlic salad dressing

Combine all ingredients and heat over low heat. Remove to chafing dish and serve with tostaditas. Serves 15–18.

Fillies Flavours

Hot Crab Dip

This is one of the best dips you will ever eat.

1 (8-ounce) package cream
  cheese
1 (7-ounce) can king crab
⅛ teaspoon garlic powder or 1
  clove garlic
½ cup mayonnaise

1 teaspoon minced onion or
  1 teaspoon juice
1 teaspoon dry mustard
1 teaspoon powdered sugar
Pinch of salt

Combine ingredients and melt over low heat. Mix until
smooth. Add two tablespoons white wine before serving.
Lower heat, keep warm for serving. An electric fondue pot
could be used for making this dip. Use potato chips or dried
bread cubes as dippers.

A Taste from Back Home

Broiled Crab Meat Canapés

3 tablespoons butter or
  margarine
3 tablespoons flour
½ cup cream
¼ cup chicken bouillon
¼ cup dry white wine
1 tablespoon minced parsley

1 tablespoon minced pimento
1 cup flaked fresh or canned
  crab meat
Salt, pepper, celery salt
Dash of cayenne
60–(½ inch) rounds of white
  bread

Melt butter and stir in flour. Add cream and chicken broth;
cook, stirring constantly, until mixture is thickened and
smooth. Remove from heat and add wine, parsley, pimento,
crab meat and seasonings. Chill mixture thoroughly. Toast
rounds of bread on one side only; spread untoasted side with
crab meat mixture; dust with paprika. Broil until delicately
browned. Serve piping hot. Makes 60 canapés.

Historic Kentucky Recipes

Pickled Shrimp
Fantastic Flavor

3 pints water
2½ pounds shrimp
⅓ cup celery tops
¼ cup pickling spice
1 bay leaf
1 medium onion, thinly sliced
1¼ cups salad oil

¾ cup white vinegar
3 teaspoons salt
2 teaspoons celery seed
2 tablespoons chopped capers
  and juice
2 teaspoons Tabasco

Drop shrimp in boiling water with celery tops and pickling spice. Boil 6 minutes. Clean and shell shrimp. Layer with bay leaf and onion. Cover with a sauce made of remaining ingredients. Refrigerate at least 24 hours. Turn occasionally.

The Cooking Book

Shrimp Salad Dip

1 cup small shrimp
1 cup water chestnuts, sliced
1 teaspoon green onion

1 cup real mayonnaise
2 teaspoons soy sauce

Combine all chopped ingredients with mayonnaise and soy sauce and chill 4 to 6 hours. Serve on crackers.

The Junior Welfare League 50th Anniversary Cookbook

Shrimp Dip

1 can shrimp, mashed
8 ounces cream cheese
16 ounces sour cream

1 package Italian dressing mix
2 tablespoons lemon juice

Mix all together and chill several hours before serving. Good with vegetables.

Favorite Recipes

Shrimp Puffs

½ cup butter or margarine
3 ounces cream cheese
1 cup flour
1 cup shrimp, cooked, cleaned, rinsed and diced
¼ cup finely diced celery

½ teaspoon lemon juice
¼ teaspoon salt
⅛ teaspoon pepper
⅛ teaspoon cayenne pepper
Dash of Worcestershire sauce
Mayonnaise (optional)

Mix butter and cream cheese; blend well. Add flour. Form into a ball and chill for at least 1 hour. Roll thin and cut with a round cookie cutter.

SHRIMP FILLING:
Mix all remaining ingredients together. Add a little mayonnaise if too thick. Put ½ teaspoon of the mixture in each puff. Spread rounds with Shrimp Filling. Fold in ½ and pinch edges together. Bake on ungreased cookie sheets in a preheated 400° oven for 10 minutes. Serve hot. Makes 40 puffs.

Variation: Baked ham, crabmeat or anchovies may be substituted for shrimp. May be heated in microwave oven to serve hot.

Best Made Better Recipes, Volume II

Hot Spiced Meat Balls

MEAT BALLS:

1 pound ground beef
½ pound hot sausage
1½ tablespoons onions, minced
½ teaspoon horseradish
5 drops Tabasco sauce

2 eggs, beaten
¾ teaspoon salt
½ teaspoon pepper
¾ cup fine bread crumbs

Combine all ingredients. Shape into walnut-size balls. Cook and pour off drippings.

SAUCE:

¾ cup catsup
½ cup water
¼ cup vinegar
1 tablespoon onion, minced
2 tablespoon brown sugar
1½ teaspoons salt

2 teaspoons Worcestershire sauce
1 teaspoon mustard
¼ teaspoon pepper
4 drops Tabasco sauce

Mix all ingredients. Pour over cooked meat balls. Cover and simmer 10 minutes. Pour into chafing dish and serve with toothpicks.

Best Made Better Recipes, Volume II

Holly Hill Inn Ham Spread

¼ cup mayonnaise
2 tablespoons prepared mustard
2 tablespoons Worcestershire sauce
2 teaspoons chili powder

½ teaspoon paprika
1 tablespoon (or more) chopped onion
1 cup ground cooked ham (country ham is not suitable)

Combine all ingredients except ham, and mix well, then add ham. Serve with crackers or as a sandwich filling. An excellent use for leftover ham.

Dining in Historic Kentucky

Country Ham Spread

2 tablespoons butter
1 tablespoon flour
1 cup half and half cream
¼ cup burgundy
1 tablespoon + 1 teaspoon
  unflavored gelatin

2½ cups country ham, cooked
  and ground
½ cup mayonnaise
2 teaspoons Dijon mustard
½ cup whipping cream,
  whipped

Make a cream sauce by melting butter in a saucepan. Add flour and cream. Cook, stirring until thickened. Dissolve gelatin in wine, add to hot cream sauce and stir well. Cool, fold in ham. Combine mayonnaise and mustard, add to cream mixture. Chill until slightly thickened. Fold in whipped cream. Pour into a 1-quart greased mold. Refrigerate until set. Unmold on a serving platter. Pass beaten biscuits or party rye.

Fillies Flavours

Sour Cream Fruit Dip

1 cup sour cream	1 teaspoon vanilla
½ teaspoon cinnamon	½ teaspoon rum extract
½ teaspoon nutmeg	2 tablespoons sugar
Dash cloves	

Mix all ingredients throughly and chill. Mixture will keep 1 month easily, if refrigerated.

Sample West Kentucky

Benedictine

Benedict's, the home of Benedictine, was made famous by caterer and cookbook writer, Jennie Carter Benedict. The opulent decor of the Fourth Street establishment is remembered by many. The Blue Ribbon Cookbook of Jennie Benedict was popular at the turn of the century. The author was a civic leader as well as an astute businesswoman.

1 large cucumber	¼ teaspoon salt
1 (8-ounce) package cream cheese, softened	1 tablespoon mayonnaise
1 small onion, grated	2–3 drops green food coloring

Pare, grate, and drain cucumber. Combine cucumber with remaining ingredients. A favorite sandwich spread or can be thinned with milk or sour cream to make a delightful vegetable or chip dip.

The Cooking Book

The first observation of Mother's Day was started by schoolteacher Mary T. Wilson in Henderson.

Les Boutiques de Noel Pâté

1 pound chicken livers
½ pound bacon, cut up
1 large onion, chopped
2 cloves garlic, minced
2 bay leaves
¼ teaspoon dried oregano
⅛ teaspoon sage

½ cup dry red wine
Salt
Pepper
Hot pepper sauce
Butter
¼ cup black olives, chopped

Wash liver. Put liver, bacon, onion, garlic, bay leaves, oregano, sage, and wine in a pan and bring to a boil. Cover pan; reduce heat and simmer for 20 minutes. While cooking, adjust flavor by adding salt, pepper, and hot pepper sauce to taste.

While simmering, place mold in the freezer briefly. When chilled, butter mold then return it to freezer. Butter a second time for a double buttered mold. This will give the pâté a golden glaze.

When mixture is cooked, drain and discard bay leaves. Blend or process mixture until smooth. After blending, add black olives. Pour pâté into buttered mold and chill at least 2 hours. Dip mold briefly into warm water to unmold. Invert onto bed of red leaf lettuce. Preparation Time: 30 minutes + chilling. Yield: 36 servings.

This recipe is very attractive when garnished with parsley and grapes. Serve with bland crackers.

CordonBluegrass

Chunky Guacamole

4 very ripe avocados
Juice of 2 large limes
1 large tomato, seeded and
  coarsely chopped
½ cup red picante sauce (recipe
  follows)
1 jalapeño, seeded and minced

Peel and cube avocados and place in a mixing bowl. Quickly coat with lime juice so avocados won't blacken. Stir in remaining ingredients with a fork, breaking up avocado cubes slightly. Chill briefly. Serve within an hour or so of preparation. Makes 3 cups.

RED PICANTE SAUCE:
4 tomatoes, seeded and chopped
1 tiny onion, diced
1 garlic clove, minced
4 pickled jalapeños, stemmed
¼ cup juice from can of pickled
  jalapeños
½ teaspoon marjoram
½ teaspoon chili powder
Salt and freshly ground pepper

Combine tomatoes, onion, garlic, jalapeños and juice in a blender or food processor. Mixture will be thick. Transfer to a small saucepan and simmer 15 minutes. Cool. Add herbs and seasoning. Chill a few hours. Makes 2 cups.

The Courier-Journal Kentucky Cookbook

Georgian Hearts

1 (14-ounce) can artichoke
  hearts
1 cup mayonnaise
1 cup fresh Parmesan cheese,
  grated
Seasoned bread crumbs

Drain and chop artichoke hearts. In a small casserole combine artichokes with mayonnaise and Parmesan. Top with bread crumbs. Bake at 325° for 15–20 minutes. Dip with crackers. Serves 6 and doubles beautifully. Can be kept warm in a chafing dish. For a special treat, add crabmeat.

The Cooking Book

Spinach Bars

½ stick butter
3 large eggs
1 cup regular flour
1 cup milk
1 teaspoon baking powder
6 medium mushrooms, chopped
1 small onion, minced

2 packages frozen, chopped
spinach, thawed and squeezed
till dry
1 teaspoon salt
1 pound Cheddar cheese, finely
grated

Melt butter in a 9 × 13-inch Pyrex dish. Combine remaining ingredients and pour over butter in pan. Bake at 350° for 35 minutes. Cool a bit before cutting into 1-inch cubes. Can be frozen and reheated.

Holy Chow

Mick Noll's Sauerkraut Balls

1 medium onion, minced
½ rib celery, minced
1 tablespoon butter
3 pounds Boston butt, ground
2 stale hard rolls, grated
1 pound sauerkraut, well
drained and ground

2 eggs, lightly beaten
1 egg, beaten, for egg wash
Milk, for egg wash
Cracker meal for breading

In large skillet, sauté onion and celery in butter; do not brown. Add pork and cook just until done, then set aside.

In large mixing bowl, mix pork mixture with grated roll crumbs, sauerkraut, and eggs, and blend to a smooth consistency, adding more egg or crumbs if necessary. Shape mixture into balls about ¾ inch in diameter; chill, dip in egg wash made of one egg beaten with a little milk, and roll in cracker meal. Deep fry at 350° until brown, and serve at once. Mick Noll suggests this amount for "a big party."

Dining in Historic Kentucky

Doug's Oyster Mushrooms

20 extra large mushrooms	**Mayonnaise**
¼ cup butter, melted	**Horseradish**
1 pint small oysters	**Worcestershire sauce**

Wash and dry mushrooms. Remove stems. Dip each mushroom in melted butter. Place mushrooms in pan. Place an oyster in each mushroom. Cover each oyster with the following: 1 teaspoon mayonnaise; 1 teaspoon horseradish; 1 drop Worcestershire sauce.

Broil oysters 6 inches from the source of heat until the tops begin to color. Serve hot. Preparation time: 30 minutes. Yield: 8–10 servings.

Plates and forks are a must!

CordonBluegrass

Marinated Mushrooms

1 can consommé	**¾ teaspoon salt**
½ can water	**Clove of garlic**
3 tablespoons wine vinegar	**1 pound mushrooms**
3 tablespoons olive oil	**1 tablespoon lemon juice**

Bring all ingredients except lemon juice to a boil, add mushrooms and cook, covered, until tender—usually about 3 minutes. Put mushrooms in a jar, add lemon juice to liquid and pour over them. They will keep a long time stored in the refrigerator. Serve at room temperature.

The Farmington Cookbook

Soups

The celebrated outdoor musical drama "The Stephen Foster Story" is performed during the summer months in My Old Kentucky Home State Park in Bardstown.

Corn Soup

6 slices breakfast bacon, cut in half

3 large onions, sliced or coarsely cut

4 good-sized potatoes, cubed

1 quart cooked fresh tomatoes (or canned)

5 good-sized ears of corn (or 6 small ones)

1 lump butter

Salt

1 small piece red pod pepper

Freshly ground black pepper (to taste)

Cook bacon in about 3 pints of water in about a 4-quart soup pot. Put the next 3 ingredients in after these are about tender. Cut off corn and add along with remaining ingredients. Cook until it is tender. Add water if necessary, to adjust quantity and richness of soup.

Larue County Kitchens

Curry Cream of Corn Soup

1 (17-ounce) can of cream-style corn

3 tablespoons butter

1 medium slice of onion, chopped

3 tablespoons flour

1 teaspoon salt

White pepper, dash

1 cup chicken broth

1 cup heavy cream

1 teaspoon curry powder

Put corn in blender or food processor; blend and reserve. Melt butter in saucepan and add onion. Cook until soft. Stir in flour, salt and pepper and mix until smooth. Add corn, chicken broth, cream and curry. Heat thoroughly, being careful not to scorch.

If serving cold, thin with additional chicken broth and chill. Serves 4.

The Kentucky Derby Museum Cookbook

Cool Benedictine Soup

3 medium cucumbers
3 cups chicken broth
3 cups sour cream
3 tablespoons white wine
    vinegar

2 teaspoons garlic salt
Several drops green food
    coloring
Chopped almonds for garnish

Peel cucumbers and cut into chunks. Pureé in food processor. Combine with chicken broth, sour cream and seasonings; tint a light green with food coloring. Chill. Serve cold, topped with almonds. Serves 6.

Fillies Flavours

Clear Mushroom Soup

Hot and tasty.

1 large onion, sliced into rings
½ cup butter
2 tablespoons flour
1 pound mushrooms, sliced

8 cups beef stock
1 tablespoon Worcestershire
Salt and pepper to taste
¼ cup sherry

Sauté onions in ¼ cup butter. Blend in flour. Sauté mushrooms in ¼ cup butter. Add mushrooms, beef stock, seasonings and sherry to onion mixture. Simmer 15 minutes. Serves 8.

The Cooking Book

Broccoli Bisque

1 cup sliced leeks
1 cup sliced mushrooms
3 tablespoons butter or
  margarine
3 tablespoons flour

3 cups chicken broth
1 cup broccoli florets
1 cup light cream or milk
1 cup grated Jarlsburg cheese

In a large saucepan, sauté leeks and mushrooms until tender (do not brown). Add flour and cook, stirring, until bubbling. Remove from heat and gradually blend in chicken broth. Return to heat; cook and stir until smooth and thick. Add broccoli; reduce heat and simmer 20 minutes or until broccoli is tender. Blend in cream and cheese and cook until cheese melts.

Bluegrass Winners

Beer Cheese Soup

2 cloves garlic, minced
2 tablespoons schmaltz or
  butter
4 cups rich chicken stock, fat
  removed
½ cup flour
1 can beer

1 pound sharp Cheddar cheese,
  grated
1 teaspoon Lawrey's Seasoned
  Salt
½ teaspoon black pepper,
  freshly ground
⅛ teaspoon cayenne pepper

In heavy saucepan, sauté garlic in schmaltz or butter. Over medium heat, add chicken stock and bring to a boil. Stir in flour that has been whisked in beer. Cook until slightly thickened, stirring constantly. Add grated cheese and seasonings; stir constantly until cheese has melted. Serves 6.

Cooking with Curtis Grace

The Shakers were the first to can food commercially in America.

Guaranteed Good Gazpacho

1 (59.2-ounce) Bloody Mary mix
1 (12-ounce) can tomato juice
3 cucumbers, peeled
1 large onion
1 bell pepper
1 celery stalk
2 large tomatoes

4–6 tablespoons wine vinegar
4–6 tablespoons sugar
2 tablespoons lemon juice
2 tablespoons Worcestershire
  sauce
2–4 tablespoons olive or
  vegetable oil

In a large container, stir together Bloody Mary mix and tomato juice. Set aside. In food processor, blend cucumbers, onion, bell pepper, celery, and tomatoes. Add vegetable mixture to juice mixture and stir. Add vinegar, sugar, lemon juice, Worcestershire sauce, and oil. Stir well. Refrigerate before serving. A committee favorite; we learned to have this on hand in the refrigerator all summer! Preparation Time: 15 minutes + chilling. Yield: 16 servings.

CordonBluegrass

Cold Chocolate Fruit Soup

It was quite difficult introducing cold soups to the general public. Now they are a favorite. This particular one can also be used as a dessert soup.

1 (6-ounce) package, semi-sweet
   chocolate chips
1 cup milk
1 (10-ounce) package frozen
   strawberries, drained
1 banana, sliced

1¼ cups heavy cream
½ teaspoon vanilla
½ teaspoon cinnamon
Whipped cream or sour cream
   (optional)

In small saucepan, place ½ package chocolate chips with milk and melt over low heat. Combine with remaining ingredients and blend until smooth. Chill until ready to serve. Place second half of chocolate chips in dry blender and chop into small particles. Set aside. When ready to serve, garnish with whipped cream or sour cream and chopped chocolate morsels. Serves 6.

Note: Morsel-milk mixture will contain flecks of chocolate. This will not be a smooth mixture.

Cooking With Curtis Grace

Kentucky is known as the "Bluegrass State" because of the abundant growth of bluegrass on its rich limestone soil. It's not really blue—it's green. But in the spring, bluegrass produces bluish-purple buds that give a rich blue cast to a large field.

Duck Soup

12 carcasses of 12 young
  ducklings
3 gallons water
1 (28-ounce) jar chicken base
Necks, skins and back bones
  from 12 young ducklings
4 carrots
6 celery ribs

1 cup flour
Fat from baked necks, skins and
  backbones to make roux
1 gallon chopped celery
1 gallon chopped carrots
½ gallon chopped Spanish
  onions
2 large boxes barley, cooked

Put the carcasses into large pot with 3 gallons water and cook at a simmer for 4 hours. Strain and add chicken base.

Take the necks, fat from skins and backbones and bake at 400° with the carrots and celery ribs for 2 hours.

Make a roux by adding enough fat from baked duckling parts to 1 cup flour to make a thick paste; save to use as thickening for soup. In fat from baked duckling parts, sauté the chopped vegetables.

Gradually add roux into stock from carcasses and blend. Cook about an hour. Collect all meat from bones and add to the stock along with the sautéed vegetables and cooked barley. Heat thoroughly. Serves 50.

The Kentucky Derby Museum Cookbook

Hearty Winter Soup

8 slices bacon
1 large onion, thinly sliced
1 pound beef shank
1 pound meaty ham hock
7 cups water
2 teaspoons salt
5 medium potatoes, diced

2 (15-ounce) cans great northern
  beans
1 clove garlic, minced
1 (4-ounce) link Polish sausage,
  thinly sliced
1 roll pepperoni, thinly sliced

Cook bacon till crisp. Drain, crumble and set aside. Add onion to 2 tablespoons of the drippings and cook until golden. Add beef, ham hock, water, and salt. Cover and simmer 1½ hours.

Remove beef from shank and ham from hock. Discard bones. Skim fat off. Return diced meat and ham to broth. Add undrained potatoes, beans, and garlic. Simmer covered 45 minutes. Add sausage, bacon, and pepperoni. Simmer another 15 minutes. Bread and a light salad make this a perfect, filling meal for a fun winter evening. Freezes well. Serves 6–8.

The Cooking Book

Potato and Swiss Cheese Soup

2 (10¾-ounce) cans chicken
  broth
1 (10½-ounce) can beef broth
3 cups water
2 large onions
4 large potatoes
2 cups chopped celery

½ pound sliced fresh
  mushrooms
⅓ cup butter
⅓ cup all-purpose flour
Salt and pepper to taste
⅓ cup chopped parsley
8 ounces shredded Swiss cheese

Slice onions. Peel and dice potatoes. In saucepan, combine broths, water, onions, potatoes, celery, and mushrooms. Cover and simmer 30 minutes or until potatoes are tender. In separate skillet, combine butter and flour. Stir over low heat until golden. Add to simmering soup to thicken. Add salt and pepper to taste. Spoon into individual soup bowls; top with parsley and shredded cheese. Serve with bacon-wrapped Pepperidge Farm bread or Waverly wafers and a green salad. Yield: 6 servings.

Seasons of Thyme

Potato Soup

6–8 slices of bacon
4 large potatoes, peeled and
  diced
1 onion, chopped
2 carrots, diced

½ cup butter
2 tablespoons flour
4 cups milk
Grated cheese

Fry bacon until crisp; crumble and set aside. To bacon grease, add potatoes, onion and carrots. Add enough water just to cover vegetables. Boil until potatoes are tender.

Meanwhile, melt butter, then add flour and stir until smooth. Cook about 1 minute. Add milk all at once, blending until smooth. Cook until mixture thickens. Add to cooked vegetables (add more milk if you like thinner soup). Just before serving, add reserved bacon. Garnish soup with grated cheese. Yield: 6–8 servings.

Lake Reflections

Heidelberg Soup

Wonderful for a soup and salad luncheon.

5 medium potatoes, diced
3 medium onions, diced
5 cups water
1 (16-ounce) package frozen
   mixed vegetables

2 cans cream of celery soup or 1
   can cream of celery and 1 can
   cream of mushroom soup
1 pound Velveeta cheese

In 5 cups of water, cook onions and potatoes until tender. Add frozen mixed vegetables; cook until hot. Add soup and Velveeta cheese. Stir until cheese melts.

A Tasting Tour Through Washington County

Lentil Soup

1¼ cups lentils
5 cups water
4 slices bacon
1 medium onion, diced
1–2 medium carrots, finely
   chopped
1 medium green pepper, finely
   chopped

1 medium tomato, peeled,
   coarsely chopped
3 tablespoons margarine
3 tablespoons all-purpose flour
1 (10½-ounce) can beef
   consommé
2 teaspoons salt
2 tablespoons vinegar

Wash lentils and cook in water for 1 hour. Cut bacon into little pieces and fry in large skillet. Place vegetables in bacon fat and cook until limp, about 5 minutes. Add vegetable mixture to lentils and continue cooking over low heat. Do not clean skillet. In same skillet in which bacon was cooked, melt margarine. Add flour, stirring to make a smooth paste. Add consommé, salt and vinegar; stirring constantly. Add this sauce to the lentils and stir well. Cook over low heat for 30 minutes or longer, until cooked to taste. Serve with crusty rolls and green salad for a satisfying meal.

Mountain Laurel Encore

Soupe au Pistou

1 (16-ounce) package navy beans
Water to cover
4 quarts water
½ pound green beans, cut into
   pieces
4 leeks, sliced
3 large tomatoes, skinned and
   chopped

3 sage leaves
1½ teaspoons salt
½ teaspoon pepper
4 potatoes, diced
4 zucchini, sliced
4 ounces vermicelli
Pistou

Wash and pick over beans. Put in a large pot and add water to cover. Bring to a boil and boil 2 minutes. Cover, remove from heat, and let stand 1 hour. Drain beans and add 4 quarts water. Bring to a boil, lower heat, partially cover, and simmer 40 minutes. Add next 6 ingredients and simmer 30 minutes, stirring occasionally. Add potatoes and zucchini and simmer, uncovered, 15 minutes or until vegetables are barely tender. Stir in vermicelli and simmer 5 minutes or until pasta is cooked. Stir in Pistou and serve.

PISTOU:
½ cup olive oil
¼ cup grated Parmesan cheese

2 cloves garlic
½ cup basil leaves

Combine ingredients in a food processor or blender.

Favorite Fare II

Star Hiker Soup
for the Cosmic Cruiser

¼ cup oil (olive is best)
2 chopped onions
1 clove of garlic (crushed)
½ teaspoon thyme
½ teaspoon marjoram
Salt to taste
1 pound tomatoes (canned)

3 cups of vegetable stock
1 cup lentils
¼ cup parsley (fresh and chopped)
¾ cup of cheese, grated (Swiss or whatever)

Sauté garlic and onions in the oil for a few minutes (3–4), add thyme, marjoram and sauté another minute. Add tomatoes, stock, lentils and parsley. Cover and cook until the lentils are soft, 45 minutes minimum. Sprinkle with cheese, or a spoon of sour cream is good. Cornbread is definitely called for.

"Bob, I called to tell you I'm leaving. A stranger walked into my camp here in the Maine woods and told me about a man in Nepal I should visit. All very mysterious and intriguing. I'm gonna do it, buddy. I'm really gonna pack up and leave! I'll come and stay with you when I get back under one condition, OK? That when I stay with you we won't have Lentil Soup again. Everytime I come and see you, all I get is lentil soup; I'm tired of it. You have to promise to feed me something else before I'll share my mystic goodies with you. OK?" That was the last communication I had with Joe for two years, until I got a letter postmarked in Nepal. It said, "I've almost died several times in the quest but I've found him, and it's much more and different from what I expected. I have much to tell you when I see you. But I want you to know, when I finally found him, the first thing he did was offer me a bowl of lentil soup! Cosmic, man, Cosmic!"

The Corn Island Cookbook

Salads

John James Audubon Memorial Museum displays priceless Audubon prints published in "The Birds of America." Henderson.

Chicken Curry Layered Salad

6 cups shredded lettuce
2 (10-ounce) packages frozen
  peas
3 cups cooked chicken or turkey
3 cups tomatoes (wedges)

2 cups cucumber slices
3 cups mayonnaise
1 tablespoon sugar
1½ teaspoons curry powder
3 cups croutons

Shred lettuce and place ½ in large salad bowl. Add cooked, drained frozen peas (chilled). Add layer of chicken and tomatoes, cucumbers; continue to layer lettuce, peas, chicken, tomatoes and cucumbers to fill bowl. Mix mayonnaise, sugar and curry powder and pour on top. Refrigerate overnight. Add croutons when ready to serve.

Campbellsville College Women's Club Cookbook

Party Chicken Salad

6 ounces lemon gelatin
2 cups boiling water
2 cups cream, whipped
1 cup stuffed olives, sliced

1 (8-ounce) package cream
  cheese
1½ cups chopped celery

Dissolve lemon gelatin in boiling water. Cool. When it reaches the consistency of egg whites, fold in whipped cream and cream cheese which has been softened with a little milk. Add remaining ingredients. Fold together gently and pour into a 9 × 12-inch pan that has been coated with mayonnaise. Chill and cut into squares.

TOPPING:
3 to 4 cups chicken or turkey,
  diced
1 pint Hellmann's mayonnaise

1 tablespoon onion, chopped
1½ tablespoons lemon juice

Mix all ingredients together. Place squares of gelatin mixture on lettuce leaves. Spoon topping on individual servings. Garnish with tomato wedges, avocado slices or both. Serves 12 to 15.

Cooking With Curtis Grace

Chicken Salad with Fruit

1 cup mayonnaise
2 tablespoons sherry
2 cups cooked chicken
¾ cup sliced celery

¾ cup seeded grapes, halved
Salt and pepper to taste
½ cup slivered almonds, toasted

Mix mayonnaise with sherry. Add chicken, celery, grapes, pepper and salt to taste. Mix well. Serve on crisp lettuce. Sprinkle with almonds. Place 6–8 strawberries around mound of chicken or similar amount of other fruit.

Lake Reflections

Nutty Bread Cups For Chicken Salad

2 cups Bisquick
½ cup sugar
¼ cup flour

1 egg
¾ cup milk
1 cup chopped nuts

Mix all ingredients with spoon. Grease and flour small muffin pans. Fill ⅔ full of batter. Bake at 350° until golden brown. When cool, scoop out the middle of muffin and butter, then fill with chicken salad.

A Taste from Back Home

Hot Chicken Salad
(Cate's)

2 cups diced chicken
1 cup diced celery
½ cup diced almonds
¾ cup mayonnaise
2 teaspoons grated onion

1 small can water chestnuts,
  diced
2 tablespoons lemon juice
½ teaspoon salt

Combine all ingredients. Put a layer of grated cheese and crushed cracker crumbs on top. Bake 15 or 20 minutes at 350°.

The Wyman Sisters Cookbook

Molded Creamed Chicken Salad

1½ teaspoons gelatin
2 tablespoons strained lemon
  juice
¼ cup boiling water
½ cup salad dressing or
  mayonnaise

½ cup whipped cream
4 cups diced chicken
1 cup diced celery

Soak gelatin in lemon juice. Dissolve in boiling water. Cool and pour over mayonnaise. Fold into whipped cream. Let mixture cool in refrigerator and when it thickens, add chicken and celery.

Add chopped parsley for color and salt to taste with perhaps a dash of Worcestershire and Angostura bitters. Fill molds and keep in refrigerator until it has set well. Unmold by dipping each mold into a pan of warm water. Serve on crisp lettuce. Garnish with egg slices, tomatoes and sliced ripe olives.

Cabbage Patch: Famous Kentucky Recipes

In the late summer of 1852 young Stephen Collins Foster of Pittsburgh visited his Rowan cousins at Federal Hill in Bardstown and was inspired to compose the beloved ballad, "My Old Kentucky Home, Good-Night."

Molded Chicken and Cranberry Salad

. . . a two-layered main dish salad with great eye appeal

FIRST LAYER:

1 envelope unflavored gelatin
¼ cup cold water
1 (16-ounce) can jellied
   cranberry sauce
½ cup orange juice
½ cup diced celery
½ cup chopped walnuts

Sprinkle gelatin on water to soften. Mash cranberry sauce and add orange juice and gelatin; place over low heat and stir until gelatin is dissolved. Remove from heat; chill to unbeaten egg white consistency. Fold in celery and walnuts; pour into an 8½-inch square dish and chill until firm.

SECOND LAYER:

1 envelope unflavored gelatin
¼ cup cold water
1 cup hot chicken broth
⅔ cup mayonnaise
½ cup half-and-half
2 cups diced cooked chicken
2 tablespoons chopped parsley
1 teaspoon lemon juice
Dash of pepper
Dash of salt

Soften gelatin in water; stir in hot broth. Chill until partially set. Fold in remaining ingredients and pour on top of first layer. Chill until firm. To serve, cut into squares and place on lettuce leaves with a dab of homemade mayonnaise, if desired.

Bluegrass Winners

Pink Arctic Freeze Cranberry Salad

2 (3-ounce) packages cream
   cheese, softened
2 tablespoons mayonnaise or
   salad dressing
2 tablespoons sugar
1 (9-ounce) can (1 cup) crushed
   pineapple, drained
1 (1-pound) can (2 cups) whole
   cranberry sauce
½ cup chopped black walnuts
1 cup whipping cream

Blend together cream cheese, mayonnaise and sugar. Add pineapple, cranberry sauce and walnuts. Whip whipping cream until stiff. Fold into cranberry mixture. Pour into 8½ x 4½ x 2½-inch pan. Freeze 6 hours then unmold and serve.

What's Cooking in Kentucky

Creamy Frozen Salad

2 cups dairy sour cream (or 1½ cups or to suit taste)
2 tablespoons Realemon or lemon juice
¾ cup sugar (granulated)
1 banana, sliced
⅛ teaspoon salt
1 (9-ounce) can crushed pineapples (drained)
¼ cup sliced maraschino cherries

Blend sour cream, lemon juice, sugar and stir in ingredients. Pour into 1-quart mold or baking cups for cup cakes. It's nicer to put in baking cups so you can serve in the cups. Put in freezer. If you have muffin pans set the paper cups in muffin pan till they freeze. Take out, put in plastic bags or wrap. Will keep in freezer 2 weeks or over. Take out a few minutes before serving.

Mountain Recipe Collection

Frozen Waldorf Salad

1 (9-ounce) can crushed pineapple
2 eggs, slightly beaten
½ cup sugar
¼ cup lemon juice
⅛ teaspoon salt
¼ cup mayonnaise
2½ cups diced apples
⅔ cup chopped celery
½ cup chopped nutmeats
⅓ cup miniature marshmallows
½ cup heavy cream, chilled

Drain pineapple, reserving juice. Mix together eggs, sugar, lemon juice, salt and pineapple juice. Cook over low heat, stirring constantly until slightly thickened, about 20 minutes. Remove and cool. Fold in mayonnaise. Combine drained pineapple, apples, celery, nuts, marshmallows; mix well. Whip cream in chilled bowl. Fold in cooled egg mixture. Pour over fruit mixture and toss to mix. Fill a 6-cup mold and freeze firm—3 to 4 hours.

Entertaining the Louisville Way, Volume II

Frozen Fruit Salad I

⅓ cup chopped nuts
3 tablespoons chopped
  maraschino cherries (well
  drained)
1 (9-ounce) can crushed
  pineapple (drained)

2 cups sour cream
¾ cup sugar
2 tablespoons lemon juice
⅛ teaspoon salt
2 bananas, diced

Mix nuts, cherries and pineapple together and set aside. Mix together the sour cream, sugar, lemon juice and salt. Blend in the fruit mixture. Gently add bananas. Spoon the mixture into lined muffin tins and freeze until firm. It is not necessary to defrost these before serving as it defrosts quite rapidly. Serves 6–8.

The Crowning Recipes of Kentucky

Winter Fruit Salad

DRESSING:

3 tablespoons fresh lemon juice
3 tablespoons honey

1½ teaspoons salad oil
¾ teaspoon poppy seed

SALAD:
4 oranges, peeled and sectioned
4 pears, cut into 1½-inch pieces
1 cup raisins

2 red apples, cut into 1½-inch
  pieces

In large bowl, whisk together dressing ingredients. Add fruit; toss with dressing. Makes ten 1-cup servings, 150 calories each.

Country Cookbook

Bibb lettuce was developed in the 1850s by John B. Bibb in Frankfort.

Raspberry Carousel

1 (3-ounce) box raspberry
  gelatin
2 cups boiling water
¾ cup cranberry juice
1 cup diced apples
¼ cup sliced celery

½ cup chopped walnuts
1 (3-ounce) box lemon gelatin
1 (4½-ounce) carton whipped
  topping
¼ cup mayonnaise (optional)

Dissolve raspberry gelatin in 1 cup boiling water. Add cranberry juice and chill until thickened, about 1 hour. Fold in apples, celery and nuts. Spoon in 6-cup mold and chill until set, about 15 minutes. Dissolve lemon gelatin in remaining boiling water. Chill until slightly thickened, about 45 minutes. Combine whipped topping and mayonnaise. Fold into gelatin. Spoon into mold. Chill until firm, at least 4 hours. Unmold on crisp salad greens.

Lake Reflections

Extra Special Salad

2 boxes lemon Jello
1 (#2) can crushed pineapple,
  drained; reserve 1 cup juice
½ cup chopped nuts
1 package whipped topping mix
1 (8-ounce) package cream
  cheese

1 teaspoon lemon juice
¾ cup sugar
2 tablespoons cornstarch
2 eggs, beaten

Prepare Jello according to package directions. Add pineapple and nuts and let set. Prepare whipped topping mix according to directions and mix in cream cheese. Spread over Jello. Combine 1 cup pineapple juice, lemon juice, sugar, cornstarch and eggs in saucepan. Cook over low heat until thick. Let cool and spread over top of cream cheese and topping mixture. Sprinkle nuts on top.

Somethin's Cookin' at LG&E

Kentucky Ambrosia Salad
(Phyllis George Brown—Former First Lady of Kentucky and Miss America 1971)

1 cup Mandarin oranges, drained (tangerines can be used also)
1 cup pineapple tidbits, drained
3 bananas, sliced

1 cup miniature marshmallows
1 cup flaked coconut
1 cup sour cream
1 tablespoon mayonnaise
Maraschino cherries, if desired

Any combination of fresh fruit can be used. Combine fruits. Mix sour cream and mayonnaise. Fold in fruit. Add coconut and marshmallows. Garnish with cherries.

"Mother used to fix ambrosia for our family in Texas. And in my new home here in Kentucky, ambrosia is a favorite dish with dinner or afterwards as a dessert. It's yummy! The more you add the more you can serve. The coconut makes it! Use a big clear glass salad bowl."

The Crowning Recipes of Kentucky

Cottage Cheese Salad

1 package lime Jello
1½ cups hot water
½ cup pineapple juice
1 cup cottage cheese
¼ teaspoon salt
½ cup mayonnaise

1 tablespoon vinegar
1 cup crushed pineapple
1½ cups diced celery
¼ cup pimiento (or omit)
¼ cup chopped nuts (or omit)

Dissolve Jello in water and add pineapple juice. When slightly thickened, whip. Add remaining ingredients and chill. May be prepared the day before using.

Larue County Kitchens

Mandarin Orange and Pineapple Salad

1 (20-ounce) can unsweetened
   pineapple chunks (save 1 cup
   juice)
2 (3¼-ounce) boxes toasted
   coconut instant pudding
2 level tablespoons mayonnaise

1 (8-ounce) carton frozen
   whipped topping
1 cup pecan pieces
1 (16-ounce) can Mandarin
   orange slices, drained
3 cups miniature marshmallows

Mix the cup of pineapple juice and pudding. Add mayonnaise, whipped topping and nuts. Slice each pineapple chunk in half. Add oranges and marshmallows; fold well into first mixture. Chill overnight in a covered dish. This can be frozen.

Country Cookbook

Whole Cranberry Salad

2 small boxes cherry Jello
2 cups boiling water
1 can whole cranberry sauce
1 (20-ounce) can crushed
   pineapple (including juice)

1 small can frozen orange juice
   (undiluted)
Nuts (as many as desired)

Mix all ingredients together; chill.

Stephensburg Homecoming Recipes

 Kentucky takes its name from the Wyandon Indian word "Kah-ten-tah-teh," which translates "land where we live tomorrow" or "land of tomorrow."

Blueberry Salad

2 (3-ounce) packages blackberry
  Jello
2 cups boiling water
1 medium can crushed
  pineapple, drained
1 can blueberry pie filling
1 cup sour cream

1 (8-ounce) package cream
  cheese
¼ cup sugar
1 large package Cool Whip
½ cup chopped pecans
1 teaspoon vanilla

Dissolve Jello in boiling water. Let set 30 minutes. Then add the crushed pineapple and blueberry pie filling. Let jell. Beat sour cream until smooth. Cream cheese and sugar. Stir in the Cool Whip, pecans and vanilla. Spread on top of the Jello mixture. Let jell in refrigerator.

Favorite Recipes

Grapefruit Aspic with Dressing

2 (¼-ounce) envelopes plain
  gelatin (soaked in ½ cup cold
  water)
1 cup boiling water
3 tablespoons lemon juice
3 large grapefruit (sectioned)

½ cup blanched almonds
  (chopped)
¾ cup celery (chopped)
1 avocado (sliced)
¾ cup sugar

Pour dissolved plain gelatin (soaked in water) into boiling water, add remaining ingredients, put into large mold and chill.

POPPY SEED DRESSING:
2 tablespoons butter
4 tablespoons sugar
2 tablespoons wine vinegar

2 eggs, slightly beaten
Poppy seeds

Melt butter, add sugar and dissolve, add vinegar, eggs. Cook in a double boiler stirring until it thickens slightly. Remove and add poppy seeds. (Dressing thickens as it cools.) Keeps well in refrigerator and can be frozen.

Holy Chow

Congealed Lemon and Pimento Cheese Salad

1 (3-ounce) package lemon
  gelatin
1 cup boiling water
½ cup sugar
1 small jar pimento cheese
  spread

1 small can crushed pineapple,
  drained
1 (9-ounce) carton Cool Whip
1 cup toasted pecans, if desired

Dissolve gelatin in boiling water. Add sugar and cheese spread. Mix well. Add drained pineapple. Let congeal to consistency of unbeaten egg whites. Fold in Cool Whip and pecans. Pour into oiled ring mold. Place in refrigerator to congeal. Serves 6 to 8.

Cooking With Curtis Grace

Ninth Street House Congealed Spinach Salad with Crabmeat Dressing

9 ounces lime gelatin
6 tablespoons vinegar
1½ cups mayonnaise
3 cups cottage cheese
4 tablespoons minced onion

1 cup diced celery
3 (10-ounce) packages frozen
  chopped spinach, thawed,
  drained, and squeezed dry
Tomato wedges for garnish

Dissolve gelatin in 3 cups boiling water; add ½ cup cold water and vinegar, then all other ingredients, and pour into 9 × 13-inch pan that has been coated with mayonnaise. Refrigerate until congealed. Cut into squares, garnish with tomato wedges, and serve with crabmeat dressing. Serves 12 to 15.

CRABMEAT DRESSING:
3 cups mayonnaise
¾ cup chili sauce
6 tablespoons horseradish

½ large onion, chopped
Tabasco (optional)
2 cups flaked crabmeat

Mix all ingredients except crabmeat. Fold in crabmeat, and spoon over squares of Congealed Spinach Salad.

Dining in Historic Kentucky

French Potato Salad

This is best served at room temperature, therefore ideal to take on an outing. There is no mayonnaise to make it unsafe.

9 or 10 small new potatoes
2 tablespoons canned
   consommé
2 tablespoons sauterne
½ teaspoon Dijon-type mustard
1 teaspoon salt

2 tablespoons wine vinegar
2 tablespoons olive oil
Plenty of freshly ground pepper
1 tablespoon parsley, minced
½ teaspoon tarragon

Boil potatoes in their skins in salted water until tender when pierced with a fork—about 30 minutes. Do not overcook. Peel as soon as cool enough to handle and slice about ¼-inch thick. There should be 3 cups. Immediately pour the consommé and wine over them. Lift gently with two forks to mix. The secret of their goodness is that they soak up the seasonings while still warm. Mix mustard and salt with oil and vinegar and pour over them. Grind on pepper and sprinkle on herbs. Mix gently until each slice is coated. Do not refrigerate unless this is to be kept overnight. Serves 4.

The Farmington Cookbook

German Potato Salad

6 slices bacon
½ cup chopped onions
2 tablespoons all-purpose flour
2 tablespoons sugar
1½ teaspoons salt
Dash of pepper
1 cup water
½ cup vinegar
6 cups sliced potatoes (cooked)

Cook bacon until crisp. Drain and crumble, reserving drippings. Cook onion in reserved drippings until tender. Blend in flour, sugar, salt and pepper. Add water and vinegar; cook and stir until thickened and bubbly. Add bacon and potatoes, tossing lightly; beat thoroughly, about 10 minutes. Trim with topping of your choice, if desired. Makes 8 to 10 servings.

The Junior Welfare League 50th Anniversary Cookbook

Green Bean Salad

1 (#303) can French-style green
   beans
1 (#303) can small English peas
1 (#303) can fancy Chinese
   vegetables (meatless)
1 jar sliced pimento
1 (6-ounce) can water chestnuts-
   thin sliced
1 (8½-ounce) can artichoke
   hearts, quartered
1½ cups thin sliced celery
3 medium onions, sliced thin
1 cup sugar
¾ cup cider vinegar
Cinnamon to taste—between
   1–3 teaspoons
1 teaspoon salt
1 teaspoon pepper

Drain all canned vegetables well, then mix together. Mix sugar, vinegar, cinnamon, salt, pepper and pour over vegetables. Cover and refrigerate at least overnight. Will keep about 3 weeks if tightly covered. You can do lots of substituting of vegetables, but everything was sliced very, very thin and the peas the smallest you can find and it is all very crisp.

Larue County Kitchens

Shoe Peg Relish Salad

1 (16-ounce) can French style
  green beans
1 (17-ounce) can very young
  small sweet peas
1 (17-ounce) can shoe peg corn
1 onion, sliced into rings
1 green pepper, cut into thin
  strips

½–1 cup chopped celery
1 (2-ounce) jar pimientos,
  chopped (optional)
½ (8-ounce) can water
  chestnuts, sliced (optional)
Marinade

Drain canned vegetables thoroughly. Place all the ingredients except the marinade in a large bowl. Add hot marinade and mix well. Cover and chill overnight in the refrigerator. Drain before serving or serve with a slotted spoon. Will keep several days in the refrigerator.

MARINADE:
1 cup sugar
¾ cup vinegar
½ cup oil

1 teaspoon salt
1 teaspoon pepper

Blend the ingredients together well. Heat almost to boiling.

Favorite Fare II

Jack Fry's Shrimp and Artichoke Pasta Salad

If you don't have freshly made fettucini for this recipe, the cooking time for the pasta will be longer. Cook al dente. The recipe for this popular pasta salad, featured in a 1984 story by Elaine Corn, comes from Jack Fry's restaurant in Louisville.

¾ pound each fresh green and white fettucini
1 quart boiling water
¼ cup olive oil
1 pound medium-to-large shrimp, peeled
1 tablespoon red pepper flakes
¼ cup white wine
1 teaspoon thyme
2 jars marinated artichoke hearts, drained
1 red onion, finely chopped
6 tablespoons fresh chopped parsley
Salt and white pepper, to taste
½ cup Vinaigrette (see recipe)

Boil fresh pasta in 1 quart boiling water with ¼ cup olive oil for 1–1½ minutes. Drain, rinse and cool under cold water. Cook the shrimp in boiling water to cover, with red pepper flakes, white wine and thyme for two minutes, starting timing when shrimp are added to water. Drain and rinse under cold water. Toss shrimp with pasta, remaining ingredients and Vinaigrette. Cover well and chill. Makes 6 servings.

VINAIGRETTE:
½ cup cider vinegar
¼ teaspoon salt
1 teaspoon white pepper
1 teaspoon dry mustard
1½ cups salad oil
1 egg

Whisk all ingredients in a mixing bowl by hand with a wire whip.

The Courier-Journal Kentucky Cookbook

Big Bone Lick State Park is the home of the world's largest natural depository of mammal bones from the Pleistocene epoch (500,000–2,000,000 years ago).

Crabacado Salad

½ cup mayonnaise
½ cup dairy sour cream
1 tablespoon Dijon-style
 mustard
1 teaspoon lemon juice
1 teaspoon Worcestershire
 sauce
¼ cup minced celery
¼ cup minced, drained capers
1 hard-cooked egg, minced
2 tablespoons minced, drained
 pimiento

1 tablespoon minced parsley
1 head leaf lettuce
2 chilled ripe avocados, halved,
 seeded and peeled
2 (6-ounce) packages crabmeat,
 drained
4 chilled artichoke hearts,
 drained
4 chilled tomatoes, peeled
16 chilled, whole, pitted black
 olives
4 chilled hard-cooked eggs

In mixing bowl, blend together mayonnaise, sour cream, mustard, lemon juice, and Worcestershire. Stir in celery, capers, minced egg, pimiento, and parsley. Chill.

Arrange leaf lettuce on four salad plates. Place one avocado half on each plate. Reserve a little crab for garnish; divide remaining between the four avocado halves. Spoon a fourth of the dressing over each avocado. Place one piece of reserved crab on top. Sprinkle each salad lightly with paprika. Cut each tomato in half lengthwise. Place one-half of the tomato on each end of the avocado. Cut each artichoke heart in half lengthwise, starting at the stem end, and place on each side of the filled avocado. Cut each hard-cooked egg in quarter wedges and place on each corner of the salad platter. Place one whole black olive alongside each quarter of egg. Serve immediately. Makes 4 servings.

Holy Chow

Lincoln's Boyhood Home is near Hodgenville. He lived there from the time he was two till he was eight. "My earliest recollection is of the Knob Creek place," Abraham Lincoln wrote in 1860.

Luscious Lentil Salad

1 pound lentils, washed
5 cups water
1 bay leaf
1½ teaspoons salt
2 onions, peeled and stuck with
   2 whole cloves each
⅔ cup olive oil
¼ cup red wine vinegar
¼ teaspoon dry mustard
¼ teaspoon sugar
1 clove garlic, minced

½ teaspoon Worcestershire
   sauce
½ teaspoon red pepper sauce
Salt and pepper to taste
½ cup finely chopped green
   onions
½ cup chopped celery
3 tablespoons chopped parsley
3 hard-boiled eggs, chopped
3 additional hard-boiled eggs
   quartered, for garnish

Place lentils, water, bay leaf, salt and onions in a heavy saucepan. Bring to a boil; cover and simmer 30 minutes. Drain lentils and remove bay leaf and onions.

Combine olive oil, wine vinegar, dry mustard, sugar, garlic, Worcestershire, and red pepper sauce. Mix well and season with salt and pepper. Pour over hot lentils and toss gently. Chill several hours or overnight.

Add green onions, celery, parsley, and chopped hard-boiled eggs. Garnish with quartered eggs. Preparation Time: 40 minutes. Yield: 12 servings.

CordonBluegrass

Marinated Vegetable Salad

¾ cup white vinegar
½ cup cooking oil
1 cup sugar
1 teaspoon salt
1 teaspoon pepper
1 tablespoon water
1 (16-ounce) can peas
1 (16-ounce) can green beans

1 (16-ounce) can whole kernel corn
1 cup green pepper, chopped fine
1 cup onion, chopped
1 cup celery, chopped
1 (4-ounce) jar pimento

In a saucepan, bring to a boil vinegar, oil, sugar, salt, pepper and water. Remove from heat and allow to cool. Drain peas, beans and corn. Add to pepper, onion, celery and pimento; mix well. Pour cooled mixture over vegetables and stir. Marinate at least 4 hours, but preferably overnight. Drain and serve. This makes a colorful salad. You may use either white or yellow corn. Yield: 8 cups.

Mountain Laurel Encore

Marinated Zucchini Salad

1 pound carrots, pared, thinly sliced
1 (16-ounce) can artichoke hearts, drained, halved

4 small zucchini, thinly sliced
2–3 ounces bleu cheese
Lettuce leaves

DRESSING:
½ cup olive oil
2 tablespoons wine vinegar
1 clove garlic, minced

½ teaspoon each sugar and salt
Several drops Tabasco sauce, to taste

Mix ingredients for dressing in a blender. Place vegetables in deep bowl; cover with dressing and let marinate overnight. Drain vegetables to serve. Arrange on lettuce leaves and crumble cheese over top. Serves 8.

The Monterey Cookbook

Cabbage Salad

1 large cabbage	1 cup vinegar
½ cup celery	1½ teaspoons salt
1 large onion	1 teaspoon prepared mustard
1 cup sugar	1 cup vegetable oil

Shred cabbage head. Cut celery in small pieces. Cut onions round and separate rings. Arrange cabbage, celery and onion rings in layers in a large bowl. Cover with 1 cup granulated sugar. Heat to boil; vinegar, salt and prepared mustard. Add vegetable oil and reheat to boiling point and pour over mixture of vegetables. Let stand 4 hours, keep well covered. Then toss. Keeps indefinitely.

Lake Reflections

Hot Slaw

3 slices bacon	¼ teaspoon pepper
1 medium onion, chopped	1 cup vinegar
1 tablespoon sugar	1 medium-sized cabbage,
1½ teaspoons flour	shredded
½ teaspoon salt	

Snip up the bacon into snibbles and fry until crisp. Take out and drain on a paper towel. Sauté the onion in the bacon drippings until it is a golden brown. Combine the sugar, flour, salt and pepper and stir into the drippings. Gradually add vinegar, and cook slowly until thickened, stirring constantly. Add the bacon to the sauce, and heat hot. Pour over the shredded cabbage and toss to mix well.

You'll find this same dressing good with lettuce, or even on potato salad.

The Courier-Journal Kentucky Cookbook

The largest stained glass window in the world, 67 feet high, is in the Cathedral Basilica of the Assumption in Covington.

Shady Lane Salad

In the heart of the bluegrass country there is an old curvy road, seldom traveled now, that goes from Frankfort to Lexington. There are vine-covered stone fences on either side of this road, forming a canopy of protection from the sun. We take this narrow old road very slowly so we can drink in the beauty of the rolling land and farm pastures where the thoroughbred horses romp. Many times, if we stop, the high-spirited mares come up to peep over the fence to see what's going on. When they decide that all is well, they toss their gorgeous heads and fly away. What elegance.

I never intended to let a spring blend into summer without a day's outing to drive along Shady Lane to Lexington. I haven't missed many.

4 heads Bibb, or 1–2 heads Boston, or other leaf lettuce
1 center slice country ham
4 hard-cooked eggs, sliced
1½ tablespoons capers, drained

⅓ cup chopped chives or tender scallion (green onion) tops
Chopped fresh marjoram, chervil, and tarragon, for garnish

VINAIGRETTE:
⅓ cup good-quality olive or vegetable oil
1½ tablespoons white or red wine vinegar

Salt and freshly ground black pepper to taste

Separate the lettuce, rinse it, and dry in a spinner. Cut the ham into slivers. Grease an iron skillet well with a piece of ham or bacon fat. Sauté the ham quickly.

In the meantime, put the lettuce in a salad bowl. Scatter the eggs and capers about. Put the hot ham slivers in the center. Add the chives or scallions and the fresh herbs. Blend the vinaigrette ingredients together with a whisk. Present the salad, then add the dressing, toss, and serve. Serves 4.

Delicious with bread, corn muffins, biscuits, or hot rolls for luncheon, or with tender ears of corn dripping with butter for a light supper on the patio.

The Heritage of Southern Cooking

Warm Asparagus Salad with Mustard Dressing

This salad of warm asparagus can be an exquisite first course, or you can serve it with the entrée. The sauce is so delicious and easy that you will enjoy serving it with many dishes instead of hollandaise.

2 pounds asparagus, stems
   trimmed and peeled
1 hard-cooked egg yolk
1 raw egg yolk
1½ teaspoons light yellow Dijon
   mustard
1½ tablespoons tarragon vinegar

½ teaspoon salt, or to taste
Cayenne pepper to taste
½ cup good-quality olive or
   vegetable oil
1 red bell pepper, cored, seeded,
   and slivered

Drop the asparagus into boiling salted water to cover and cook until tender but still crisp, 5 to 7 minutes. Drain and keep warm.

In the meantime, put the hard-cooked egg in a blender or small bowl along with the raw yolk. Add the mustard, vinegar, salt, and cayenne pepper. Gradually add the oil to the blender as it is running, or beat in briskly but gradually with a whisk, until the dressing is smooth and looks like thin mayonnaise.

Divide the asparagus among 4 salad plates. Spoon the dressing over the asparagus and garnish with the red pepper strips. Serves 6.

This dressing may be made with tepid melted butter instead of the oil, if you desire. Save the hard-cooked egg white for a tossed salad.

The Heritage of Southern Cooking

Bluegrass music, a synthesis of many musical and cultural influences, got its name and basic musical form from Kentuckian Bill Monroe and his Blue Grass Boys, most famous and influential of the Bluegrass bands.

Overnight Layer Salad

1 medium head lettuce, torn
4 ribs celery, chopped
1 bunch green onions, chopped
1 (10-ounce) box frozen peas,
  thawed but not cooked
3 hard-cooked eggs, chopped
6–8 slices bacon, fried crisp,
  crumbled

1½ cups sour cream
1½ cups mayonnaise or Miracle
  Whip
3 or 4 tablespoons sugar
½ teaspoon garlic salt
½ cup grated Parmesan cheese

Place lettuce pieces in bottom of a large glass or wooden bowl. Sprinkle the celery over lettuce, the green onions over celery, peas over the green onions, then eggs and half of the bacon. Make a dressing by combining the sour cream, mayonnaise, sugar and garlic salt. Pour dressing over salad. Sprinkle Parmesan cheese and remaining bacon over top. Chill overnight before serving. Serves 6 to 8.

Somethin's Cookin' at LG&E

Thousand Island Dressing

1 cup mayonnaise
1 cup chili sauce
1 tablespoon chopped ripe
  olives
1 tablespoon chopped green
  pepper

1 tablespoon pimiento
1 hard-boiled egg, put through
  sieve
½ cup tomato catsup
1 teaspoon chopped parsley

This will keep for days in covered jar.

The Junior Welfare League 50th Anniversary Cookbook

Berea College Crafts began with fireside weaving in 1893. Today over 200 students and craftsmen work in a variety of craft medium including the beauty and softness of Churchill weavings.

Bread and Breakfast

Appalachian Museum. Berea.

Sour Cream Cornbread

1 cup self-rising cornmeal
2 eggs
1 (8¼-ounce) can cream-style
  corn, undrained

½ cup salad oil or bacon
  drippings
½ teaspoon salt
1 cup sour cream

Combine and mix all the ingredients well. Pour into a greased 9-inch pan. Bake in a 400° oven 20–30 minutes. Serves 4 to 6. Can be frozen after baking; reheats well.

Entertaining the Louisville Way, Volume II

Iron Kettle Hot Pepper Cornbread

2 cups milk
2 eggs
½ cup sugar
2 cups self-rising white
  cornmeal

½ cup hot jalapeño peppers,
  chopped while wearing
  gloves
1 cup grated Cheddar cheese

Grease and heat 9-inch black iron skillet until very hot. In large bowl, mix milk, eggs, sugar, and cornmeal. Stir in peppers and cheese. Pour into hot skillet and bake at 400° until firm and crusty around edges. Serves 8.

Note: Use extreme caution when handling peppers.

Dining in Historic Kentucky

Berea Kentucky Corn Sticks

½ cup flour
2 cups white cornmeal
½ teaspoon salt
1 teaspoon baking powder

½ teaspoon baking soda
2 cups buttermilk
2 eggs, well beaten
4 tablespoons melted lard

Sift flour, cornmeal, salt, baking powder together. Mix soda with buttermilk. Add to dry ingredients. Mix. Add eggs and beat. Add lard. Mix well. Pour into well-greased, hot corn stick pan. Place on lower shelf of oven at 450°–500° for 8 minutes. Move to upper shelf and bake 5 to 10 minutes longer. Yield: 1 dozen large corn sticks.

A Taste from Back Home

Firecracker Corn Sticks

2 cups self-rising cornmeal
2 teaspoons sugar
1½ teaspoons crushed red
  pepper

1 egg, beaten
¼ cup margarine, melted
1 cup milk
¼ cup buttermilk

Combine dry ingredients; mix well. Add remaining ingredients and stir until batter is smooth. Place 2 well-greased cast-iron corn stick pans in a 450° oven for 5 minutes or until very hot. Remove pans from oven; spoon batter into pans. Bake at 450° for 12–15 minutes or until lightly browned. Yield: 14 corn sticks.

Lake Reflections

Cracklin' Bread

2 cups plain cornmeal
1 cup buttermilk
1 tablespoon baking powder
Warm water

1 heaping teaspoon salt
½ teaspoon soda
¾ cup cracklins

Mix all ingredients with enough warm water to make the right consistency. Pour into a hot greased iron skillet. Bake at 400° until done.

Mountain Recipe Collection

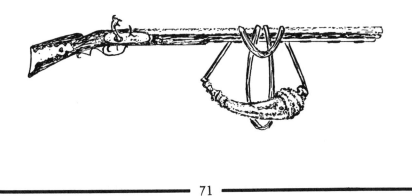

Corn Meal Battercakes

1 cup buttermilk
½ teaspoon baking soda
1 egg, beaten slightly
⅔ cup white cornmeal

¾ teaspoon salt
3 tablespoons melted bacon fat
   or butter
¼ cup water

Stir soda into buttermilk and add to egg. Stir in other ingredients. Heat an ungreased electric griddle to 380°. It is ready when a drop of water bounces over the surface. (To make lace edged cakes, cook in hot fat in a heavy skillet, adding more fat after each batch.) Pour the batter from the tip of a large spoon. Turn cakes when broken bubbles appear over the surface and the center seems dry. Turn only once. Makes 16–18 four to five-inch cakes.

The Farmington Cookbook

Village Hush Puppies
(Kentucky Dam Village)

1 cup self-rising cornmeal
½ cup self-rising flour
1 teaspoon salt
1 teaspoon garlic powder
¼ teaspoon paprika

2 tablespoons dry chives,
   chopped
¼ cup onions, minced
¾ cup buttermilk

Mix together the above ingredients. Drop hush puppy mixture into fryer, heated to 300°, with very small ice cream scoop or iced tea spoon. Cook for approximately 5 minutes or until golden brown. Yield: 12–16 hush puppies.

Sample West Kentucky

Kentucky is the nation's largest coal producer. Mining is the leading industry in the state.

Chili Bean Spoonbread

½ pound dried beans	½ jalapeño pepper
1 bay leaf	4 cloves garlic, chopped
1 teaspoon salt	1 teaspoon cumin
1 onion, chopped	1 teaspoon chili powder
Oil	1 tablespoon parsley, chopped
2 cups tomatoes, chopped	Salt to taste

Soak beans in water overnight or approximately 8 hours. Add bay leaf and 1 teaspoon salt. Cook until done. Add more water if necessary. Cut up 1 medium onion and sauté in oil. Add tomatoes, ½ jalapeño pepper, garlic, cumin, chili powder, parsley, and salt to taste. Simmer for 15 minutes.

TOPPING:

2 cups milk	4 tablespoons oil or butter
½ teaspoon salt	4 eggs
⅔ cup cornmeal	

Combine milk and salt in saucepan. Heat to almost boiling and add cornmeal gradually, stirring constantly. When mixture has thickened, remove from heat. Stir in oil (or butter) and eggs. Turn bean and tomato mixture into greased skillet or 1½-quart baking dish. Cover with cornmeal mixture. Bake in 350° oven for 30 minutes until firm and golden.

The Monterey Cookbook

Spoonbread

Far back into the Virginia past, almost as far as Mary Randolph in 1824, there were dishes that came close to this rich, light delicacy. In fact, the Indian porridge called suppone or suppawn is considered by some food historians to be the true ancestral source of spoonbread. But the butter, milk, and eggs that make spoonbread such a special dish came later, much later—probably after the Civil War. John F. Mariani, in *The Dictionary of American Food & Drink*, says the term was not used in print until 1906. Whether it belonged first to Virginia, Maryland, the Carolinas, Kentucky, or Tennessee (those are the most likely candidates, with Virginia having the edge), it is claimed now by those states and others as a highly prized and appreciated dinner-table specialty.

The ingredients in spoonbread are very much the same from one recipe to the next, the major difference being that about half use baking powder and/or sugar and the rest use neither. The following recipe can be considered fairly typical. It was a specialty in the country kitchen of Elizabeth Carpenter Wilson in western Kentucky more than fifty years ago.

1 cup white cornmeal	1 cup cold sweet milk
2 cups water	2 well-beaten eggs
1 teaspoon salt	2 tablespoons melted butter

In a large saucepan, combine 1 cup of white cornmeal with 2 cups of water and then add 1 teaspoon of salt. Bring to a boil, then lower the heat and cook for 5 minutes, stirring constantly. (The mixture will be very stiff at first, but the proportions are right, so keep stirring and don't add more water.) Remove from heat and very gradually stir in 1 cup of cold sweet milk, followed by 2 well-beaten eggs and 2 tablespoons of melted butter. Pour the thoroughly mixed batter into a hot, greased baking dish and bake it in a preheated 400° oven for about 40 minutes, or until firm in the middle and well-browned over the top. Serve it hot, straight from the dish. This quantity provides 4 to 6 small servings; for more, double the recipe.

CONTINUED

CONTINUED

Spoonbread is the lightest, richest, most delicious of all cornmeal dishes, a veritable cornbread soufflé. It is an excellent companion to country ham and red-eye gravy—to any meat and gravy, for that matter—and it is also well-matched with seafood, fresh garden vegetables, hot fruit dishes, and salads. Like very few dishes, it is a welcome and suitable menu item for any meal—breakfast, lunch, or dinner.

Southern Food

French Bread Deluxe

1 long loaf French bread
½ pound butter (the real thing!)
1 cup finely chopped onions
2 tablespoons poppy seed

1 tablespoon dry mustard
2 (8-ounce) packages sliced processed Swiss cheese

Remove crust from bread, leaving a 1-inch runner along bottom. Slice bread into ¾-inch pieces and set on foil bed with sides of foil large enough to cover bread. Melt butter and add next 3 ingredients, cooking gently until onions are softened. Meanwhile, cut cheese squares diagonally, making triangles. Place 1 triangle in each cut, peak up. Spoon butter mixture over top of loaf, pulling sides of foil up to catch butter. Seal foil. Bake at 350° for 20 to 30 minutes. Can be prepared ahead of time and refrigerated until ready to bake.

Favorite Fare II

Sourdough Starter

1 envelope yeast
2½ cups warm water
2 cups flour

2 teaspoons salt
1 tablespoon sugar

Sprinkle yeast in ½ cup warm water and let stand 5 minutes. Stir in 2 cups warm water, flour, salt, and sugar. Put in a large crock or bowl, starter will bubble to about 4 times its volume. Cover loosely with a towel. Let stand in a warm place, 80–90 degrees stirring down daily. In 3 or 4 days, it is ready to use. When starter is withdrawn from the container, replace it with equal amounts of water and flour. Take some out each week and replace it, even if you do not make any bread at the time. Put it in the refrigerator after 4–5 hours.

Favorite Recipes

Sourdough Bread

1 tablespoon melted butter or
   margarine
2 cups starter
½ teaspoon soda

1 teaspoon sugar
2 cups flour
1 teaspoon salt

Add the butter to the starter. Add all the other ingredients and stir into the starter, adding enough flour to make a thick dough. Turn out on a board and work in enough additional flour to keep the dough from being sticky. Knead until smooth, put in a greased bowl and allow to rise in a warm place until almost doubled. Form it in a loaf, put in a greased tin and allow to double in width. Bake in a 375° oven for 30 minutes or until brown.

Favorite Recipes

No-Knead Golden Loaves

1½ cups lukewarm water
1 package of active dry yeast
1 tablespoon sugar

2 teaspoons salt
4 cups sifted all-purpose flour
Slightly beaten egg white

Combine water with yeast, sugar and salt in a bowl. Gradually add flour to form a stiff dough. Mix well until blended. Place in a greased bowl and cover. Put in warm place and let rise until doubled in bulk—about 1½ hours. Toss lightly on a well-floured board about a minute to coat dough with flour. Divide in half. Shape into 2 round loaves. Place in two 6-inch round casseroles which have been greased and sprinkled with cornmeal or place on a greased baking sheet. Let rise in a warm place until doubled in bulk—30 to 60 minutes. Brush with slightly beaten egg white. Preheat oven to 400° and bake 40 to 45 minutes.

The Courier-Journal Kentucky Cookbook

Dinner Rolls

½ cup warm water
2 packages dry yeast
2 cups warm milk
½ cup soft shortening

½ cup sugar
1 tablespoon salt
2 eggs, slightly beaten
7–7½ cups flour

Dissolve yeast in warm water. Set aside. Combine milk, shortening, sugar and salt in large bowl. Add eggs and yeast mixture. Stir in flour. Mix with spoon until dough is stiff enough to handle. Turn out onto floured board and knead slightly (dough should be soft). Placed in greased bowl, turning dough so as to grease the other side. Cover. Let rise in warm place until doubled in bulk (about 1½ hours). Punch down. Let rise again until doubled in bulk. Punch down again. Form into balls about ⅓ size desired for dinner rolls. Let rise again (about ½ hour).

Bake 12 to 15 minutes in 400° oven until golden brown. Dough can also be used for cinnamon rolls.

What's Cooking in Kentucky

Monticello Rolls

This is a lovely, velvety dough and is typical of the fine hot breads that are made in the South. Yeast doughs rich in eggs and butter are not kneaded as heavily as lean doughs (flour, yeast, shortening, and water), and they keep longer better before baking.

1 package dry yeast	2 eggs
¼ cup lukewarm water	1½ teaspoons salt
1 large mealy potato	3½ cups all-purpose flour, sifted
4 tablespoons (½ stick) butter, cut into pieces	6 tablespoons (¾ stick) butter, melted
2 tablespoons sugar	

Dissolve the yeast in the water. Peel and coarsely chop the potato. Place it in a small saucepan, cover with water, and cook over medium heat until soft, 20 to 25 minutes. Drain the potato but reserve the cooking water; keep it warm.

While it is still hot, sieve or rice the potato into a large bowl (not a food processor—it will turn the potato gummy). Add 4 tablespoons butter and ¼ cup of the warm potato water. Mix by hand or with an electric mixer until the butter has melted. Add the sugar and eggs and mix well. Add the dissolved yeast and the salt. Beat in 3 cups of the flour, 1 cup at a time, until you have a malleable dough.

Lift the dough onto a lightly floured surface. Knead it lightly, adding enough extra flour to keep the dough from being overly sticky, about 2 minutes. This is a soft dough and too much flour will make the rolls dry instead of light and moist.

Put the dough in a greased bowl and turn it to coat the surface. Cover the bowl with plastic wrap, and leave it in a warm spot until the dough has doubled in bulk, about 1 hour. (After it has doubled, the dough can be punched down, covered, and refrigerated until well chilled, or overnight if desired, before forming it into rolls.)

Place the dough on a lightly floured surface. Knead it gently for 1 minute. Roll out the dough ¼ inch thick. Cut it into circles with a 2½-inch biscuit cutter. Brush the tops with the

CONTINUED

CONTINUED

melted butter. With the dull edge of a knife, press a crease just off-center in each round. Fold the dough over, so that the larger part overlaps the smaller.

Place the folded rolls, barely touching each other, on a non-stick or lightly greased baking sheet, and put it in a warm spot free of drafts. Cover with plastic wrap and allow the dough to double in bulk again. It should spring back at once when lightly touched, about 45 minutes.

Preheat the oven to 375°. Place the baking sheet on the middle shelf of the oven and bake until the rolls are golden brown, and a skewer inserted in the center of a roll comes out clean, 15 to 20 minutes. Brush immediately with more melted butter. Serve piping hot. Makes 36 rolls.

If the rolls do not touch, they are likely to spring open when rising or baking.

The Heritage of Southern Cooking

Poppy Seed Bread

3 cups all-purpose flour	½ teaspoon salt
1½ teaspoons baking powder	3 eggs
1⅛ cups cooking oil	2¼ cups sugar
1½ cups milk	1½ tablespoons poppy seeds
1½ teaspoons almond extract	1½ teaspoons vanilla
1½ teaspoons butter flavoring	

Mix all ingredients for 1–2 minutes; pour into 2 buttered loaf pans lined with wax paper. Bake 1 hour at 350°. Let cool a few minutes; remove from pan. Top with glaze. Yield: 2 loaves.

GLAZE:

2 tablespoons orange juice	½ teaspoon butter flavoring
¾ cup confectioners' sugar	½ teaspoon vanilla extract
½ teaspoon almond extract	

Mix and spoon over bread.

Seasons of Thyme

Pumpkin Bread

3½ cups flour (plain)
3 cups sugar
2 teaspoons soda
1 teaspoon baking powder
2 teaspoons salt
2 teaspoons cinnamon
1 teaspoon nutmeg

1 teaspoon allspice
½ teaspoon cloves
½ teaspoon ginger
1 (16-ounce) can pumpkin
4 eggs, well beaten
1 cup oil
⅔ cup water

Mix dry ingredients; add rest and mix well. Bake in loaf pan at 350° for about 1 hour. (Can also use Bundt pan or muffin tins; adjust time accordingly.)

CREAM CHEESE FROSTING:

1 (8-ounce) package cream
  cheese, softened
1 stick butter, softened
1½ teaspoons vanilla

1 teaspoon lemon juice
2–3 cups powdered sugar (to
  taste)

Cream first 4 ingredients. Add sugar a little at a time until smooth and spreading consistency. Add nuts if desired.

Kentucky Kitchens

Chocolate-Almond Zucchini Bread

1 teaspoon butter or margarine
1 ounce unsweetened chocolate
½ cup vegetable oil
2 eggs, well beaten
1 cup sugar
1 teaspoon vanilla
½ cup chopped blanched
  almonds
1 cup finely grated unpeeled
  zucchini
¼ teaspoon baking powder
½ teaspoon baking soda
½ teaspoon cinnamon
1½ cups flour
½ teaspoon salt

Over low heat melt butter and chocolate. Combine oil, eggs and sugar, beat well. Stir in vanilla, melted chocolate, almonds, and zucchini. Sift together dry ingredients, add to zucchini mixture. Stir only until all ingredients are well blended. Do not overstir. Pour into greased 9x5-inch loaf pan. Bake on middle rack of 350° oven about 1 hour and 10 minutes or until toothpick tests done. Cool in pan 10 minutes. Turn out onto wire rack and cool thoroughly. Note: This bread is a nice alternative to fruit cake for a Christmas gift.

What's Cooking for the Holidays

Zucchini Bread

3 cups all-purpose flour
2 teaspoons baking soda
1 teaspoon salt
½ teaspoon baking powder
¾ cup finely chopped pecans
3 eggs
2 cups sugar
1 cup vegetable oil
2 teaspoons vanilla extract
2 cups shredded zucchini
1 (8-ounce) can crushed
  pineapple, well drained

Combine flour, soda, salt, baking powder, and pecans; set aside. Beat eggs lightly in a large mixing bowl; add sugar, oil and vanilla; beat until creamy. Stir in zucchini and pineapple. Add dry ingredients, stirring only until dry ingredients are moistened. Spoon batter into 2 well-greased and floured 8x4x3-inch loaf pans. Bake at 350° for 50–55 minutes or until done. Cool 10 minutes in pans; turn out on rack, and cool completely. Yield: 2 loaves.

Bell Ringing Recipes

Banana Brunch Bread

½ cup butter
1 cup sugar
2 eggs
1 cup mashed bananas
½ teaspoon vanilla

½ cup sour cream
2 cups sifted flour
1 teaspoon baking powder
¼ teaspoon salt
1 teaspoon soda

Preheat oven to 350°. Heavily grease three loaf pans. Cream butter and sugar until light. Beat in eggs, one at a time. Mix in bananas, vanilla and sour cream. Sift together flour, baking powder, salt and soda. Fold into creamed mixture, stirring only enough to moisten. Sprinkle half of topping on bottoms of prepared loaf pans. Spoon in batter and sprinkle with remaining topping. Bake at 350° for 45 minutes.

TOPPING:
½ cup chopped nuts
½ cup sugar

½ teaspoon cinnamon

Combine all ingredients and use as directed. Topping may be doubled if desired. Bread may be frozen after baking. Makes 3 loaves.

The Crowning Recipes of Kentucky

Strawberry Nut Bread
Blue Ribbon 1975 Kentucky State Fair

1 pint fresh strawberries,
  washed and hulled
1¾ cups unsifted flour
1 teaspoon baking soda
¼ teaspoon baking powder
¾ teaspoon salt
½ teaspoon pumpkin pie spice
  or cinnamon

1 cup sugar
⅓ cup shortening
2 eggs, beaten
⅓ cup water
½ cup chopped nuts

Pureé strawberries in blender; then pour into a small sauce-pan and heat to boiling over medium heat and cook 1 minute, stirring constantly. Cool.

Combine flour, baking soda, baking powder, salt and spice in large bowl. Mix together sugar, shortening and eggs; beat until very light. Alternately add flour mixture and water to sugar mixture, mixing at low speed of mixer. Stir in strawber-ries; fold in nuts. Spread batter in a greased 9x5-inch loaf pan. Bake in 350° oven for 1 hour or until toothpick inserted in center comes out clean; very important. Cool 10 minutes before removing from pan. Bread tastes better next day, so wrap in foil and store at room temperature. This bread freezes well.

Entertaining the Louisville Way, Volume II

Kentucky has the world's largest concentration of thoroughbred horse farms, located in the Bluegrass region around Lexington.

Bourbon Pecan Bread

¾ cup raisins	6 eggs, separated
⅓ cup bourbon	2¼ cups flour
1¼ sticks butter, softened	1¼ teaspoons vanilla
1½ cups sugar	1 cup coarsely broken pecans

Soak raisins in bourbon for 2 hours. Drain, reserving bourbon. If necessary, add more bourbon to make ⅓ cup. Generously grease two 8½x4½x3-inch loaf pans and line pan bottoms with greased wax paper. Preheat oven to 350°.

In a bowl, cream butter and ½ cup sugar until fluffy. Add egg yolks, one at a time, beating well. Add flour in thirds, alternating with bourbon, mixing until well blended. Stir in raisins, vanilla and pecans.

In a large bowl, with clean beaters, beat egg whites until soft peaks form when beaters are raised. Gradually beat in remaining 1 cup sugar and beat until stiff. Gently fold egg whites into batter. Turn batter into prepared loaf pans and bake for 1 hour or until done. Makes 2 loaves. Lovely gift bread, very similar to a pound cake. Delicious toasted.

The Cooking Book

No Sugar—Spicy Oat Muffins

1 cup self-rising flour
1 teaspoon cinnamon
½ teaspoon nutmeg
1 cup quick-cooking oats

½ cup milk
¼ cup egg substitute
¼ cup Parkay
½ cup raisins

Add cinnamon and nutmeg to flour and mix well. Add oats and mix. Add milk, egg substitute and melted Parkay. Add raisins. Mix until blended. Bake in muffin tins at 400° until brown.

Campbellsville College Women's Club Cookbook

Pecan Muffins

Quickly made and quickly eaten.

1½ cups flour
½ cup sugar
2 teaspoons baking powder
½ teaspoon salt

½ cup chopped pecans
1 egg, slightly beaten
½ cup milk
¼ cup vegetable oil

Sift together dry ingredients. Stir in pecans. Make a well in center. Combine egg, milk, and oil. Add to dry ingredients, stirring just until moistened. Fill paper-lined muffin pans ⅔ full. Bake at 400° for 20 minutes. Remove from pan immediately. Yield: 10 muffins.

To Market, To Market

Jefferson Davis, who became the only President of the Confederate States of America, was born June 3, 1808, in the fertile countryside of southwestern Kentucky.

Pineapple Coffee Cake

2 cups flour
1¾ cups sugar
2 teaspoons soda
2 eggs

1 (20-ounce) can crushed
   pineapple with juice
½ cup chopped nuts
2 teaspoons vanilla

Mix flour, sugar, soda and eggs by hand and add remaining ingredients. Pour into greased 9 × 13-inch pan and bake at 350° for 35–40 minutes.

TOPPING:
1 (8-ounce) package cream
   cheese
1 stick butter

1¾ cups powdered sugar
1 teaspoon vanilla

Combine all ingredients until well blended and spread over cooled cake.

Somethin' s Cookin' at LG&E

Bund Kuchen

This is a moist coffee cake that keeps well and also freezes well. A Jewish friend from Pikeville, Kentucky gave me this recipe years ago.

½ cup butter
1½ cups sugar
3 eggs
1 cup sour cream
2 teaspoons baking powder

1 teaspoon baking soda
½ teaspoon salt
2½ cups plain flour
1 teaspoon vanilla

FILLING:
½ cup granulated sugar
¼ cup brown sugar
¼ cup melted butter
1 teaspoon cinnamon

3 tablespoons flour
½ cup chopped nuts
2 teaspoons cocoa

Cream butter and sugar until light and fluffy. Add eggs and sour cream; mix well. Sift baking powder, baking soda, and salt with flour. Add these dry ingredients and mix well. Add vanilla. Set aside. Mix all ingredients of filling.

In greased and floured Bundt pan, pour ½ of batter. Add filling, then rest of batter. Bake at 350° for 50 to 55 minutes.

A Tasting Tour Through Washington County

Golden Puffs

2 cups flour
¼ cup sugar
3 teaspoons baking powder
1 teaspoon salt
1 teaspoon nutmeg

¼ cup salad oil
¾ cup milk
1 egg
½ cup sugar
1 teaspoon cinnamon

Heat enough oil in pan to deep fry. Sift flour, ¼ cup sugar, baking powder, salt and nutmeg into a bowl. Add oil, milk and egg; beat until smooth. Drop batter by teaspoon into oil. Fry only 4 or 5 at a time until golden brown, 2 or 3 minutes. Drain, then roll warm puffs in the ½ cup sugar and cinnamon mixed together. Makes 2½ dozen.

Best Made Better Recipes, Volume II

Whole Wheat Breakfast Loaf

3 cups whole wheat flour	1 cup chopped pecans
⅔ cup sugar	1 egg
¾ teaspoon salt	1¾ cups buttermilk
1 teaspoon soda	3 tablespoons molasses
1 cup golden raisins	1 tablespoon grated orange rind

Mix together the first 4 ingredients. Mix in the raisins and pecans. Add remaining ingredients. Stir as little as possible to mix well. Bake in 2 small or 1 large well-greased loaf pan. Bake at 325° for 50 to 55 minutes. This loaf has a dense, moist texture and will keep 2 weeks in the refrigerator. Delicious for breakfast or brunch lightly toasted with butter.

Favorite Fare II

Homemade Butter

Put 1 gallon, 3 quarts of sweet milk with cream in a 2 gallon churn. Add more cream for more butter. Set milk in a warm place (people used to set it by the fireplace) for a day and night. Churn for about 1 hour. When butter is done, it will float to the top and collect. Dip out with a spoon and wash through 2 cold waters. Remove as much water as you possibly can from the butter. Add salt and put in butter mold.

Note: My grandmother was known for her good butter. She used to load her butter and eggs in baskets and ride horseback to Blackey, Kentucky, and sell them.

Mountain Recipe Collection

Derby Breakfast Yeast Biscuits

1 cup warm buttermilk (I use
  powdered buttermilk mix)
1 package yeast (or cake)
½ teaspoon soda

1 teaspoon salt
2 tablespoons sugar
2½ cups flour (self-rising)
½ cup shortening

Dissolve yeast in warm buttermilk; set aside. Sift soda, salt, sugar and flour in a bowl; cut in shortening. Add yeast mixture. Stir until blended. Knead and roll ½ inch thick. Cut biscuits and dip in melted butter. Place on greased pan. Let rise 1 hour. Bake at 400° for 12 minutes.

Kentucky Kitchens

Cheese Biscuits

2 cups flour
4 teaspoons baking powder
1 teaspoon salt

4 tablespoons Crisco
1 cup grated cheese
⅔ cup milk (or more)

Sift dry ingredients; add shortening and cheese. Mix into a wet dough with milk. Place on floured board and work only enough to handle well. Cut biscuits and bake in 425° to 450° oven. These are delicious served with a salad meal. This is a raised biscuit.

The Junior Welfare League 50th Anniversary Cookbook

Tangy Butter Fingers

2 cups buttermilk biscuit mix
1 egg
½ cup whole milk
½ cup margarine
1 teaspoon minced onion

1 teaspoon garlic powder
1 teaspoon parsley flakes
½ teaspoon celery seed
½ teaspoon sesame seed
1 teaspoon paprika

Combine biscuit mix, egg and milk, beat vigorously. Turn out onto a lightly floured board, knead lightly. Roll out in 1 12 × 1-inch rectangle, cut with a floured knife into 4 × 1-inch fingers. Melt margarine in jellyroll pan. Lay fingers in melted margarine, turning once to coat. Sprinkle a mixture of onion, garlic powder, parsley flakes, celery seed, sesame seed and paprika over top of fingers. Bake at 450° for about 12 minutes or until brown. Yield: 2 dozen.

Mountain Laurel Encore

Pineapple French Toast with Coconut

4 eggs
1 (8-ounce) can crushed
  pineapple, drained
¼ cup milk
1 tablespoon sour cream
1 tablespoon maple syrup
1 tablespoon sugar

1 tablespoon vanilla
6 tablespoons (¾ stick) butter or
  margarine
8 slices day-old egg bread
Powdered sugar
Toasted shredded coconut

Combine first seven ingredients in blender and whip until smooth. Transfer to shallow dish. Melt 4 tablespoons butter in large heavy skillet over medium heat. Cut bread diagonally, dip quickly into egg mixture covering completely. Arrange bread in skillet and cook until browned, about 3 or 4 minutes per side. Repeat with remaining bread, adding more butter to skillet as necessary. Top with powdered sugar and/or toasted coconut, if desired.

Sample West Kentucky

Smack-Your-Lips Waffles

2 cups sifted cake flour
¼ teaspoon salt
4 teaspoons baking powder
2½ cups milk

2 egg yolks, beaten
2 egg whites, beaten until stiff
8 tablespoons butter, melted

Combine flour, salt and baking powder; add milk gradually, beating until smooth. Stir in egg yolks until well blended. Fold in egg whites, then melted butter and stir. Heat waffle iron. Cover grid surface about ⅔ full; close lid and wait about 4 minutes. When waffle is ready, all steam will have stopped emerging. If lid is difficult to lift, wait another minute.

Note: Batter may be made in advance, omitting egg whites and butter, and refrigerated. Add the 2 ingredients when ready to cook waffles.

Bluegrass Winners

The Rat Takes the Cheese Grits

1 quart milk
½ cup butter
1 cup grits (uncooked)

½ teaspoon pepper
3 squares gruyère cheese
½ cup grated Parmesan cheese

Bring milk to boil, add butter and grits, stir until creamy. Remove from heat and add cheese. Beat with mixer until very creamy. Pour into a greased casserole. Top with butter and Parmesan cheese. Bake at 400° 35 minutes.

I was raised in the South and, during good times and bad, grits were put on our table. When I grew up, I raised my brood of 12 kids on grits. Now the staple dish has been dressed up. It is now served at parties and banquets all over the land.

The Corn Island Cookbook

Mammoth Cave is the longest known cave system in the world with over 300 miles of mapped passageways.

Sawmill Gravy

It is rare to find in any cookbook a recipe for this quite common and popular companion to hot biscuits. The reasons probably have more to do with social and economic class than anything else; sawmill gravy is commonly thought of as a subsistence food of the poor, and cookbooks seldom focus on such fare. That's too bad, since breakfast lovers regardless of income would probably find it a tasty and satisfying dish. The barest scraps of meat and a little milk are enough to make a delicious gravy, and in lean times, many a family has gotten by on a combination of meat grease, flour, and water.

Even the name suggests poverty. By some accounts, it derives from the fact that backwoods sawmill crews often subsisted on little more than coffee, biscuits, and gravy. In some parts of Kentucky, the dish was called poor-do—a little something on which the poor made do. Native Kentuckian Jane Brock Woodall recalls that her grandmother in Casey County made the gravy from sausage or chicken dregs, and when there was not enough food to go around, the men ate first and got whatever meat there was and the women and children got by on the poor-do. Elsewhere, people who would have shunned anything called poor-do or even sawmill gravy ate essentially the same thing and called it white gravy or cream gravy. By whatever name, it was and is a flavorful and familiar dish on many Southern tables. This is how Charles F. Bryan, Jr., learned to make sawmill gravy from his elders when he was growing up near McMinnville, Tennessee.

Several slices sausage	**1 cup sweet milk**
3 tablespoons flour	**Salt and pepper to taste**

After cooking sausage in a black skillet, leave behind the sediment or dregs and about 2 or 3 tablespoons of grease. Over medium heat, slowly sift in 3 tablespoons of flour, stirring constantly until the mixture is well-browned. Then, pour in a cup of sweet milk, add salt and pepper to taste, and continue stirring as the gravy cooks and thickens. (As an alternate

CONTINUED

method, the milk and flour can be blended in a shaker and poured into the skillet.) A piece or two of cooked sausage crumbled into the gravy adds substance as well as flavor. After it has simmered and blended for 2 or 3 minutes, pour the gravy into a separate bowl and serve it with biscuits, potatoes, or whatever. This recipe makes about 1½ cups.

Southern Food

Eggs Derby

6 eggs, hard-boiled
¾ cup minced country ham
2–3 tablespoons heavy cream
Salt and pepper to taste
2 tablespoons butter
2 tablespoons flour
1½ cups milk, scalded

1½ cups heavy cream, scalded
6 large mushrooms, sliced
¼ cup butter
¼ cup grated Parmesan
2 tablespoons butter
½ teaspoon paprika

Halve eggs. Mix yolks with ham, cream, salt and pepper. Return yolks to whites and place in buttered casserole.

Melt 2 tablespoons butter; stir in flour until smooth. Remove from heat. Add scalded milk and cream, stirring until smooth. Add salt and pepper. Simmer 10 minutes. Sauté mushrooms in ¼ cup butter. Season with salt and pepper and add to the cream sauce. Pour over eggs. Top with Parmesan, butter, and paprika. Bake at 450° 8–10 minutes, until golden. Serves 6.

The Cooking Book

The Kentucky Derby, held annually the first Saturday in May at Churchill Downs in Louisville, established in 1875, is the oldest continuously contested horse race in America.

Enchiladas de Huevos

8 hard-cooked eggs, chopped
1½ cups Cheddar or Monterey
  Jack cheese, shredded
1 cup picante sauce
¼ cup sour cream
⅓ cup green onion and tops,
  sliced

⅓ cup green pepper, chopped
¾ teaspoon cumin
½ teaspoon salt
8 flour tortillas (6-8-inches)
Avocado slices and sour cream,
  optional

Combine eggs, ½ cup cheese, ¼ cup picante sauce, sour cream, green onion, green pepper, cumin and salt; mix well. Spoon about ⅓ cup of mixture in center of tortillas. Place seam side down in 11 × 7-inch dish. Spoon remaining picante sauce evenly over casserole. Cover dish tightly with aluminum foil. Bake in a preheated 350° oven for 15 minutes. Uncover. Sprinkle with remaining cheese. Continue baking uncovered about 10 minutes until hot and cheese is melted. Garnish with avocado and sour cream. Serve with additional picante sauce. Serves 4. A wonderful luncheon or brunch dish, which can be prepared the night before.

Holy Chow

Scrambled Eggs and Cornbread

Squares of cornbread, sliced and
  buttered
4 eggs
Salt and pepper to taste

¼ cup milk
2 tablespoons butter or bacon
  fat

Put the cornbread squares under broiler or near a fire until butter is melted and surface is golden brown. While bread is browning, break eggs into a bowl, add salt, pepper, and milk. Stir with fork until blended, but do not beat. Put butter or bacon fat in heavy skillet, add egg mixture and cook over medium heat. Stir eggs constantly until done. Served with sliced tomatoes and milk, this makes a delicious meal.

More Than Moonshine: Appalachian Recipes and
Recollections

Poultry and Game

America's favorite pioneer, Daniel Boone. Harrodsburg.

Skillet Chicken Stew

6 slices bacon
2½-3½ pounds chicken pieces
1 cup onions, chopped
1 cup celery, chopped
2 cups cabbage, chopped

1 (16-ounce) can tomatoes, cut
  in quarters
1 teaspoon salt
⅛ teaspoon pepper

In large electric skillet, cook bacon on medium heat until crisp. Remove bacon and turn heat to high. Add chicken and cook about 10 minutes, browning on all sides. Push chicken to one side of skillet; add onions, celery and cabbage and stir for 5 minutes more. Remove any excess oil. Add tomatoes, salt and pepper, bring to a boil. Cover and simmer over low heat for about 20 minutes or until fork can be inserted in chicken with ease. Crumble bacon on top. May be served over rice. Serves 4.

Cooking With Curtis Grace

Cassoulet

A Kentucky adaptation of the French dish—and a good way to use up the leftover dark meat of a turkey.

1 pound country sausage
3 medium onions, chopped
2 cloves garlic, minced
1 can (1¾-pounds) tomatoes
Chopped parsley
1 bay leaf
Pinch of thyme
1 teaspoon sugar
½ teaspoon salt
½ teaspoon basil

Several dashes Tabasco
2 cans great northern beans
8 chicken thighs, cooked, or 4
 cups dark turkey meat
2 teaspoons beef concentrate
1½ cups hot chicken stock
¼ cup wine vinegar
1½ cups dry bread crumbs
¼ cup olive oil

Make sausage into small balls and fry. Remove from pan and pour off all except 1 tablespoon fat. Brown onions and garlic in this. Add tomatoes and seasonings and cook until almost dry. In a buttered casserole, put a layer of beans, sausage, fowl, tomatoes, ending with beans on top. Mix beef concentrate with a little stock, add vinegar and pour over casserole. Add enough more stock to come to the top layer. Cover thickly with crumbs, drizzle with olive oil and bake, uncovered in 325° oven for about 1½ hours. Cook until liquid is absorbed but cassoulet is still moist. Sprinkle with parsley before serving. Serves 8. Menu suggestion: serve with heated French bread with a crock of sweet butter, green salad . . . a fruit dessert.

The Farmington Cookbook

Colonel Sanders Original Kentucky Fried Chicken Restaurant is in Corbin. Colonel Harland Sanders developed his famous recipe in this restaurant in the 1940s.

Chicken and Rice Supreme
(Microwave)

1¼ cups uncooked long-grain rice
1 thinly sliced onion
1 (10½-ounce) can mushroom soup
1 soup can water
1 large green pepper, chopped
1 teaspoon salt
2–3 pound fryer chicken (serving pieces or parts)
2 tablespoons melted butter
Paprika
2 finely chopped green onions

In 3-quart glass casserole, blend rice, onion, soup, water, green pepper and salt. Arrange chicken with large ends around edges and small in the center over rice. Brush each piece with butter. Sprinkle with paprika and green onions. Microwave (HIGH), covered, 30 to 35 minutes, rotating ¼ turn half way through cooking. Rest, covered, 10 minutes. Check rice and chicken for doneness. Add a few minutes more if needed. Serves 4 to 6.

Note: Serve with steamed carrots and broccoli, a spinach or tossed salad, and whole wheat rolls. We usually use 3 or 4 chicken breasts instead of a whole chicken.

Mountain Laurel Encore

Chicken Keene

⅓ cup butter
⅓ cup flour
1 cup chicken broth
1½ cups milk or cream
2 teaspoons salt
⅛ teaspoon pepper
Meat from 1 cooked hen
½ pound mushrooms
1 pimento, in strips
1 green pepper, in strips
Sherry to taste

Melt butter in double boiler; stir in flour slowly. Gradually add chicken broth, then milk or cream. Cook until thickened, stirring constantly, season. Add cubed chicken, mushrooms, pimento, green pepper and sherry. Serve in tart shells and sprinkle with paprika before serving.

Historic Kentucky Recipes

Chicken Almond Bake

1 can cream of celery soup
¼ cup milk
1 (6-ounce) can boned chicken
  or 1 cup diced, cooked
  chicken
½ cup celery

1 small minced onion
½ cup almonds
¼ teaspoon Worcestershire
  sauce
1 (3-ounce) can Chinese noodles

Blend celery soup and milk. Add diced chicken, celery, onion, almonds, and Worcestershire sauce. Cover bottom of baking dish with half a can of Chinese noodles. Pour in chicken mixture; top with remaining noodles. Bake in a 350° oven for 30 to 35 minutes. makes 4 servings. (Calories per serving, 343. Suggested menu: Chicken Almond Bake, broccoli, grapefruit, salad, rolls.)

Stephensburg Homecoming Recipes

Spanish Chicken
(Nelle's)

Inexpensive and easy to use for large groups. Aunt Nelle served this many times to her Sunday School class.

1 (3½-pound) chicken, or 3
  pounds chicken breasts
Milk, if needed
Salt and pepper

2 medium-sized cans green peas
8 ounces noodles, cooked
1 can pimento, chopped
2 small cans mushrooms

Simmer chicken until tender. Cut into bite-sized pieces. Make a thick sauce with 1 pint broth and milk. (Use all broth unless milk is needed to make 2 cups liquid.) Season with salt and pepper. Mix all ingredients and place in two large casseroles. Bake 45 minutes at 350°. Cover with buttered crumbs during the last few minutes of cooking. Makes 16 servings.

The Wyman Sisters Cookbook

Chicken and Spinach Casserole

1 clove garlic, minced
1 tablespoon butter
1 tablespoon flour
⅓ cup milk
2 (10-ounce) packages frozen chopped spinach, cooked and drained
2 (2½-pound) frying chickens, cooked, boned and cubed
3 tablespoons butter
3 tablespoons flour
¾ cup cream
¾ cup chicken stock
Salt and pepper to taste
1 cup grated Parmesan cheese

Sauté garlic in 1 tablespoon butter for 1 minute; blend in flour and cook 1 minute. Add milk and boil 1 minute, stirring constantly; stir in spinach. Spread mixture on the bottom of a casserole; cover with chicken. Melt 3 tablespoons butter; add flour, blending well. Stir in cream and broth slowly; season with salt and pepper. Simmer and stir with a wire whisk until thick and smooth. Pour sauce over chicken; sprinkle with cheese. Bake at 400° for 20 minutes or until bubbly. Serves 6 to 8.

Note: This may be frozen. Thaw and bring to room temperature before baking.

Bluegrass Winners

Chicken in Lemon Sauce

Out of this world!

6 chicken breasts, skinned, boned and halved
½ cup butter
Salt and pepper
2 tablespoons sherry
2 teaspoons lemon rind, grated
2 tablespoons lemon juice
1 cup heavy cream
Parmesan cheese

Sauté chicken breasts in butter until light brown. Salt and pepper chicken. Place in baking dish. Add sherry, lemon rind and juice to butter. Cook and stir for a few minutes. Correct seasoning. Stirring constantly, slowly add cream to sauce. Remove from heat, and pour over chicken. Sprinkle cheese over breasts, and bake at 350° for 20 to 30 minutes. Serves 6–8.

The Cooking Book

Chicken and Artichoke Casserole

1 (3-pound) chicken
3 chicken breast halves
1 cup butter
½ cup flour
3½ cups sweet milk
3 ounces Gruyère or Swiss
  cheese
⅛ pound rat cheese

1 tablespoon Accent
2 cloves garlic, pressed
½ tablespoon red pepper
2 (8-ounce) cans button
  mushrooms, drained
2 (14-ounce) cans artichoke
  hearts, drained and quartered
Hot buttered noodles

Boil chicken in well-seasoned water until tender. Cut meat into large pieces and set aside. Melt butter in skillet and blend in flour; add milk slowly, stirring constantly, until thickened. Cut cheeses into small pieces and add to sauce, stirring until melted. Add chicken, seasonings, mushrooms and artichoke hearts. Pour into a greased casserole; bake at 350° for 30 minutes. Serve over buttered noodles. Serves 12.

Bluegrass Winners

Country Fried Chicken

1½ cups all-purpose flour
1½ teaspoons salt
½ teaspoon pepper
1 broiler-fryer chicken, 2 to 3
  pounds, cut up

1 cup buttermilk
4 tablespoons lard
4 tablespoons butter

Put flour into flat dish or plate and mix in salt and pepper with fingers. Dip each piece of chicken into buttermilk and then dredge in flour and set aside. Put lard and butter in heavy skillet and place on hot burner; heat until near smoking point, then quickly put in pieces of chicken and carefully brown on both sides, then reduce heat and cover with tight lid. Fry for about 20 minutes or until tender. Yields 4 to 6 servings.

More Than Moonshine: Appalachian Recipes and
Recollections

Oriental Chicken and Rice Casserole

2 cups cooked chicken
1 tablespoon soy sauce
2 tablespoons lemon juice
1 pound can bean sprouts,
  drained
1 cup finely chopped celery
¾ to 1 cup mayonnaise
¼ cup finely chopped green
  onion

1 (8-ounce) can water chestnuts,
  drained and sliced
½ teaspoon salt
⅛ teaspoon black pepper
3 cups cooked rice
1 (3-ounce) can chow mein
  noodles

Sprinkle chicken with soy sauce and lemon juice. Add bean sprouts, celery, mayonnaise, onion, water chestnuts, and salt and pepper. Add the rice. Mix well.

Pour into a buttered 2-quart dish. Bake, uncovered, at 375° for 15 to 20 minutes. Sprinkle with noodles. Bake 5 minutes more.

A Tasting Tour Through Washington County

2 chickens or parts

SAUCE:
½ cup brown sugar, firmly
  packed
½ teaspoon ground ginger

⅓ cup sesame seeds, toasted

1 cup sherry
2 tablespoons soy sauce

Marinate chicken in sauce ingredients, then season with salt and pepper. Cook in sauce, uncovered, in the oven until tender and brown. Sprinkle sesame seeds over cooked chicken just before serving.

Oven temperature: 350°. Cooking time: 1 hour or longer.

Menu Suggestion: with Chicken Bombay serve rice, celery and cabbage casserole.

The Farmington Cookbook

Tasty Chicken Wings

3 pounds chicken wings
Salt and pepper to taste
½ teaspoon paprika
½ cup honey

¼ cup soy sauce
4 tablespoons brown sugar
1 crushed clove of garlic
¼ cup catsup

Place cleaned, disjointed wings in foil-lined 9 × 13-inch pan. Sprinkle with salt, pepper and paprika. Combine honey, soy sauce, brown sugar, garlic and catsup. Pour over wings and bake uncovered turning and basting every 15 minutes with sauce. Bake at 400° for 1 hour. Serves 10–12.

The Crowning Recipes of Kentucky

Moo Goo Gai Pan
(Stir-Fried Chicken and Mushrooms)

1 cup regular long grain rice
2 large whole chicken breasts, boned and skinned
2 tablespoons soy sauce
2 tablespoons cooking or dry sherry
2 teaspoons cornstarch
1 teaspoon minced ginger root or ¼ teaspoon ground ginger
¼ teaspoon sugar
⅛ teaspoon garlic powder
1 pound medium mushrooms
2 cups chopped broccoli
4 green onions
¼ cup sliced water chestnuts
3 to 4 tablespoons oil
1 cup snow peas, thawed

Prepare rice as package directs; keep warm. Cut each chicken breast into 1-inch thick slices. In medium bowl, mix chicken, soy sauce, sherry, cornstarch, ginger root, sugar and garlic powder; set aside. Thinly slice mushrooms and broccoli; cut each green onion crosswise into 3-inch pieces.

In 12-inch skillet or wok, over medium high heat, in oil, cook mushrooms, green onion, broccoli and water chestnuts; stirring quickly and frequently until mushrooms are tender, about 3 or 4 minutes. With spoon, remove mushrooms and broccoli mixture to bowl. In same skillet or wok, over high heat, in 3 tablespoons hot oil, cook chicken mixture; stirring quickly and frequently, until chicken is tender, about 4 to 5 minutes. Return mushroom mixture to skillet; add peas, heat through. Serve with rice. Yield: 4 servings.

Mountain Laurel Encore

Party Chicken

3 or 4 chicken breasts, halved, boned and skinned
1 or 2 packages dried chipped beef
6 to 8 slices thin bacon
1 can mushroom soup, undiluted
½ pint commercial sour cream
⅔ cup white wine

Grease an 8x12x2-inch baking dish. Flatten each half breast with hand; lay slices of beef on top (I use 2 or 3 slices of dried beef on each half breast. If beef is too salty, soak 5 minutes and dry.); roll up and wrap bacon slices around; flatten. Pin with toothpicks. Mix soup, sour cream and wine; pour over all. Let it marinate in refrigerator several hours or overnight. Bake at 275° for 3 hours, uncovered. Delicious served with rice, almond green beans and Waldorf salad.

Holy Chow

Chicken Breast with Bacon

6 whole chicken breasts
1 (8-ounce) package cream cheese
10 or 12 young green onions
24 slices bacon

Split, skin and bone chicken breasts, using very sharp knife, or buy them prepared in this manner. It will save you some time. Salt lightly, bacon will add salt. Combine softened cream cheese and onions, chopped fine, including a great deal of the green. Form into 12 walnut-sized balls. Wrap half a chicken breast around each one. Then wrap 2 slices of bacon around the chicken, covering as much of the chicken as possible. Secure with toothpicks, which can be removed after baking. Bake uncovered in 350° oven for 1 hour or until chicken is tender. Serves 6.

Note: This recipe may be made ahead and refrigerated until time to bake.

What's Cooking in Kentucky

Gourmet Chicken Breast

5 whole chicken breasts, halved
  and boned
2 cups commercial sour cream
1½ tablespoons Worcestershire
  sauce
2 teaspoons salt
¼ teaspoon garlic powder, scant
1 tablespoon dry sherry, scant
1¼ teaspoons paprika
Fine dry bread crumbs
Parsley for garnish

Place boned chicken breasts in a non-metal bowl or baking pan. Mix together sour cream, Worcestershire sauce, salt, garlic powder, sherry and paprika. Pour over chicken, coating each piece thoroughly. Cover and refrigerate overnight. To bake, first dip each piece of chicken in the bread crumbs, coating well, and place in shallow, lightly greased baking pan. Bake uncovered in a preheated 325° oven for 1 hour and 15 minutes. Carefully remove to serving platter and garnish with parsley. Serves 10.

Larue County Kitchens

Prospect Points

1 (3-ounce) package cream
  cheese
2 tablespoons butter
1 cup chicken, cooked and
  chopped
⅓ cup mushrooms, chopped
1 teaspoon lemon juice
Salt to taste
1 can refrigerated crescent rolls
¼ cup butter, melted
⅓ cup seasoned croutons,
  crushed
⅓ cup pecans, chopped

Cream cheese and butter. Fold in chicken, mushrooms and seasonings. Separate crescent rolls into 8 triangles. Place 2 tablespoons chicken mixture on each triangle. Roll jelly roll fashion starting at short side of triangles and roll to point. Tuck sides under to seal. Place melted butter in one bowl. Place croutons mixed with pecans in another. Dip each roll in melted butter, then roll in pecan mixture. Place on a cookie sheet and bake at 375° for 20 minutes. Serve hot.

Fillies Flavours

The Downs

3 cups chicken breasts, cooked and diced
2 hard-cooked eggs, chopped
¼ cup black olives, chopped
¼ cup celery, chopped
½ cup mayonnaise
1 tablespoon lemon juice
Salt to taste
12 slices white bread, crusts removed
1 (10¾-ounce) can cream of chicken soup, undiluted
1 cup sour cream
1 cup Cheddar cheese, grated

Combine chicken, egg, olives and celery. Blend in mayonnaise and lemon juice. Salt to taste. Spread chicken on bread to make a sandwich. Place 6 sandwiches in a 9 × 13-inch casserole. Combine soup and sour cream. Pour over sandwiches. Cover and refrigerate overnight. Bake at 325° uncovered for 20 minutes. Add grated cheese and bake until cheese melts. Serves 6.

Fillies Flavours

Louisville Hot Brown

This is an adaptation of Cissy Gregg's two-sauce recipe—a simpler and quicker recipe. Its authorship is unclear, and it has been printed a number of times over the years.

4 tablespoons butter
1 small onion, chopped
3 tablespoons flour
2 cups milk
½ teaspoon salt
¼ teaspoon white pepper
¼ cup shredded Cheddar

¼ cup grated Parmesan
8 slices trimmed toast
Slices cooked chicken or turkey
   breast
Crisp-fried bacon, crumbled
Mushroom slices, sautéed

Sauté onion in butter until transparent, add flour and combine. Add milk, salt and pepper and whisk until smooth. Cook on medium heat until sauce thickens, stirring occasionally. Add cheeses and continue heating until they blend. Remove from heat.

Put one slice of toast in each of four oven-proof individual serving dishes. Top each piece of toast with slices of chicken or turkey. Cut remaining toast slices diagonally and place on sides of sandwiches. Ladle cheese sauce over sandwiches. Place sandwiches under broiler until sauce begins to bubble. Garnish with crumbled bacon and sautéed mushroom slices and serve immediately.

The Courier-Journal Kentucky Cookbook

Hot Brown Sandwich

One hen, cooked in water seasoned with peppercorns, salt, and bay leaf and allowed to cool in broth. Slice thin, preferably the white meat.

SAUCE ONE OR BÉCHAMEL:

⅓ cup butter or margarine
½ medium onion, minced
⅓ cup flour
3 cups hot milk

1 teaspoon salt
Dash of red pepper
Parsley (optional)
Dash of nutmeg

Melt butter in saucepan; add onions and cook until light brown. Add flour and blend until a smooth paste. Add milk and other seasonings and cook 25 to 30 minutes, stirring constantly until sauce is thick and smooth and then occasionally. Strain.

SAUCE TWO OR MORNAY:

2 cups of Sauce One
2 egg yolks
½ cup grated Parmesan cheese

1 tablespoon butter or
  margarine
¼ cup whipped cream

In the top of a double boiler, heat the Sauce One and combine with egg yolks. When hot and thick, add cheese and butter. Sauce must not boil or it will curdle. Fold in whipped cream.

Fry one strip of bacon for each sandwich and clean one mushroom cap for each sandwich, if desired.

To assemble, cut crusts from 2 slices of bread; toast the bread. Place one slice on oven-proof shallow dish and cover with chicken slices. Spoon sauce over and place in a very hot oven or under the broiler until sauce is a golden tan. Cut the second piece of toast diagonally and place at each end of the dish. Top the sandwich with bacon slice and mushroom and sprinkle with more grated cheese mixed with bread crumbs, if desired.

Favorite Fare II

Cornbread Dressing

There are many names for this venerable companion dish with roast turkey and chicken: turkey stuffing, onion dressing, cornmeal stuffing, bread dressing. It appears in a multitude of Southern cookbooks under Meat, Poultry, or Bread, but it is none of these. It is a highly seasoned mixture of crumbled cornbread (often with biscuits or light bread added), fortified with onions and a rich poultry broth, then either stuffed into the cavity of the bird or baked separately. (We prefer it as a separate dish, shaped into patties the size of eggs and baked to a crusty brown on a cookie sheet.) Lettice Bryan gave directions for making a turkey stuffing in her *Kentucky Housewife* in 1839. This particular recipe is not that old, but it does have a documented history of almost a century in Kentucky and Tennessee.

1 cup white cornmeal	1½ cups buttermilk (about)
1 cup flour	4 tablespoons bacon grease
¾ teaspoon baking soda	1 medium-sized onion
2 teaspoons baking powder	1 rib celery
1½ teaspoons salt	1 teaspoon poultry seasoning or
¾ teaspoon black pepper	sage
1 beaten egg	Turkey or chicken broth

Mix together 1 cup of white cornmeal, 1 cup of flour, ¾ teaspoon of baking soda, 2 teaspoons of baking powder, 1½ teaspoons of salt, and ¾ teaspoon of black pepper. Stir in 1 beaten egg and add up to 1½ cups of buttermilk—just enough to give the mixture a thick, pouring consistency. Heat 2 tablespoons of bacon grease in a large black skillet; when smoking hot, pour the batter in and set on the bottom rack of a preheated 350° oven. Bake 5 minutes there, then move up to middle rack for 15 or 20 minutes more, or until crispy brown. Turn out on a cake rack. When cold, crumble thoroughly in a large pan or bowl. Next, mince 1 medium-sized onion and 1 rib of celery and sauté in 2 tablespoons of bacon grease. When the vegetables are soft, add them to the cornbread crumbs and sprinkle in 1 teaspoon of poultry seasoning or sage (or more, to suit your taste). Moisten the mixture with broth (from the

CONTINUED

CONTINUED

roaster or the giblets), making it just sticky enough to shape into patties. Taste and adjust seasonings if necessary. Spoon the dressing into the turkey's cavity to cook along with the bird, or shape it into about 20 small patties and bake at 350° until rich brown and crusty (20 to 30 minutes). Serve hot with the turkey and giblet gravy. For 4 or more holiday diners, a double recipe may be advisable.

Southern Food

Dressing Balls

¾ stick butter
2½ tablespoons chopped celery
2 teaspoons chopped parsley
1 small chopped onion
6½ cups stale bread crumbs
Chicken broth

1 beaten egg
Black pepper
Poultry seasoning
Salt
Seasoning salt

Sauté celery, parsley and onion in butter. Add bread crumbs. Add chicken broth until consistency is right for molding mixture into 2-inch balls. Stir in egg and add seasonings to taste. Bake at 350° for about 20 minutes. Serve immediately. Makes 10 balls.

Historic Kentucky Recipes

Roast Goose

Choose a young goose of 8–10 pounds, allowing 1¼ pounds per person. Wash and dry the goose. If you have any doubts as to the youth and tenderness of your bird, it is wise to parboil it in water for an hour before roasting. Turn the goose once, if required.

Dry the goose and rub the skin with salt and pepper and, if desired, a clove of garlic. Stuff the cavity loosely and fasten with skewers or string. Prick the skin well to let the fat run off. Place the bird on a rack in a roasting pan, if you have no rack, prop the goose on two wooden spoons to prevent its sticking to the pan. Put in a 450° oven for 20–25 minutes to brown, then pour off the fat and reduce the heat to 300°. Pour a cup of hot cider or wine over the bird and cook uncovered, allowing 20 minutes per pound for the total roasting time.

Serve the bird on a large platter garnished with glazed fruits, crab apples, spiced pears or stuffed prunes, with bunches of parsley or watercress. Stewed apples are excellent with roast goose.

My Old Kentucky Homes Cookbook

Cajun-Style Chicken or Quail

6 to 7 chicken breasts or 8 to 9 quails
Salt and red pepper to taste
Floured (1 tablespoon) and Pam sprayed roasting bag
1 cup diced onion
½ cup sweet green pepper, chopped
½ cup dried parsley
4 chopped garlic cloves
Grated lemon
1 pound mushrooms, soaked in salt water and drained
½ cup water
1 cup Sauterne or your favorite light wine

Salt and pepper each breast and place in roasting bag. Poke 12 holes in bag with 2 prong fork. Cover breasts with remaining ingredients and bake at 350° for 1½ hours.

Note: The salt and pepper will have to be your own decision. Danny likes things "spicy," so 2 tablespoons red pepper will clear the sinuses, I guarantee.

The Junior Welfare League 50th Anniversary Cookbook

Quail, Kentucky Style

4–5 quail	2–2½ cups chicken stock
4–5 tablespoons butter	½ cup sherry
2½–3 tablespoons flour	Salt and pepper to taste

Preheat oven at 350°. Wash and truss quail; tie legs and wings close to body. Brown quail in butter in skillet. Place quail in casserole (1½-quart). Add flour to remaining butter in pan. Slowly stir in stock and sherry. Blend well. Add salt and pepper. Pour over quail. Cover and bake for one hour. Delicious over rice. Serves 2–4.

Wine: Serve with a light Rhone or California Blanc de Noir.

The Kentucky Derby Museum Cookbook

Stuffed Rock Cornish Hens

1½ cups wild rice	1 teaspoon poultry seasoning
¼ cup melted butter	Salt and pepper to taste
½ cup celery, chopped fine	3 Cornish hens
1 small onion, chopped fine	¼ cup lemon juice
¼ cup green pepper, chopped fine	2 teaspoons slivered almonds

Cook rice according to directions on package. Sauté celery, onion and green pepper in butter 5 minutes. Stir in poultry seasoning. Add salt and pepper to taste. Season inside and outside of hens with butter, salt and pepper. Combine rice and sautéed vegetables. Add lemon juice and almonds.

Stuff inside of hens lightly with mixture. Brush hens with melted butter or margarine. Place in roasting pan. Bake uncovered in 400° oven 30 minutes. Cover and bake 45 minutes, or until tender. *Note:* You may use a brown-and-bake bag if desired. Follow instructions.

What's Cooking for the Holidays

Baked Doves With Fruit Juices

6–12 doves or quail
Olive oil
Dry mustard
Curry powder
Celery salt
Garlic salt
Salt

Pepper
¾ cup white wine
3 teaspoons Worcestershire
  sauce
Juice of 2 oranges
Juice of 1 lemon

Grease doves or quail well with olive oil. Sprinkle dry mustard, curry powder, celery salt, garlic salt, salt, and pepper on birds and place in a Dutch oven. Add white wine and a little water to Dutch oven.

Bake at 250° for 2½ to 3 hours. Add Worcestershire sauce, orange juice, and lemon juice. Cook for 15 minutes or longer until birds are tender. Wine Selection: Semi-sweet German Riesling.

To Market, To Market

Doves in Tomato Sauce

1 cup boiling water
1 beef bouillon cube
3 stalks celery, chopped
1 medium onion, chopped
1 (8-ounce) can tomato sauce

2 tablespoons flour
½ cup water
Salt and pepper to taste
12 dove breasts, skinned
6–7 slices bacon, halved

Preheat oven to 350°. Dissolve bouillon cube in boiling water. Add celery and onion and simmer until soft. Add tomato sauce. Make thickening with 2 tablespoons flour and ½ cup cold water. Season and wrap dove breasts with half slice bacon. Pour sauce over doves. Cook uncovered for an hour. Serve with wild rice. Serves 4–6. Wine: Serve with a Rhone or an Italian white.

The Kentucky Derby Museum Cookbook

Meats

A half-mile track, one of many facilities for sports events at Kentucky Horse Park in Lexington.

Marinated Beef Tenderloin

1 cup ketchup
2 teaspoons prepared mustard
½ teaspoon Worcestershire
  sauce
2 (0.7-ounce) envelopes Italian
  salad dressing mix

1½ cups water
1 (4–6 pound) beef tenderloin,
  trimmed
Watercress (optional)
Red and green grapes

Combine ketchup, mustard, Worcestershire sauce, salad dressing mix and water together. Mix well. Spear meat in several places and place in zip-top, heavy-duty plastic bag. Pour marinade over meat and seal bag tightly. Place bag in a shallow pan and refrigerate 8 hours, turning occasionally. Drain off and reserve marinade. Place tenderloin on a rack in a baking pan. Insert meat thermometer. Bake at 425° for 30–45 minutes or until thermometer registers 140° (rare). Bake until thermometer registers 150° for medium rare or 160° for medium. Baste occasionally with marinade while baking. Remove to serving platter and garnish with watercress and grapes, if desired. Serve remaining marinade with meat.

Somethin's Cookin' at LG&E

Horseradish Sauce

4 tablespoons grated horseradish
  (ours came from the bottle)
6 tablespoons thick cream
2 tablespoons vinegar

1 teaspoon salt
¼ teaspoon pepper (we used red)
1½ teaspoons prepared mustard,
  the yellow kind

Mix altogether, taste and reseason, until it's so good it could be eaten on shoe leather. Serve with hot or cold beef.

The Courier-Journal Kentucky Cookbook

Tenderloin with Brie and Spinach

2 pounds beef tenderloin, cut
    into 1-inch slices and
    pounded slightly
4 handfuls fresh, raw spinach
Glace de Viande, optional*

Brie slices, ¼–½ pound
4 tablespoons unsalted butter
Shallots, mushrooms, thyme to
    taste
White wine

Sauté meat in butter lightly on both sides with shallots, mushrooms and thyme. Season with pepper, Glace de Viande and wine. Cover meat with Brie slices, (at room temperature) and place spinach on top. Cover and steam till spinach wilts. Remove meat, Brie and spinach; place on warm plate. Reduce pan liquids and sauce plates. Serves 4.

*Glace de Viande: Reduce brown stock slowly until the stock forms an even coating on a spoon inserted into it. Remove from heat and cool, at which point the mass solidifies and becomes very glutinous. Covered and refrigerated, a meat glaze will last for several weeks.

Entertaining the Louisville Way, Volume II

Magic Beef Stew

2½ to 3 pounds lean stew beef
6 large carrots, cut into 2-inch
  pieces
3 large potatoes, quartered
3 large onions, sliced
5 stalks celery, cut into 2-inch
  pieces
1 tablespoon salt
1 teaspoon pepper
¼ cup tapioca
2 tablespoons sugar
1½ cups tomato juice
1 cup water

Layer first 5 ingredients in casserole. Sprinkle with mixture of salt, pepper, tapioca and sugar. Pour mixture of tomato juice and water over all. Seal with foil and lid. Bake at 275° for 4 hours or until beef is tender. Serve with salad and corn bread. Yields: 5 to 6 servings.

Capital Eating in Kentucky

Beef Burgundy
(Crock Pot)

1–2 pounds beef round steak,
  cut in ¾ inch cubes
¼ cup all-purpose flour
½ teaspoon salt
3 tablespoons butter or
  margarine
1 cup burgundy
½ cup chopped onion
2 tablespoons snipped parsley
⅛ teaspoon pepper
¾ cup beef broth
1 (3-ounce) can whole
  mushrooms, drained
2 bay leaves
1 clove garlic, minced
Hot cooked noodles

Coat beef with mixture of flour and salt. In skillet melt butter; brown meat on all sides. Transfer meat to crockery cooker. Combine remaining ingredients except noodles. Stir into meat. Cover; cook on high heat setting for 3 hours. Meat may be held longer by turning to a low heat setting. Remove bay leaves; discard. Serve over noodles. If desired, sprinkle with paprika and garnish with parsley. Makes 6–8 servings.

Bell Ringing Recipes

J. D.'s Kabobs

MARINADE:

½ cup oil

2 tablespoons red wine vinegar

1 clove garlic, minced

2 tablespoons Dijon mustard

¼ teaspoon salt

¼ teaspoon pepper

Combine oil, red wine vinegar, garlic, Dijon mustard, salt, and pepper to make marinade. Pour over beef, cover and refrigerate 2 hours or more.

2 pounds beef tenderloin or
  sirloin, cubed

1 cup beef broth

12 medium fresh mushrooms

4 slices bacon, cut into fourths

2 zucchini, sliced ½-inch thick

Heat broth to boiling, add mushrooms. Reduce heat, cover, and simmer 2 minutes. Remove from heat. On skewers, alternate beef cubes, bacon, zucchini, and mushrooms. Broil 7 minutes. Brush with remaining marinade. Broil an additional 7 minutes. Preparation Time: 20 minutes + marinating + cooking. Yield: 4 servings.

Delicious grilled. Serve with baked or hash browned potatoes and a tomato or Caesar salad.

Wine: Light to medium-bodied red such as Beaujolais, Merlot or young Zinfandel.

CordonBluegrass

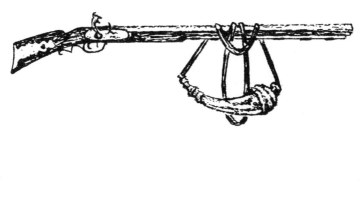

119

Barbecue Ribs

Cut ribs into serving pieces, place on a rack in broiler pan. Salt and pepper. Place under broiler and brown on both sides. This takes away a lot of grease.

When the ribs are nice and brown, sprinkle with Liquid Smoke, place in a crockpot and pour barbecue sauce over them. Set the dial at low and cook for 12 hours.

BARBECUE SAUCE:

1½ cups tomato catsup
½ cup vinegar
1 large onion chopped
2 tablespoons brown sugar

Dash Tabasco sauce
1 teaspoon mustard
½ teaspoon salt
¼ teaspoon black pepper

Mix all ingredients and cook for about 7 minutes. This sauce may also be used for barbecue chicken by adding ½ cup butter or salad oil.

My Old Kentucky Homes Cookbook

Barbecue Shredded Beef

3 pounds chuck roast
2 tablespoons shortening
1 cup chopped onions
2 teaspoons paprika
1 teaspoon pepper
1 teaspoon dry mustard
Dash of cayenne pepper

½ teaspoon salt
3 tablespoons vinegar
3 tablespoons sugar
3 tablespoons Worcestershire
  sauce
1 clove garlic, minced
1 (6-ounce) can tomato paste

Cook meat until very tender in a small amount of water to which 3 teaspoons salt have been added. While meat is cooking, melt shortening and add onions. Cook until tender, but not brown. Add remaining ingredients and cook over low heat for 20 minutes. When meat is done, shred it fine. Add meat and liquid to the sauce; mix well.

Cover and cook very slowly for 30 minutes. If necessary, add a little water if mixture becomes too thick. Serve on hamburger buns. Yields 10 to 12 servings or 1½ quarts.

Best Made Better Recipes, Volume II

Barbecue Sauce

4 (28-ounce) cans tomato sauce
1 (5-ounce) bottle
  Worcestershire sauce
6 ounces white vinegar
4 tablespoons dry mustard
1 box dark brown sugar

1 pint jar dark molasses
1 (8-ounce) bottle ReaLemon
  juice
1 tablespoon salt
2 (16-ounce) bottles Robusto
  Italian dressing

Mix all above ingredients and pour over cooked beef or pork. Simmer about 2 hours or more. Makes about one gallon of sauce. Good used in crockpot.

Campbellsville College Women's Club Cookbook

Slow Cooker Barbecued Pot Roast

2–3 pounds beef chuck roast   ½ cup barbecue sauce
2 tablespoons oil   1 large onion, sliced

Brown meat in hot oil in skillet, then transfer to slow cooker. Add sauce and onion. Cover. Cook at high heat 4–5 hours, or until tender. Slice and serve with sauce. Serves 6–8.

Favorite Recipes

Finger Lickin' Spareribs

6 pounds country-style   ½ cup each, sherry and water
   spareribs

SAUCE:
1 teaspoon each chili powder   ¼ cup each vinegar and
   and celery seed   Worcestershire
2 cups water   ¼ lemon, sliced thin
½ cup chopped onion   ⅛ teaspoon pepper
1 teaspoon salt   ½ cup brown sugar
1 cup catsup

In a large frying pan, brown spareribs (without flour). Then add sherry and ½ cup water and cook, covered for one hour. In another pan, combine all sauce ingredients and cook for an hour. Let ribs cool in liquid long enough to skim off fat. Then remove ribs and drain. Lay drained ribs in large casserole, cover with sauce and bake one hour at 300°.

Historic Kentucky Recipes

Honest to goodness Kentucky hickory-smoked barbecue must be made in a hickory pit, an enclosed, furnace-like cinder-block structure that allows the meat to cook over low heat, surrounded by hickory smoke. The favorite meat is mutton, and hickory smoke and hot fire produce mutton fit for kings.

Barbecued Lamb

4–5 pounds leg of lamb
1 pod garlic
Flour, salt, and pepper
2 onions, chopped
2 cups water

¼ cup vinegar
½ teaspoon dry mustard
2 tablespoons catsup
2 tablespoons sugar
4 tablespoons Worcestershire

Rub lamb with garlic, salt, pepper and flour. Put in roaster and add chopped onions. Pour all other ingredients over meat. Bake at 350° for 3–4 hours until tender. Remove top and brown for 30 minutes at 400°. Skim grease from gravy and thicken with flour and water. Serves 8.

Cabbage Patch: Famous Kentucky Recipes

Meat Quiche

¾ pound ground beef, cooked
  and drained
½ cup mayonnaise
½ cup whole milk
2 eggs, beaten
Salt and pepper to taste
1 tablespoon cornstarch

1½ cups shredded Cheddar
  cheese
⅓ cup chopped onion
⅓ cup chopped green pepper
⅓ cup sliced ripe olives
1 deep-dish pie shell, unbaked

Mix all ingredients except ¾ cup Cheddar cheese. Pour into unbaked pie shell. Sprinkle remaining Cheddar cheese over top of meat mixture. Bake at 350° for 40 to 45 minutes or until set. Yield: 8 to 10 servings.

Mountain Laurel Encore

Meat Loaf
Jim's Favorite

1½ pounds ground beef
1 cup cracker crumbs
2 stalks celery, chopped
½ cup cubed American Cheddar
  cheese
1 large onion, chopped
1½ teaspoons salt
American cheese slices
1 egg

½ (10½-ounce) can condensed
  tomato soup
½ medium green pepper,
  chopped
¼ teaspoon pepper
¼ cup water
½ (10½-ounce) can condensed
  tomato soup

Combine first 10 ingredients. Mix well and form into one large or two small meat loaves. Freeze, if desired, and bake without thawing. Just unwrap, place in greased baking dish and top with cheese slices. Combine water and tomato soup and pour over cheese slices. Bake 350° for 45 minutes.

Larue County Kitchens

Microwave Meatloaf

1½ pounds ground beef
½ cup bread crumbs
2 eggs
½ cup onions
½ cup green pepper

⅓ cup chopped water chestnuts
2 tablespoons catsup
2 tablespoons soy sauce
½ teaspoon salt
¼ teaspoon pepper

Combine preceding ingredients and shape into loaf in baking dish. Cover with wax paper; microwave on HIGH for 18–20 minutes. Drain off drippings.

MIX TOGETHER:
2 tablespoons catsup
1 tablespoon soy sauce

1 tablespoon brown sugar
½ teaspoon dry mustard

Spoon over meatloaf and cook for 2 minutes on MEDIUM setting. Let stand 5 minutes before serving.

Stephensburg Homecoming Recipes

Hamburger and Noodles Stroganoff

½ package (4-ounce) noodles
½ cup finely chopped onion
½ pound mushrooms, or 1 (6-ounce) can sliced mushrooms
1 (8-ounce) can tomato sauce
1 (10½-ounce) can beef bouillon, undiluted
1 cup dairy sour cream

¼ cup butter or margarine
1 clove garlic, finely chopped
1 pound ground chuck
1 tablespoon flour
¼ cup Burgundy
1 teaspoon salt
¼ teaspoon pepper
½ cup grated Parmesan cheese

Preheat oven to 375°. Cook noodles as package label directs, drain. Meanwhile, in hot butter in large skillet, sauté onion, garlic, and mushrooms until onion is golden, about 5 minutes. Add beef; cook, stirring until it is browned. Remove from heat. Stir in flour, tomato sauce, Burgundy, bouillon, salt and pepper. Simmer 10 minutes, stirring occasionally. Blend in sour cream.

   In lightly greased 2-quart casserole, layer ⅓ of the noodles, then ⅓ of the meat mixture. Repeat twice. Sprinkle with cheese. Bake uncovered, 25 minutes.

Larue County Kitchens

Pizza Pop Up

1 pound ground beef	1 tablespoon butter
1 onion, chopped	¼ teaspoon oregano
1 (16-ounce) jar of spaghetti	Salt to taste
sauce	1 (6-ounce) package mozzarella
½ pound fresh mushrooms,	cheese, sliced
sliced and sautéed	

Sauté beef and onion, drain. Add to sauce, add sautéed mushrooms. Blend in seasonings. Pour into a 9 × 13-inch casserole dish. Top with mozzarella cheese. Bake at 400° for 10 minutes. In the meantime, make pop-up batter:

1 cup flour	1 tablespoon vegetable oil
½ teaspoon salt	½ cup fresh grated Parmesan
2 eggs	cheese for topping
1 cup milk	

Place flour and salt in a deep bowl. Make well in center of flour. Combine eggs, milk and oil. Pour into well of flour. Whisk thoroughly. Remove casserole from oven, pour batter over meat mixture. Sprinkle with Parmesan cheese. Bake at 400° for 30 minutes more. Serve immediately. Serves 6–8.

Fillies Flavours

Burger Bundles

1 pound ground beef	1 cup Pepperidge stuffing
½ cup evaporated milk	1 can golden mushroom soup

Mix milk and ground beef; divide into 4 or 5 patties, 6 inches in diameter. In the center of each patty put ¼ cup stuffing, prepared as directed. Mold the meat around the stuffing to form a ball. Put in an 8 × 8-inch pan and add soup. Bake at 350° for 1 hour. Baste several times. Easy preparation in 20 minutes. Will freeze.

Holy Chow

Juicy Hamburgers

2 pounds ground beef
2 teaspoons garlic salt
1 cup fine bread crumbs
½ cup tomato catsup
½ teaspoon salt

2 teaspoons Worcestershire
  sauce
2 teaspoons onion salt
2 eggs
1 teaspoon pepper

Combine all ingredients; form into patties and broil 4 minutes on each side. Yield: 12 servings.

Historic Kentucky Recipes

Mary D's Hot Sweet Mustard

1 cup dry mustard
1 cup sugar

3 eggs, beaten
1 cup cider vinegar

Mix mustard and sugar. Place into heavy saucepan. Add beaten eggs and vinegar. Cook over medium heat, stirring constantly until thickened. Keeps well stored in refrigerator.

Very good served with cold baked ham or cold sliced turkey. Also, a must for hamburgers.

Cooking With Curtis Grace

Mac Attack

1 cup Miracle Whip
⅓ cup creamy French dressing
¼ cup sweet pickle relish

1 tablespoon sugar
¼ teaspoon pepper
1 teaspoon dry minced onions

Mix all together. Refrigerate covered. Spoon over hamburgers on a sesame seed bun. Yields 2 cups.

Fillies Flavours

Sausage and Broccoli Lasagne

1 pound pork sausage
1 large onion, chopped
1 (15-ounce) can tomato sauce
1½ teaspoons sugar
1 teaspoon crushed oregano
1 teaspoon crushed marjoram
¼ teaspoon garlic

10 ounces frozen broccoli
4 ounces lasagne noodles
2 beaten eggs
2 cups cottage cheese
½ cup Parmesan cheese
8 ounces sliced mozzarella
cheese

In skillet, cook sausage and onion until meat is browned. Drain off fat; stir in tomato sauce, sugar, oregano, marjoram and garlic. Simmer gently, uncovered, for 10 minutes; stir occasionally. Cook broccoli until tender; drain well. Cook noodles according to package directions; rinse in cold water and drain.

Combine eggs, cottage cheese, Parmesan cheese and broccoli. Layer in following order in 13 × 9 × 2-inch baking dish: ½ noodles, ½ cottage cheese mixture, ½ meat and ½ Mozzarella cheese. Repeat layers except last cheese. Cover with foil and bake in 375° oven for 25 minutes. Uncover; add cheese and bake 10 minutes more. Let stand 10 minutes; serve. Makes 10 servings or more.

Best Made Better Recipes, Volume II

Pigs in Blanket

1 pound ground beef
2 eggs
1 cup rice
1 onion, chopped
1 teaspoon celery salt

1 teaspoon salt
½ teaspoon pepper
6 cabbage leaves
2 cups tomato juice

Mix beef, eggs, rice, green pepper, onion, celery salt, salt and pepper thoroughly; form into 6 patties. Wrap each pattie in a cabbage leaf. Place in a pan; cover with tomato juice. Bake for 1 hour at 350°. Serves 6.

Historic Kentucky Recipes

Uncle Julio's Spaghetti

3 cans Red Gold tomato purée
1 medium onion, chopped
1 green pepper, chopped
1 pound bacon, fried crisp and
crumbled

1 (7-ounce) box spaghetti
½ pound American cheese, torn
in pieces

Mix tomato purée, onion, green pepper and bacon together as a sauce. Cook spaghetti and layer spaghetti, sauce and cheese in a greased deep casserole dish or Pyrex bowl. Bake at 350° for 30 minutes.

Note: Uncle Julio was a chef at the Brown Hotel many years ago.

Somethin's Cookin' at LG&E

Billy Goat Strut Alley Stew Au Vin

4 pounds of billy goat meat
Water
Soy sauce
Wine vinegar
Olive oil

2 cups Sauterne wine
2 (8-ounce) cans cream of
mushroom soup
One mint leaf
Ground red pepper

Marinate for one hour in mixture of water, wine vinegar and soy sauce. Remove and lightly rinse. Cover bottom of baking pan with olive oil. Place meat in pan after red peppering. Add mint leaf and cream of mushroom soup. Cover pan and place in preheated oven (200°) for 30 minutes. Add wine and cook approximately 2 hours. Baste every 15 minutes to brown. Set table while cooking. Serves 4 to 6 people.

Mrs. Gretchen Kloppner of Billy Goat Strut Alley, Louisville, Ky. cooked this dish for relatives from Ohio on Derby day 1926. She didn't know what to call it but it tasted good under any name. She prepared it later for the Quilters at her Church and they put the recipe in their 1927 "Knit-wit Cook Book".

The Corn Island Cookbook

Bowl of Red

This recipe calls for "pure" chili powder, and when she wrote about several variations on chili in 1983, Elaine Corn noted that some commercial brands of chili powder contain not just the powder of chili pepper pods but also cumin, oregano and cayenne.

¼ pound suet
4 cloves garlic, minced
6 pounds round steak or sirloin, trimmed and cut into 1-inch cubes
9 dried red chili pods
¼ cup pure chili powder

¼ cup oregano
¼ cup ground cumin
¼ cup paprika
2 tablespoons salt
⅛ cup cayenne
3 quarts water

In a large kettle, sauté the suet until browned and curled. Add steak and garlic and stir until meat is browned on all sides. Add remaining ingredients. Bring to a boil. Place cover askew and simmer 1 hour. Remove cover and simmer 30 minutes more, or until chili thickens. Serve with cornbread. Serves 16.

The Courier-Journal Kentucky Cookbook

Julian's Chili

2 pounds ground beef
1 medium onion, chopped
1 package spaghetti
2 (7-ounce) cans chili beans
¾ cup sugar
2 cans tomato paste

1 quart home-canned tomato
  juice
4–6 tablespoons chili powder
½ cup red wine
Salt and garlic to taste

Brown ground beef and onion together. Cook spaghetti in 3 quarts of salted water. Retain water for part of liquid. Add other ingredients. Simmer for 1½ hours. Add red wine 30 minutes before done. Except for the addition of the wine, which is Charlann's suggestion, this is the recipe Governor Carroll used when he cooked for his brothers and sisters as a boy. Yield: 6–8 servings.

Seasons of Thyme

Kentucky Chili
(Crockpot)

1 pound ground beef
Onion flakes, salt, pepper
1 cup chili meat
1 medium can tomatoes
1 medium can tomato juice

1 medium can chili hot kidney
  beans
2 ounces spaghetti (broken)
2 teaspoons chili powder

Brown beef in skillet. Add onion flakes, salt and pepper to taste. Mix chili meat with beef. In crockpot or slow cooker empty tomatoes, tomato juice and beans. Add beef mixture. Stir together and add chili powder. Cook on HIGH 3½–4 hours. Then add dry spaghetti. Cook on low for 1 more hour and serve.

Campbellsville College Women's Club Cookbook

Kentucky Burgoo

2 pounds pork shank
2 pounds veal shank
2 pounds beef shank
2 pounds breast of lamb
1 (4-pound) hen
8 quarts water
1½ pounds Irish potatoes
1½ pounds onions
1 bunch carrots
2 green peppers
2 cups chopped cabbage
1 quart tomato pureé

2 cups whole corn, fresh or
  canned
2 pods red pepper
2 cups diced okra
2 cups lima beans
1 cup diced celery
Salt and cayenne to taste
Chopped parsley
Tabasco
A-1 Sauce
Worcestershire sauce, to taste

Put all the meat into cold water and bring slowly to a boil. Simmer until it is tender enough to fall from the bones. Lift the meat out of the stock. Cool and chop up the meat, removing the bones. Pare potatoes and onions. Dice. Return meat to stock and add potatoes and onions and all other vegetables. Allow to simmer along until thick. Burgoo should be very thick, but still "soup." Season along but not too much until it is almost done. Add chopped parsley just before the stew is taken up.

Stir frequently with a long-handled wooden paddle or spoon during the first part of the cooking and almost constantly after it gets thick. We made ours in a 4-gallon water bath kettle and all in all it cooked approximately 10 hours. Serves about 25.

Cabbage Patch: Famous Kentucky Recipes

Burgoo, a slow-cooked stew of meat and vegetables, is said to have originated with a French chef accompanying Morgan's Raiders during the Civil War.

Burgoo

Many have enjoyed David's burgoo at the Monterey Fair or at the Monterey Beach. This recipe makes 50 gallons of rich stew in a 60-gallon kettle.

40 pounds beef	**100 ears field corn, shelled**
25–30 pounds deer meat	**1 bushel tomatoes**
10 squirrels	**3–4 heads cabbage**
5 wild rabbits	**10 pounds green beans**
6–8 chickens	**18–20 quarts tomato juice**
2 ground hogs	**6 ounces black pepper**
5 pounds beef suet	**1½ ounces red pepper**
25 pounds potatoes	**6 jalapeño peppers, chopped**
20 pounds onions	**6 cayenne peppers, chopped**
10 pounds carrots	**1 pound salt**

Cook meat with water to cover for 4 hours. Remove bones from meat. Bring back to boil and add your hard vegetables (potatoes, onions, carrots and corn). Let that boil for 2 hours. Let fire die down and add remaining vegetables. Add tomato juice. Add salt and pepper, red pepper, jalapeño pepper and cayenne pepper. Let simmer for 1 hour very slowly. You can almost let the fire go out as the kettle has enough heat to simmer the burgoo. Stir constantly while you are cooking it.

The Monterey Cookbook

Pork-Stuffed Leg Of Lamb
A sensational party dish!

1 tablespoon dry mustard
1 tablespoon lemon juice
2 teaspoons salt
½ teaspoon crushed dried
  thyme leaves
½ teaspoon crushed dried
  rosemary leaves
½ teaspoon crushed dried
  marjoram leaves

¼ teaspoon pepper
1 clove garlic
1 leg of lamb, 6–8 pounds,
  boned (not tied)
1 pork tenderloin, about one
  pound
¼ cup water
2 tablespoons flour

Mix mustard, lemon juice, salt, thyme, rosemary, marjoram, pepper, and garlic. Brush mixture inside leg of lamb. Place tenderloin inside lamb. Wrap lamb around tenderloin and tie securely. Insert meat thermometer so tip is in center of pork tenderloin. Place meat on rack in open shallow roasting pan. Do not cover. Roast at 325° until thermometer registers 170 degrees (2½ to 3½ hours).

Remove roast from oven; let stand while preparing gravy. Skim off fat. Add enough water to meat juices to measure 1¾ cups. Shake an additional ¼ cup water and 2 tablespoons flour until smooth. Stir into drippings. Heat to boiling, stirring constantly. Boil one minute.

To Market, To Market

Kentucky Baked Pork Chops

6 pork chops
Salt and pepper
1 teaspoon cooking oil
½ cup chopped celery

2 tablespoons dry mustard
¾ cup water
1 (8-ounce) can tomato sauce

Brown chops in oil, after browning place in shallow baking dish. Combine remaining ingredients and pour over the chops. Cover. Bake at 350° for 1 hour. Serves 6.

The Crowning Recipes of Kentucky

Orange Pork Chops

Delicious served with fried rice.

6 thick pork chops
1 can (11-ounces) Mandarin
   oranges
4 tablespoons brown sugar
½ teaspoon cinnamon

3 whole cloves
½ teaspoon salt
1 teaspoon prepared mustard
¼ cup catsup
1 tablespoon vinegar

Brown chops on both sides in large skillet. Add drained oranges to skillet, reserving juice. Combine ½ to ¾ cup of reserved liquid with remaining ingredients. Pour over pork chops. Cover and simmer gently until chops are done (about 45 minutes).

To Market, To Market

How to Cook a Country Ham

Scrub a large ham, removing all mold and dirt, and place it in a large container. I recommend a lard can. Cover ham with water and heat to a slow, rolling boil slowly, for 30 minutes. Secure lid on can; remove from heat and place on floor on a pallet composed of a blanket, heavy quilt and many layers of newspaper. Wrap can in newspaper then cover with blanket and let it set. After 24 hours, lift ham out of can (water will still be very hot). Remove skin and bones while it is hot.

Make about 1 cup of paste from sweet pickle juice, meal, brown sugar, ground cloves and ground mustard and spread on top of ham. With fat side up, bake at 300° for 20 minutes and score and decorate with whole cloves.

Your ham remains moist and is not dried out using this recipe.

Country Cookbook

Festive Baked Ham

1 can (3–4½ pound) ham
½ cup brown sugar, firmly
   packed
½ cup honey

Remove ham from can; place ham, fat side up, on shallow pan. Combine brown sugar and honey; spoon over ham. Bake in slow oven (325°) 1¼ to 2 hours. Baste occasionally with drippings.

CHERRY SAUCE:
1½ tablespoons cornstarch
¼ cup sugar
¼ teaspoon allspice
¼ teaspoon ground cloves
1 can red sour pitted cherries

Combine dry ingredients; slowly add juice from cherries. Cook until thick and clear. Add cherries and red food coloring. Serve hot, spooned over baked ham. Serves 4.

Bell Ringing Recipes

Country Ham

A more modern version, and my favorite method of baking ham is to baste it with sherry or fruit juices. I like the slightly sweet taste this gives the crust.

1 (12 to 14-pound) country ham	Brown sugar
1 cup firmly packed brown sugar	Cloves
1 tablespoon whole cloves	Sherry, apple cider, or fruit juice

Soak ham in cold water overnight to remove excess salt; drain. Scrub ham thoroughly with stiff brush and rinse thoroughly. Place ham, skin side down, in a large kettle and cover with cold water. Cover and simmer 20 to 25 minutes per pound. Add hot water as necessary to keep ham covered during cooking. Ham is done when shank bone pulls loose from meat. Remove ham from water and cool slightly.

While ham is still warm, remove skin carefully and trim excess fat, leaving about a half-inch layer. With a sharp knife score fat; sprinkle with brown sugar, stud with cloves, and bake at 375° for 20 minutes or until ham is browned, basting frequently with sherry, cider, or fruit juice.

Remove ham to serving platter and garnish with spiced peaches and parsley, or a garnish of your choice. Yields about 20 servings.

More Than Moonshine: Appalachian Recipes and Recollections

Country Ham Slices

Cured ham slices, cut ¼-inch thick	Brown sugar
	Black pepper

Sprinkle both sides of ham with brown sugar and black pepper. Brown on both sides. Cover 5 minutes to tenderize.

Mountain Recipe Collection

Ham Fried Rice

1⅓ cups long grain rice, soaked
    in cold water for 30 minutes
    and drained
2 cups water
1 teaspoon salt
1 tablespoon butter
2 eggs, lightly beaten

¼ cup vegetable oil
4 ounces green beans, cut into
    1-inch lengths
10 ounces cooked ham, diced
½ teaspoon black pepper
4 scallions
6 average mushrooms

Put the rice into a saucepan; pour over the water and 1 teaspoon of salt. Bring to boil; reduce the heat to low and cover the pan. Simmer for 15 to 20 minutes or until the water has been absorbed and the rice is cooked and tender. Remove from heat.

Melt butter in a large frying pan. Add the eggs and cook for 2 to 3 minutes or until they are set on the underside. Stir eggs and cook 2 to 3 minutes more or until they are just set. Remove from heat and transfer eggs to a bowl, breaking them up with a fork. Set aside. Add oil to the frying pan and heat over moderately high heat. Add the cooked rice, beans, ham and pepper. Cook for 2 minutes, stirring constantly. Reduce heat to moderately low and add the scallions, eggs and mushrooms. Cook for 2 minutes, stirring constantly, or until mixture is very hot. Transfer the mixture to a warmed serving dish and serve at once.

Kentucky Kitchens

Whistle Stop Ham and Asparagus Rolls

Fresh asparagus spears, cooked
Margarine or butter, melted
Salt
Nutmeg
Center-cut slices of baked
  country ham

Hollandaise or mild cheese
  sauce
Fresh pineapple wedges

Toss asparagus spears with small amount of margarine or butter; sprinkle with salt and nutmeg to taste.

Place two asparagus spears on each ham slice and roll up. Top with sauce, garnish with pineapple, and serve.

Dining in Historic Kentucky

Kentuckians ordinarily are agreeable folk, but there is one query guaranteed to start a debate among them. Ask the proper way to cure a Kentucky country ham, and the fist pounding begins.

Frozen Ham Sandwiches

2 sticks margarine
3 tablespoons prepared mustard
1 small onion, grated
1½ tablespoons poppy seeds
1 tablespoon Worcestershire
  sauce

Sesame buns
Ham slices
Swiss cheese slices

Melt margarine and add mustard, onion, poppy seeds, and Worcestershire sauce. Mix and refrigerate until mixture is spreadable. Cover tops and bottoms of buns with butter mixture. Add ham slices and cheese slices.

Wrap individually in foil. Freeze until needed. Remove as many sandwiches as needed and bake at 350° for 30 minutes.

A Tasting Tour Through Washington County

Rolled Pork Loin with Parsley-Herb Stuffing

1 4- to 5-pound boneless pork loin	1 egg white

Have your butcher cut half a pork loin from the rib end, leaving the "lip" intact and defatting the top. It should weigh about 4 to 5 pounds. Then have the butcher split the loin open from the lip end, in butterfly fashion, and continue splitting until the loin lies flat.

Paint unfurled loin with egg white. Set aside while you prepare the filling.

FILLING:

2 cups water	1 teaspoon summer savory
½ cup raw rice	½ teaspoon thyme
2 tablespoons butter	1 egg yolk
2 tablespoons minced shallots	Sesame seeds
3 cloves garlic, minced	1 egg, lightly beaten
⅓ pound fresh mushrooms, coarsely chopped	Salt and pepper, to taste
4 cups packed parsley (curly or flat Italian), leaves only	

Bring 2 cups water to a rolling boil. Add rice. Boil 5 minutes, lid off. Strain rice and reserve.

Heat the butter in a wide skillet. Sauté shallots and garlic a minute or two over medium heat, stirring a little. Add mushrooms. Place parsley leaves into skillet. Turn the leaves over and over with a spatula, rather than stir, until the mixture moistens enough to manage it. Sauté a total of 8 minutes. Mixture will decrease in volume by more than three-fourths. Purée just until small lumps remain. Transfer mixture to a mixing bowl. Mix in herbs and egg yolk. Stir in cooked rice. Add salt and pepper, to taste.

Spread filling evenly over surface of prepared pork loin, leaving a ½-inch border. Roll up. Tuck seam underneath, or slightly at the side, depending on how your piece of meat looks best. Secure with fishing line. (It doesn't show at the

CONTINUED

CONTINUED

table, but be sure guests don't eat it.) Roll may be refrigerated overnight at this point.

Place roll on rack set in a roasting pan. Roast at 400° for 30 minutes. Reduce heat to 325° and roast 50 minutes to 1 hour more. Internal temperature of pork should reach between 140° and 160° for a barely pink center. Remove from oven. Let cool slightly. Increase oven temperature to 500°.

Near serving time, paint top of roll with beaten egg. Press sesame seeds into place. Bake at 500° for 10 to 12 minutes. Seeds should turn golden brown. Remove. Reserve 2 table-spoons drippings for sauce. Slice roll on the diagonal.

Place a little lagoon of about ¼-cup Tinted Wine-Thyme Sauce per plate, then center meat on top of sauce. Serve with steamed asparagus.

TINTED WINE-THYME SAUCE:

2 tablespoons pan drippings	¼ teaspoon thyme
2 tablespoons butter	2 teaspoons tomato paste
2 cloves garlic, minced	½ cup stock or water
1 tablespoon minced shallot	Salt and white pepper, to taste
1 tablespoon flour	Additional 2 tablespoons butter
¾ cup dry white wine	

Heat pan drippings and butter. Add garlic and shallots and sauté 1 minute. Stir in flour. Cook 1 minute, stirring and keeping mixture bubbling. Add wine gradually. Add thyme. Bring to boil. Boil 5 minutes. Strain. Return sauce to pan. Blend in tomato paste. Add stock or water, salt and pepper. Bring to a boil again. With pan off the heat, finish with butter, swirling until melted and sauce thickens slightly. Makes about 2¼ cups.

The Courier-Journal Kentucky Cookbook

Pork Tenderloin Hazelet

All the flavors in this dish blend so beautifully, and it is an easy dish for a buffet—no carving. This makes Pork Tenderloin Hazelet fabulous for a dinner party.

6 pork tenderloin filets (6–7 ounces each)
Salt and freshly ground black pepper to taste
2 tablespoons butter or vegetable oil
1 large Spanish onion, sliced
3 large tomatoes, sliced
12 slices smoked bacon
1 teaspoon dried marjoram
1 cup chicken stock
3 tablespoons heavy or whipping cream
Watercress or parsley, for garnish

Flatten the tenderloins a bit with the flat side of a mallet. Season with salt and pepper to taste. Preheat the oven to 400°.

Heat the butter or oil in a heavy skillet and brown the filets quickly over medium-high heat. Do not allow them to cook through.

Place the filets in a shallow casserole or a baking pan and cover each one with a slice of onion and a slice of tomato. Sprinkle the tomato with salt to taste. Cover each tomato slice with 2 strips of bacon laid crisscross over the top. Secure with toothpicks. Cook uncovered in the oven until the bacon is done, 20 to 25 minutes. Remove the bacon and set it aside. Discard the toothpicks. Reduce the oven heat to 325°.

Sprinkle the filets with the marjoram, and add the stock. Return the pan to the oven and bake until the meat is tender, basting often to keep it moist.

When the filets are tender, place the meat on a warmed platter. Stir the cream into the sauce and pour over the filets. Garnish with the bacon and watercress or parsley. Serves 6.

Variations: Thick pork chops may be prepared this way for a family supper. Sautéed whole mushrooms may be added as an elegant garnish.

The Heritage of Southern Cooking

Pork Loins and Fried Apples

Flour
Salt
Pepper
4 pork loins

Bacon drippings or butter for
  browning
3 or 4 tart apples
½ cup brown sugar

Mix flour, salt, and pepper, and dredge each piece of meat in this mixture. Melt fat in heavy skillet and brown each piece of meat on both sides. Turn heat low. Cut unpeeled apples into quarters and place around the meat. Sprinkle with brown sugar, cover, and simmer 45 to 60 minutes. Serves 4.

More Than Moonshine: Appalachian Recipes and
Recollections

Stir-Fry Wild Rice, Snow Peas and Pork

½ pound pork tenderloin, sliced
  ¼ inch thick
3 tablespoons vegetable oil
3 cloves garlic
1 cup sliced celery
1 cup sliced green onion
1 cup sliced fresh mushrooms
1 (8-ounce) can water chestnuts,
  sliced

½ pound snow peas
1 tablespoon fresh ginger root,
  grated
2 cups cooked wild rice
1 tablespoon cornstarch
1 tablespoon dry sherry
3 tablespoons soy sauce
½ teaspoon garlic salt
½ cup cashews

Slice pork and set aside. Heat oil and garlic in heavy skillet for 30 seconds. Add pork and stir-fry over high heat for 2 minutes until meat is no longer pink. Add celery, green onions, mushrooms, water chestnuts, pea pods and ginger. Stir-fry for 5 minutes over high heat until vegetables are tender-crisp. Toss in the wild rice until evenly blended.

Mix cornstarch with sherry, soy sauce and salt. Add to the juices in the pan and cook about 1 minute until thickened. Toss mixture together to coat everything with the glaze. Garnish with cashews.

Somethin's Cookin' at LG&E

Henry Bain Sauce

Henry Bain went to work for the Pendennis Club in 1881, and he was head waiter when he created his famous sauce. Cissy Gregg printed this recipe in 1962, calling it a "modified" version "because we never make it twice the same way. It will be good with either Master Pig or Ribs of Beef." This particular version of the sauce, she wrote, came "from another well-known and popular Louisville waiter, Livingston Whaley."

1 (12-ounce) bottle chili sauce
1 (14-ounce) bottle catsup
1 (11-ounce) bottle A-1 sauce
1 (10-ounce) bottle Worcestershire

1 (1 pound, 1-ounce) bottle chutney
Tabasco or hot pepper sauce
Chopped watercress, as desired

Mix together and add the hot sauce according to taste. It takes more than you think. If the chutney comes with large pieces of mangoes or other chutney fruit in it, chop finely. Chopped watercress may be added as you like.

The sauce will keep indefinitely refrigerated, and it has many uses. Any left may be used for French fried potatoes. Thinned with oil and herb vinegar, it snuggles up to Bibb lettuce.

The Courier-Journal Kentucky Cookbook

Inverness Sauce
(Wedgewood Farm)

A marinade for steaks, pork or lamb on the grill.

2 cloves garlic, minced
½ cup oil (or olive oil)
3 tablespoons soy sauce

2 tablespoons catsup
1 tablespoon vinegar
½ teaspoon fresh ground pepper

Mix all ingredients well. Pour over meat. Cover and refrigerate overnight for best flavor; 2–3 hours of marinating will do in a pinch. Makes 1 cup.

The Kentucky Derby Museum Cookbook

Seafood

Elkhorn Creek. Breaks Interstate Park in Eastern Kentucky.

Josh's Shrimp
At the Drawbridge Inn

6 ounces butter
1½ teaspoons crushed garlic
Flour
24 large peeled, deveined
   shrimp

⅔ cup white wine
1 tablespoon chopped parsley
Cooked rice

Sauté garlic in butter. Dust shrimp with flour, add to garlic and sauté for a few minutes on each side. Then add wine and parsley. Cook 2 minutes longer. Place 6 shrimp on each plate in a bed of cooked rice. Spoon the wine sauce over the shrimp.

What's Cooking for the Holidays

Shrimp and Artichoke Casserole

6½ tablespoons butter
4½ tablespoons flour
1 cup whipping cream
½ cup half-and-half
Salt and pepper to taste
1 (14-ounce) can artichoke
   hearts
½ pound fresh mushrooms

¼ teaspoon flour
¼ cup dry sherry
1 tablespoon Worcestershire
   sauce
¼ cup Parmesan cheese, grated
Paprika
1½ to 2 pounds shrimp, cooked
   and cleaned

Melt 4½ tablespoons butter. Stir in 4½ tablespoons flour, add creams, stirring constantly. When thick, add salt and pepper. Set aside. Drain artichokes and cut in half. Place on bottom of casserole. Place shrimp over artichokes. Sauté mushrooms in remaining butter. Sprinkle ¼ teaspoon flour over mushrooms. Stir, then scatter mushrooms over shrimp. Add sherry and Worcestershire sauce to cream sauce. Pour over casserole. Top with cheese and paprika. Bake at 375° for 20 mintues. Serves 6. You cannot get enough of this dish!

Holy Chow

Shrimp Stuffed Peppers

6 bell peppers
2 cups shrimp, cooked, cleaned
1 cup bread crumbs
2 eggs, beaten
½ cup milk
3 tablespoons butter or
  margarine

3 tablespoons chopped celery
1 tablespoon chopped onion
1 teaspoon salt
⅛ teaspoon pepper
1 tablespoon Worcestershire
  sauce

Cut off tops and remove seeds from peppers. Cook pepper shells in boiling water for 5 minutes and plunge in cold water. Chop shrimp slightly. Combine with eggs, crumbs and milk. Melt butter, cook onion and celery for about 3 minutes and add to shrimp mixture with remaining ingredients. Stuff mixture into peppers. Dot tops with butter. Bake in a moderate oven (350°) 30 minutes. Makes 6 servings.

Historic Kentucky Recipes

Shrimp Stew

This recipe is from Big Sink Farm chef, Morgan Bradley.

½ cup flour
3 tablespoons cooking oil
2 medium onions, chopped
2 ribs celery, chopped
½ cup chopped green bell
  pepper
4 small cloves garlic, mashed
  and centers removed
1½ quarts water

2 (6-ounce) cans tomato paste or
  2 fresh tomatoes, chopped
2 bay leaves
2 pounds raw medium shrimp,
  peeled and deveined
  (approximately 40)
Salt and pepper
Hot cooked rice

Make a roux by combining flour and oil in a heavy 4-quart saucepan. Brown over medium heat, stirring constantly to prevent scorching. Add onions, celery, green pepper and garlic; stir and cook until vegetables are softened. Add water, tomato paste and bay leaves; simmer slowly for 1½ hours. Remove bay leaves after first 30 minutes. Add shrimp and simmer for 15 minutes; do not overcook. Season to taste with salt and pepper; serve immediately over hot cooked rice. Serves 6 to 8.

Bluegrass Winners

Creole Shrimp and Okra
(Microwave)

¼ pound bacon
1 medium onion, sliced
1 small green pepper, halved, seeded and chopped
1 large clove garlic, minced
2 teaspoons seafood seasoning
¼ teaspoon crushed red pepper

1 can tomatoes in juice (14 or 16-ounce)
¼ cup tomato paste
1 cup hot water
1 box okra, frozen
1 pound shrimp, shelled and deveined
3 cups cooked rice

In microwave-safe 2-quart casserole, combine bacon, onion, green pepper, garlic, seafood seasoning and red pepper. Cover with plastic wrap, turning back a corner to vent. Microwave on HIGH 5 minutes, stirring once after 3 minutes. Stir in tomatoes with their juice, the tomato paste and water. Cover and vent; microwave on HIGH 8 minutes. Stir okra into tomato mixture. Cover and vent; microwave on HIGH 5 minutes, stirring once after 3 minutes. Add shrimp; cover and vent; microwave on HIGH 2 minutes. Stir; let stand 2 minutes. Serve with rice.

Campbellsville College Women's Club Cookbook

Shrimp Curry

¼ cup oleo
½ medium onion
4 tablespoons flour
2 tablespoons curry powder
2 teaspoons salt

⅛ teaspoon pepper
1 cup milk
1 cup light cream
1 cup cooked shrimp
8 ounces mushrooms

Melt oleo and sauté onion, thinly sliced, till soft. Blend in flour, curry powder, salt and pepper. Add milk and cream. Cook, stirring frequently, till mixture thickens. Add shrimp and mushrooms. Cover and cook 5 minutes. Serve over rice. (I top serving with crushed cashews or peanuts.) May use ½ cup milk and ½ cup mushroom liquid.

Holy Chow

Merrick Inn Crab Cakes

1 pound fresh backfin crabmeat
2 hard-cooked eggs, finely grated
1 tablespoon finely chopped
  parsley
½ cup mayonnaise

1 teaspoon prepared mustard
1 teaspoon salt
White pepper to taste
6 soda crackers, crushed

Clean crab, removing all cartilage and bone. In bowl, mix remaining ingredients, except crackers; add crabmeat. Mix lightly and refrigerate. Form mixture into eight cakes and roll in crushed crackers. Deep fry at 340° or sauté until golden. Serve plain with lemon or with a sauce. Serves 4.

Dining in Historic Kentucky

Coquilles St. Jacques Provençal

12 sea scallops or 24 bay scallops
¼ cup all-purpose flour
3 tablespoons olive or peanut oil
3 tablespoons butter
1 large tomato, diced
2 shallots, chopped

2 small cloves garlic, minced
1 teaspoon finely chopped mixed herbs: thyme, rosemary, oregano
Salt and pepper
¾ cup grated Swiss cheese
3 tablespoons chopped parsley

Dredge scallops in flour and brown in oil. Remove immediately from pan. Sauté tomatoes, shallots, garlic and herbs in butter. Combine scallops with vegetables in one large casserole or in 8 individual ramekins. Top with cheese and parsley. Broil 1 minute. Serve immediately. Good as entreé or can be served as a first course.

Entertaining the Louisville Way, Volume II

Swiss Baked Scallops

2 pounds fresh bay scallops
1 lemon
½ teaspoon white pepper
½ teaspoon celery salt

½ stick butter
8 slices Swiss cheese
Fresh parsley
Paprika

Place scallops in individual baking dishes. Season with lemon juice, white pepper, celery salt and melted butter. Bake in 350° oven for 15 minutes. Remove from oven and pour off a portion of the excess butter and lemon juice. Place slices of cheese on top of scallops and place under broiler until cheese bubbles. Garnish with sprigs of parsley and a sprinkle of paprika. Serves 4.

Sample West Kentucky

Louisville Rolled Oysters

This recipe was printed in the Cook's Corner column in response to requests for information about rolled oysters, the Louisville invention that is associated with Mazzoni Oysters.

½ cup flour
1 teaspoon baking powder
¼ teaspoon salt
1 well-beaten egg
¼ cup milk or more if needed
18 medium-sized oysters, drained

1 cup or more white cornmeal or cracker meal, enough in which to roll batter-coated oysters
Lard or vegetable shortening for frying oysters

Sift the flour, baking powder and salt together. Beat the egg and milk and add to flour mixture. It should be stiff, but if too stiff to coat the oysters, add a little more milk. Beat smooth. Put all the oysters in this and coat them well.

Take three batter-coated oysters at a time and form them in the hand into a croquette. Then quickly roll the croquette in the meal, covering completely. The trick is to prevent the individual oysters from escaping the roll and separating when fried. I find it best to coat them a second time, putting the rolled croquettes back once more into the batter, then giving them another dusting of cornmeal or cracker meal.

The six rolled oysters are now ready for frying. They do not suffer one whit if made up in the morning and fried in the evening. When ready to fry, treat the oysters as you would doughnuts. Have a pan of deep lard on the stove. Heat to 375°, put the oysters in a basket and lower them into the fat. Do not cook too quickly, as they should be cooked through. I lower the heat as soon as they hit the fat. They should cook on both sides at once if enough fat is in the pan. If not, cook on one side, turn with pancake turner and cook on the other.

This will take about three to four minutes all together. Drain on absorbent paper. Cook only three of these oysters at a time and leave space around them so that they can brown evenly. Serve hot. Makes 6 servings.

The Courier-Journal Kentucky Cookbook

Oysters Casino

3 slices bacon, chopped
4 tablespoons chopped onion
2 tablespoons chopped green
  peppers
2 tablespoons chopped celery
1 teaspoon lemon juice

½ teaspoon salt
⅛ teaspoon pepper
½ teaspoon Worcestershire
  sauce
2 drops Tabasco sauce

Fry bacon, add onion, green pepper, celery and cook until tender. Add seasonings and mix well. Arrange drained oysters on buttered baking dish. Spread bacon mixture over oysters. Bake in a moderate (350°) oven about 10 minutes or until browned. Makes 4 to 6 servings.

Historic Kentucky Recipes

Kentucky's impressive number of navigable streams and man-made lakes create a navigation network second only to Alaska in number of navigable miles (1,090) open to commercial traffic.

Baked Flounder with Crabmeat

3 or 4-pound flounder
Salt to taste

1 stick butter

STUFFING:

2 tablespoons bacon drippings
1 medium onion, chopped
2 cloves garlic, crushed
2 tablespoons celery, chopped
2 tablespoons green pepper,
  chopped
1 teaspoon salt

½ teaspoon pepper
⅛ teaspoon thyme
1 tablespoon chopped parsley
1 egg
¾ cup bread crumbs
1 cup crabmeat

Cut big pocket in cleaned fish. Place generous amount of stuffing, made by sautéing vegetables in bacon drippings, then mix with remaining ingredients. Melt butter in pan and lay fish in pan. Place fish dark side down.

Bake at 375° for 30 minutes, covered. Uncover last 5–10 minutes. Serves 4.

The Crowning Recipes of Kentucky

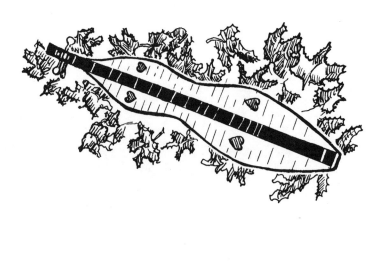

Billy's Baked Bass
This gives you time to tell tall tales.

½ cup butter
⅔ cup crushed crackers
¼ cup Parmesan cheese
½ teaspoon basil

½ teaspoon oregano
½ teaspoon salt
¼ teaspoon garlic powder
8 bass fillets

Melt butter in 9 × 13–inch baking dish.

Mix together next six ingredients. Dip fish in cracker batter, breading both sides. Place in baking dish and sprinkle extra crumbs over fish. Bake at 350° for 15 to 20 minutes.

To test fish, flake with fork. Yield: 4 to 6 servings.

To Market, To Market

Baked Almond Fillets

1 medium onion, sliced
1 bay leaf
4 fish fillets
¼ teaspoon salt
Dash of pepper
Pinch of thyme
¼ cup blanched almonds,
   slivered

1 tablespoon oil
1 small onion, grated
1 teaspoon grated lemon rind
1 tablespoon minced parsley
1 tablespoon white wine
1 chicken bouillon cube
¼ cup boiling water

Place onion slices and bay leaf in shallow baking dish. Season fish fillets with salt, pepper and thyme; place on top of onion slices. In a small skillet, brown almond slivers lightly in oil. Add onion, lemon rind, parsley and wine. Dissolve bouillon cube in ¼ cup boiling water and add to sauce. Blend thoroughly and pour over fish. Bake in a moderate oven (350°) 30 minutes. Makes 4 servings.

Historic Kentucky Recipes

Elizabethtown, Kentucky Trout

5 fresh Rainbow Trout
½ pound crabmeat, picked over
1 red Delicious apple, chopped
8 ounces Kentucky country
   ham, finely chopped
3 ounces black walnuts, finely
   chopped

3 eggs
Pepper to taste
20 bacon strips
1 small bag of sassafras or
   mesquite wood
Watercress for garnish

Skin trout from the back of the tail to the head, leaving filets connected at the dorsal fin. Remove head and tail, then slice off dorsal fin. Cut trout in half. In a bowl, mix the crabmeat, apple, ham, walnuts and eggs. Season with pepper (these ingredients may be chopped and mixed in a food processor.) Stuff trout and wrap tightly with bacon.

Grill trout on medium heat until bacon is brown and crisp and bake in 325° oven until done. Serve with Bourbon Apple Sauce underneath. Garnish with sautéed watercress. Serves 10.

Wine: Serve with a Riesling, a Zinfandel or a Blanc de Noir.

BOURBON APPLE SAUCE:
3 red Delicious apples, diced
1 onion, diced
3 ounces Kentucky Bourbon
2 cups veal stock or veal bercy
   sauce (or 1 cup chicken broth
   and 1 cup beef broth)

3 ounces cream
2 ounces pinenut butter (made
   from a few crushed pinenuts
   and softened butter)

Sauté apples and onions for five minutes until soft. Add bourbon and flambé, being careful not to have bourbon near flame when pouring. Add chicken and beef broth to other ingredients and bring to a simmer for 5 minutes. Then add cream and reduce sauce until it begins to thicken. Finish sauce by adding pinenut butter and then strain.

Courtesy of Sixth Avenue Restaurant, Louisville, Kentucky.

The Kentucky Derby Museum Cookbook

Potted Lobster

2 large onions, finely chopped
3 cloves garlic, finely minced
6 lobster tails in shell, thawed if frozen (see note)
½ cup cooking oil
½ stick butter
½ cup brandy
3 tablespoons tomato paste
1 fish bouillon cube dissolved in 2 cups hot water
1 cup dry white wine
Salt and ground black pepper, to taste
1 to 2 teaspoons cayenne pepper
3 egg yolks
¼ cup fresh chopped parsley

Place onions and garlic in a pot with water to cover and simmer, covered, for 30 minutes. Meanwhile, slice lobster according to natural divisions in tails. Heat the oil and butter in a wide, heavy skillet over medium-high heat. Add lobster, shells down, and sauté without disturbing until shells turn red, about 15 minutes. Transfer lobster with a slotted spoon to heated Dutch oven or heavy kettle. Pour in brandy and immediately light with match. Remove from heat and let flame extinguish itself. Keep warm.

Drain onions and garlic. Add to skillet where lobster was sautéed. Add paste, fish stock and wine, stirring until heated through. Add salt, black and cayenne pepper. Sauce should be spicy. Combine a little sauce with egg yolks, then add yolks to skillet, stirring over low heat until slightly thickened. Pour sauce into pot with lobster. Sprinkle with parsley. Serve hot or warm. Serves 10.

Note: Dish may be made with 3 pounds of peeled medium shrimp. Reduce skillet cooking time to 8 minutes, turning shrimp once.

The Courier-Journal Kentucky Cookbook

Rock Lobster Tetrazzini

2 (6-ounce) rock lobster tails
⅓ package thin spaghetti
2 tablespoons butter or
  margarine
2 tablespoons flour
¾ teaspoon salt
1 teaspoon paprika
⅛ teaspoon nutmeg

1 teaspoon grated onion
2 cups milk and mushroom
  stock
2 tablespoons melted butter or
  margarine
1 (4-ounce) can sliced
  mushrooms
Cooked asparagus spears

Cook lobster tails according to directions. Remove meat and dice. Cook spaghetti according to directions on package. Melt butter, stir in flour and seasonings. Add milk and mushroom stock; cook, stirring constantly, until thickened. Add lobster and mushrooms. Drain spaghetti and toss with melted butter. Line 4 shallow casseroles with spaghetti. Place lobster mixture in center and garnish with cooked asparagus. Makes 4 servings.

Historic Kentucky Recipes

Vegetables

Authentically costumed "Traipsin Women" bring history to life in one of the many restored homesites throughout Kentucky.

Saucy Artichokes

PER SERVING:

1 fresh artichoke
1 tablespoon olive oil
1 slice fresh lemon

½ teaspoon salt
1 small clove garlic

Select artichokes carefully. Leaves should not be spreading or discolored. Turn down and break off bottom leaves. Snip tops off remaining leaves. Cut off stems about 1 inch from base. Stand artichokes upright in deep saucepan. Add ingredients (per serving) to boiling water, enough to cover by 1 inch. Boil gently, covered, 20 to 45 minutes until stem can be pierced with fork or until outside leaves pull off easily. Serve hot or chilled with Sauce (below) for dipping leaves.

SAUCE:

1 cup sour cream
2 teaspoons grated lemon rind
8 drops hot pepper sauce

½ teaspoon salt
1 tablespoon minced onions

Combine above ingredients.

What's Cooking for the Holidays

Asparagus and Tomatoes

3 slices bacon
½ cup green onions, sliced
3 tablespoons vinegar
1 tablespoon water
2 teaspoons sugar
¼ teaspoon seasoned salt

Pepper to taste
1½ pounds asparagus, cut in
  1½-inch pieces
2 medium tomatoes, cut in
  eighths

Cook and crumble bacon. To the drippings, add onion and cook until tender. Add vinegar, water, sugar, seasonings, and bacon. Bring to a boil, add asparagus, cover and cook until just crispy. Toss in tomato wedges and heat through, about 3 minutes. As pretty as it is tasty! Serves 6.

The Cooking Book

Sesame Broccoli Steamed

1 bunch broccoli
4 tablespoons butter
½ cup water
1 tablespoon soy sauce

1 cup thinly sliced celery
1 can water chestnuts, drained
   and sliced
1½ tablespoons sesame seeds

Trim outer leaves and ends from broccoli. Cut stalks and flowerets into 2-inch lengths, then slice thin lengthwise. Combine butter, water and soy sauce in large frying pan; heat to boiling. Stir in broccoli, celery and chestnuts; heat again; cover, steam 10 minutes or until broccoli is crisply tender. While broccoli cooks, heat seeds in heavy pan to toast. Stir in broccoli. Pass soy sauce at table.

A Taste from Back Home

Baked Eggplant

1 large eggplant
Butter, about 2 tablespoons
½ medium-size onion (chopped)
3 tablespoons chopped parsley
   (more or less)
1 can condensed mushroom
   soup (½ can, if eggplant is
   small)

Worcestershire sauce
Salt and pepper
Ritz cracker crumbs
Butter

Cut top off of eggplant, lengthwise, scoop out inside, leaving about ¼ inch of the meat around the sides and bottom of the shell. Parboil meat in salt water until just tender. Drain thoroughly.

Sauté the onion in butter and add chopped parsley. Mix all with the mushroom soup. Season with Worcestershire sauce and salt and pepper to taste. Then add enough Ritz cracker crumbs to make eggplant filling the consistency of stuffing. Return to shell, cover with cracker crumbs, dot with butter and bake in 375° oven for 30 or 35 minutes.

Cabbage Patch: Famous Kentucky Recipes

Aubergines Farcies Duxelles
(Eggplant Stuffed with Mushrooms)

3 (3 × 6-inch) eggplants
1 tablespoon salt
2 tablespoons olive oil
1 cup minced yellow onion
1½ tablespoons olive oil
Salt and pepper to taste
1 pound fresh mushrooms,
  minced
3 tablespoons butter
1 tablespoon olive oil

4½ ounces cream cheese,
  softened
¼ cup minced parsley
½ teaspoon basil
3 tablespoons grated Swiss
  cheese
3 tablespoons fine dry white
  bread crumbs
2 to 3 tablespoons melted butter

Preheat broiler to 500°. Remove stems from eggplant; cut in half lengthwise. Make cuts in flesh 1 inch apart and to within ¼ inch of skin. Sprinkle with salt. Place cut side down on paper towel. Let stand for 30 minutes. Squeeze to remove liquid; pat dry. Drizzle with 2 tablespoons oil. Place cut side up in roasting pan. Add ⅛ inch water. Broil 4 to 5 inches from heat source for 10 to 15 minutes or until tender and light brown. Scoop out pulp; chop. Reserve skins. Set aside.

Sauté onion in 1½ tablespoons oil over low heat for 10 minutes or until very tender; do not brown. Season with salt and pepper. Add to eggplant. Place mushrooms in towel; twist to extract juices. Sauté in mixture of 3 tablespoons butter and 1 tablespoon oil for 5 to 6 minutes. Season with salt and pepper. Add to eggplant.

Combine cream cheese, parsley and basil in bowl. Beat until fluffy. Add to vegetables; mix well. Spoon into eggplant skins. Sprinkle with mixture of Swiss cheese and bread crumbs. Drizzle with 2 to 3 tablespoons melted butter. Place in roasting pan. Add ⅛ inch water. Bake for 25 minutes or until brown.

Yield: 6 servings. Preheat: 375°.

Capital Eating in Kentucky

Swiss-Stuffed Mushrooms

½ cup shredded Swiss cheese
1 hard-boiled egg, finely grated
3 tablespoons fine dry bread
  crumbs
1 clove garlic, minced

2 tablespoons butter, softened
1 pound fresh mushrooms, each
  about 1 to 1½ inches in
  diameter
4 tablespoons butter, melted

In a mixing bowl combine cheese, egg, bread crumbs, garlic, and 2 tablespoons softened butter; blend thoroughly.

Remove stems from mushrooms. Place unfilled mushrooms, rounded side up, on baking sheet. Brush tops with melted butter. Broil 3 to 4 inches from heat for 2 to 3 minutes until lightly browned. Remove from broiler. Turn mushrooms over; fill each with cheese mixture. Return filled mushrooms to broiler. Broil 1 to 2 minutes more. Yield: 3 dozen.

Hint: May be prepared early in day and broiled before serving.

To Market, To Market

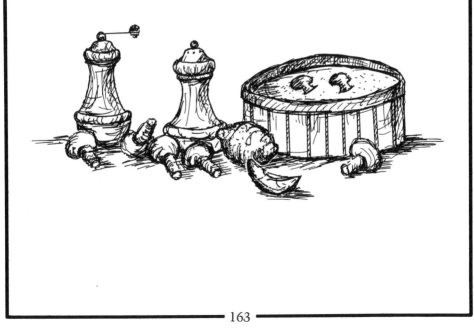

Scalloped Mushrooms

1 pound fresh mushrooms
¼ cup butter or margarine
Salt and pepper to taste
½ pint whipping cream

2 tablespoons very dry sherry
¼–½ teaspoon instant onion
Dash hot sauce (optional)

Sauté mushrooms in butter. Season with salt and pepper. Spread in shallow baking dish, rounded side up. Combine whipping cream, sherry and onion. Add a dash of hot sauce if desired. Pour over mushrooms. Bake uncovered in 325° oven until cream has been reduced to half and mushrooms are golden.

This can be used for meat sauce. For appetizer, bake until almost dry and serve in chafing dish with toothpicks.

What's Cooking in Kentucky

Dilled Green Beans

4 pounds green beans
¼ teaspoon crushed red pepper
  per pint jar
½ teaspoon whole mustard seed
  per pint jar

½ teaspoon dill seed per pint jar
1 clove garlic per pint jar
5 cups white vinegar
5 cups water
½ cup uniodized salt

Wash beans thoroughly; drain and cut into lengths to fit pint jars. Pack beans into clean hot jars; add pepper, mustard seed, dill seed and garlic. Combine vinegar, water and salt; heat to boiling. Pour boiling liquid over beans, filling the jars to within ½ inch of the top. Adjust jar lids. Process in boiling water bath for 5 minutes.

The Monterey Cookbook

Logan County Green Beans

2 (16-ounce) cans green beans
1 onion, sliced
1 cup mayonnaise
4 slices bacon, fried and
  chopped
2 hard-cooked eggs, chopped
1 heaping tablespoon
  horseradish

1 teaspoon Worcestershire sauce
⅛ teaspoon garlic powder
⅛ teaspoon celery salt
⅛ teaspoon onion salt
¼ teaspoon salt
1 teaspoon parsley flakes
1 lemon, juiced

Cook beans with sliced onion for 20 minutes. Blend mayonnaise with remaining ingredients and set aside at room temperature. When beans are ready to serve, drain and spoon mayonnaise mixture over beans.

A Taste from Back Home

Curry Green Bean Casserole

3 cups frozen cut green beans
1 cup celery, cut slantwise
½ cup thinly sliced onion
1 cup sliced water chestnuts

½ cup sour cream
¼ cup mayonnaise
⅛ teaspoon curry powder
Salt and pepper to taste

Cook the beans, celery, and onions all together; drain. Add water chestnuts. Mix in sour cream, mayonnaise, and curry powder. Season to your taste. Pour into a shallow casserole and bake at 300° until hot. Brown under broiler. Yield: 6 servings.

Seasons of Thyme

Green Bean Casserole

1½ sticks butter or margarine
¼ cup onion, chopped
2 tablespoons flour
Salt and pepper

8 ounces sour cream
1 quart green beans, drained
5 slices Swiss cheese
5 slices toasted bread, cubed

Melt ½ stick butter; sauté onion until tender. Add flour, salt and pepper. Add sour cream and heat until warm. Add green beans and simmer 10 minutes. Pour into casserole dish. Top with broken up Swiss cheese. Melt 1 stick butter. Stir toasted bread cubes into butter. Pour on top of cheese. Bake 10 minutes at 400°.

Campbellsville College Women's Club Cookbook

Granny Brock's Greens

Sheep sorrel, dandelion, poke, dock, lamb's quarters, and other favorites

4 cups early greens
4 slices bacon
3 green onions, chopped
3 tablespoons vinegar

2 teaspoons sugar
½ teaspoon salt
¼ teaspoon dry mustard
Dash of pepper

Gather greens early in the day if possible. Wash in pure spring water until all grit is removed. Fry bacon and remove from skillet, leaving fat to cool. Mix chopped onions and greens together in large bowl and then put in individual bowls if desired. Crumble bacon over greens. To the fat in skillet, add vinegar, sugar, salt, mustard, and pepper. Heat and pour over greens. Toss until wilted. Serve immediately.

More than Moonshine: Appalachian Recipes and
Recollections

Green Pepper Casserole

This is an original recipe and has always been a family favorite.

3 large green peppers, chopped
1 cup bread crumbs
1 cup shredded sharp Cheddar
  cheese
1½ tablespoons melted butter or
  margarine

1½ tablespoons all-purpose
  flour
1 cup milk
1 teaspoon salt
⅛ teaspoon pepper

Combine peppers, bread crumbs and ⅓ cup cheese. Stir lightly and set aside. Combine butter and flour in a medium saucepan; cook until bubbly. Gradually add milk. Cook over low heat until thick, stirring constantly. Add ⅓ cup cheese, salt and pepper, stirring until cheese melts. Add green pepper mixture and mix well.

Spoon into a well-greased 1-quart casserole. Top with remaining ⅓ cup cheese. Bake at 350° for 1 hour. Yield: 4 servings.

A Tasting Tour Through Washington County

Broccoli Ring

3 tablespoons butter	2 cups cooked chopped broccoli
3 tablespoons flour	6 tablespoons chopped celery
1 cup milk	3 tablespoons onion juice
¼ teaspoon salt	Juice of ½ lemon
6 eggs, separated	1 cup mayonnaise

Melt butter over low heat; blend in flour. Slowly stir in milk; add salt and cook, stirring constantly, until sauce is smooth. Beat egg yolks, and stir into sauce; add broccoli, celery, onion juice and lemon juice. Cool; add mayonnaise and mix thoroughly. Beat egg whites until stiff and fold into broccoli mixture. Spoon into a ring mold; set in a pan of water in oven. Bake at 350° for 1 hour.

Bluegrass Winners

Early Peas With Potatoes

Fresh early peas (about 1½–2
  pounds)
¼ pound salt pork
7 small early potatoes

1 tablespoon fat
Salt to taste
Sugar to taste

Wash and string peas. You can break the peas or leave them as they are. Put peas, salt pork, fat and salt in a kettle with water to cover. Cook until almost tender. Scrape potatoes and add to peas. Cook until potatoes are done.

Note: This is one of the first vegetable dishes to be cooked in spring. Peas are the first crop to be planted by mountain people.

Mountain Recipe Collection

Shaker Village of Pleasant Hill near Harrodsburg is beautifully restored. The Shakers were a 19th century religious sect known today for lovely craftsmenship and practical design in their tools, furniture and buildings.

Harvard Beets

12 small beets, cooked and cut
  in cubes or slices
½ cup sugar
½ tablespoon cornstarch

¼ cup vinegar
2 tablespoons oil or butter
¼ cup water

Mix sugar and cornstarch. Add vinegar, oil and water and boil 5 minutes. Add beets and let stand over low heat 30 minutes.

Mountain Recipe Collection

Carrots Vichy
(Diabetic)

1 tablespoon reduced-calorie
  margarine
3 cups sliced carrots
¾ cup boiling water
1 teaspoon salt
¼ teaspoon nutmeg
⅛ teaspoon pepper

¼ cup parsley
½ teaspoon monosodium
  glutamate
Sugar substitute to equal 2
  teaspoons sugar
1 tablespoon lemon juice

Place margarine in saucepan. Add carrots, boiling water, salt, nutmeg and pepper. Cover; simmer 8 to 10 minutes or until crisp-tender. Stir in remaining ingredients and serve. Yield: 6 servings. Each serving: ½ cup. Each serving may be exchanged for one vegetable.

Country Cookbook

Zesty Carrots

6 to 8 carrots
2 tablespoons horseradish
2 tablespoons grated onion
¼ cup carrot liquid
½ teaspoon salt
¼ teaspoon pepper

½ cup mayonnaise
¼ cup fine bread or cracker
  crumbs
1 tablespoon melted butter
Dash of paprika

Pare and cut carrots lengthwise. Cook until tender in water to cover. Reserve liquid. Arrange in shallow baking dish. Combine horseradish, grated onion, carrot liquid, salt, pepper and mayonnaise. Blend thoroughly. Pour over carrots. Combine bread crumbs, butter and paprika. sprinkle over top of carrots. Bake 15 to 20 minutes in 375° oven. This dish can be refrigerated for later baking. Add extra time for cold dish.

What's Cooking in Kentucky

Asparagus au Gratin
(Cabbage Patch Circle Bazaar Luncheon Dish)

1 (No. 2½) can asparagus tips (or pieces, for economy)
1 small can mushrooms (or pieces, for economy)
4 eggs (hard-boiled and sliced)

Cheese sauce (made by adding 1 cup grated Cheddar cheese to 1½ cups white sauce)
Bread crumbs (about 1 cup)

Place asparagus, mushrooms and egg slices in layers in a buttered casserole dish, pour cheese sauce over all, put buttered bread crumbs on top, add salt, pepper and paprika. Bake at 305° until brown on top and bubbly—about 20 or 30 minutes. Serves 6.

Cabbage Patch: Famous Kentucky Recipes

"Moonbow," a rainbow-like spectrum produced from a combination of moonlight and mist at Cumberland Falls, is the only one in the Western Hemisphere.

Zucchini Casserole

2 cups sliced zucchini
1 medium onion, chopped
½ cup green pepper
1 egg, beaten

½ cup mayonnaise
1 cup Parmesan cheese
Salt and pepper
Ritz cracker crumbs

Cook zucchini, onion and pepper until just tender. Drain well. Add remaining ingredients. Top with Ritz cracker crumbs. Bake 40 minutes at 350°.

Best Made Better Recipes, Volume II

"Mrs. Wiggs" Boiled Cabbage

1 good-size head of cabbage
1 chunk of seasonin' meat, or
  ham hock is mighty good

1 red pepper pod
Some salt and pepper

Put the cabbage, meat, red pepper and salt and pepper in a kettle and cover with water. Cook down real slow. It's mighty good het up agin' and be sure to have some cornbread.

Cabbage Patch: Famous Kentucky Recipes

Stuffed Acorn Squash

2 acorn squash
½ cup bread crumbs
¼ cup chopped onion
¼ cup chopped green pepper
2 tablespoons melted butter

4 ounces grated sharp Cheddar
  cheese
Salt and pepper to taste
Paprika

Cut squash in half and scrape out seeds. Place in greased baking dish with skin side up and bake at 350° until tender (about 30 minutes).

Scrape pulp into bowl, being careful to keep shell intact. Mix pulp with bread crumbs, onion, green pepper, butter, and Cheddar cheese. Season with salt and pepper.

Stuff shells with mixture and sprinkle with paprika. Heat in 350° oven until hot. Yield: 4 servings.

To Market, To Market

Mixed Vegetable Casserole
(Cate's)

1 (20-ounce) package frozen
   mixed vegetables (cook as
   directed)
1 cup chopped celery
1 cup chopped onions

1 stick oleo, melted
1 cup grated cheese (cheddar)
½ cup mayonnaise
1 tube of crackers

Put cooked vegetables in greased casserole. Sauté onions and celery in part of the oleo. Mix with cheese and mayonnaise and spread over vegetables. Mix crushed crackers with rest of oleo. Spread over casserole. Bake 30 minutes at 350°.

The Wyman Sisters Cookbook

Spinach-Artichoke Casserole

2 (14-ounce) cans artichoke
   hearts, drained and halved
3 (10-ounce) packages frozen
   leaf spinach, cooked
Freshly ground pepper

3 (3-ounce) packages cream
   cheese, softened
¼ cup margarine, softened
¼ cup + 2 tablespoons milk
⅓ cup grated Parmesan cheese

Arrange artichokes on the bottom of a greased 1½-quart casserole. Cover with spinach and season with pepper. Beat next 3 ingredients together. Spread over spinach. Refrigerate about 24 hours. Sprinkle top of casserole with Parmesan cheese and bake at 375° for 40 minutes. Serves 6 to 7.

Favorite Fare II

Château Potatoes

6 cups mashed potatoes (cooked fresh or prepared with instant)
3 cups creamy cottage cheese
¾ cup sour cream
1½ tablespoons chopped chives or green onions
1 teaspoon salt
1 teaspoon Mrs. Dash
⅛ teaspoon pepper
Melted oleo
Slivered almonds

Combine first 7 ingredients until smooth (may use mixer). Place in 2½-quart casserole. Cover with almonds and melted oleo. Bake at 350° 30 minutes.

Campbellsville College Women's Club Cookbook

Friday Potatoes

5 or 6 medium potatoes
1 large onion
Dollop of butter
Salt and pepper

This is an "approximate" recipe. Decrease or enlarge according to the number at the table.

For four people, peel and dice 5 or 6 medium potatoes and 1 large onion. Add just a little salted water—about ½ inch. Bring to a boil and cook until both potatoes and onions are done. This does not take long—7 or 8 minutes. Drain, or take lid from kettle so the excess water will evaporate. Add a liberal dollop of butter and a hearty sprinkle of pepper.

This is an excellent dish for a "meat and potatoes and gravy" family when there is no gravy.

Years ago, Catholics did not eat meat on Friday. The problem of how to serve potatoes without gravy was met in several ways. This is a favorite of my family. Irish-Catholics, of course, were strong on potatoes for the big meal. Poor Irish-Catholics had more meatless days than meatless Fridays. There was never a complaint when Friday potatoes were served on more days than Friday. My aunts tell me that this dish was used in their home at the turn of the century. Their father used to tell them, "Pare the potatoes thin—the sweetest part is under the skin."

The Corn Island Cookbook

Ronnie Combs' Potatoes

7 or 8 medium potatoes
2 onions (medium) sliced
Sliced bacon

Parmesan cheese
Garlic salt
1 stick butter

Peel potatoes and slice roundways. Place 2 sheets of aluminum foil together for secure wrapping. First put a layer of sliced potatoes in foil then a layer of bacon and a layer of onions. Repeat until potatoes are used up. Sprinkle with Parmesan cheese and garlic salt. Place stick of butter on top and wrap foil tightly around potatoes. Cook on a grill or in oven. While cooking turn potatoes over without opening foil. Make sure foil is wrapped securely enough to not leak.

Mountain Recipe Collection

Zippy Buttered Potatoes
(Microwave)

4 medium potatoes
3 tablespoons butter or margarine

½ teaspoon garlic salt
½ teaspoon paprika
3 tablespoons Parmesan cheese

Scrub potatoes; microwave (HIGH) butter in 8-inch square glass baking dish 1–2 minutes or until melted. Blend in garlic salt, paprika and cheese. Quarter potatoes lengthwise (leave skin on).

Dip in butter mixture. Arrange cut-side down in dish. Cover with waxed paper. Microwave (HIGH) 12–14 minutes or until potatoes are tender. Rearrange once or twice. Makes 5–6 servings.

Lake Reflections

Low-Calorie Baked Potato Dressing

Most of the calories in a baked potato come from the butter or sour cream we slather on it to moisten it. Try using this dressing instead. It is also good on broccoli and other vegetables.

¼ cup mayonnaise	3 tablespoons Parmesan cheese
1 cup yogurt	

Put mayonnaise in a bowl or jar and stir it up to make it creamy. Add a little yogurt and stir again. Mix in the remaining yogurt and the Parmesan cheese. Makes about 1½ cups.

The Monterey Cookbook

Linda's Baked Potato Casserole

6 large potatoes	¼ cup parsley flakes
1 pint sour cream	1 teaspoon garlic powder
1 cup grated sharp cheese	Paprika
½ stick margarine	Salt, pepper to taste
1 small onion, grated	Cheddar cheese

Boil potatoes (already peeled) on stove until tender. Drain water; add all ingredients. Mix together with mixer. Pour into greased casserole. Sprinkle grated Cheddar cheese on top and cover. Bake 350° for 30 minutes, covered.

Entertaining the Louisville Way, Volume II

Fancy Potatoes

10 medium potatoes
1 package cream cheese
1 carton sour cream
4 tablespoons butter

½ cup chopped chives
Salt and pepper to taste
Paprika

Boil potatoes. Beat sour cream and cream cheese together, add peeled hot potatoes and beat until smooth. Add butter, chives and salt and pepper to taste. Pour into a well-greased (2-quart) casserole. Dot with butter and sprinkle with paprika. Bake at 350° for 25 minutes. Serves 8–10. Wonderful do-ahead dish for company.

The Crowning Recipes of Kentucky

New Potatoes with Caper Sauce

1 dozen new potatoes, small,
  scrubbed clean
½ cup butter
Salt and pepper to taste
1 teaspoon vinegar
2 tablespoons capers, minced

2 tablespoons fresh parsley,
  minced
⅓ cup grated Parmesan cheese
1 tablespoon green onion,
  minced

Boil potatoes until tender. If fairly large, cut in quarters before cooking. Combine remaining ingredients and add to hot potatoes after draining. Heat through. Serve potatoes covered with sauce.

The Monterey Cookbook

Man o' War's achievements on the racing oval are unparalleled even to this day. He won 20 of 21 starts, coming in second only once to a horse appropriately named Upset.

Ham 'n' Cheese Potatoes
(Microwave)

1 large potato, peeled and cubed (about 2 cups)
2 tablespoons chopped onion
1 tablespoon water
¼ pound cooked ham, cut in strips
½ cup shredded Cheddar cheese
¼ cup milk or half and half
1 tablespoon minced green pepper
¼ teaspoon dry mustard
1 drop Tabasco sauce

In 1-quart microwave casserole dish, place potato cubes, onion, and water. Cover with lid or plastic wrap, turning back one corner to vent. Microwave at HIGH (100% power) for 5 to 8 minutes, stirring after 3 minutes, until all potato pieces are almost tender. Add ham, cheese, milk, green pepper, mustard, and Tabasco sauce, gently stir to blend. Microwave at MEDIUM (50% power) for 4 to 7 minutes, just until the cheese begins to melt, stirring gently every 2 minutes. Let stand about 5 minutes, and stir again before serving. Makes about 2 servings.

Bell Ringing Recipes

Sweet Potato Casserole

3 cups cooked sweet potatoes (fresh or canned)
½ cup brown sugar
2 eggs, beaten
½ teaspoon salt
½ stick margarine, melted
½ cup evaporated milk
1½ teaspoons vanilla

TOPPING:
½ cup brown sugar
⅓ cup plain flour
1 cup pecans, chopped
⅓ stick margarine, melted

Mash sweet potatoes. Add sugar, eggs, salt, margarine, milk and vanilla. Put mixture into casserole dish. Mix topping ingredients and spread over sweet potato mixture. Bake at 325° for 30 minutes. Serves 6.

Sample West Kentucky

Creamed Sweet Potatoes

3 large baked potatoes
1 cup milk
1 cup sugar
1 tablespoon butter, melted

1 egg
Chopped nuts and dates
1 teaspoon vanilla

Mash potatoes; add milk, sugar, melted butter, slightly beaten egg, chopped dates, chopped nuts and vanilla. Bake in a buttered casserole or in orange shells. Cook 30 to 40 minutes in casserole, less time for orange shells.

The Junior Welfare League 50th Anniversary Cookbook

Sweet Potato-Honey Balls

2½ cups mashed, cooked sweet potatoes
¾ teaspoon salt
5 tablespoons butter or margarine, melted and divided

½ cup miniature marshmallows
½ cup honey
1 cup chopped pecans

Combine sweet potatoes, salt, and 2 tablespoons butter or margarine; stir in marshmallows. Chill.

Shape potato mixture into balls, using ¼ cup for each. Combine 2 tablespoons melted butter or margarine and honey in a heavy skillet. Add potato balls one at a time, quickly coating each with glaze. Roll potato balls in pecans; place in a greased shallow casserole. Drizzle with remaining butter or margarine. Bake at 350° for 15 to 20 minutes. Yield: 10 servings.

Stephensburg Homecoming Recipes

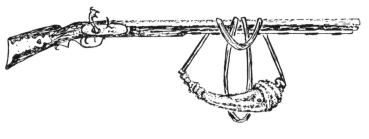

Sweet Potatoes

1 (20-ounce) can pineapple
 slices (or crushed pineapple)
2 (17-ounce) cans yams or sweet
 potatoes
¼ cup flour

3 tablespoons brown sugar
½ teaspoon cinnamon
⅛ teaspoon salt
3 tablespoons margarine
1 cup miniature marshmallows

Drain pineapple, reserving ¼ cup syrup. Line baking dish with pineapple. Arrange yams or sweet potatoes in center. Pour remaining syrup over them. Combine flour, brown sugar, cinnamon and salt in a small bowl. Cut in margarine until mixture resembles coarse crumbs. Sprinkle over sweet potatoes. Bake at 350° for 25 minutes. Top with marshmallows. Broil lightly until brown. Serves 6 to 8.

Somethin's Cookin' at LG&E

Fried Green Tomatoes

6 medium tomatoes (green, but
 turning pink)
1 cup cornmeal
½ teaspoon salt

¼ teaspoon pepper
½ teaspoon oregano
Bacon drippings

Cut tomatoes horizontally into ¼-inch thick slices, discarding the top and bottom slices. Mix cornmeal with seasonings. Coat the tomatoes well. In hot skillet containing bacon drippings, add tomato slices in one layer. Lower heat to medium and fry for about 6 more minutes, or until golden brown. Drain on paper towels. Repeat with remaining tomato slices. Serves 8.

The Kentucky Derby Museum Cookbook

Bourbon Baked Beans

My favorite way to prepare baked beans.

4 cans Boston baked beans
1 tablespoon molasses
⅓ cup strong coffee
¾ teaspoon dry mustard
½ cup chili sauce

⅓ cup bourbon
12 slices canned pineapple
  (optional)
Brown sugar (optional)

Place all ingredients except pineapple and sugar in a large baking dish. Cover, let stand 3 to 4 hours at room temperature. Preheat oven to 350°; bake, covered, about 35 to 40 minutes. Uncover, arrange pineapple on beans, brush liberally with brown sugar and continue baking about 30 minutes.

A Taste from Back Home

The home of Heaven Hill and Evan Williams bourbon is the largest family-owned distillery operation in the United States: Near Bardstown.

French Fried Cauliflower

1 large head cauliflower
2 eggs, beaten

¼ cup milk
Seasoned flour

Separate cauliflower in flowerets, mix eggs and milk together, then dip cauliflower in mixture and then into the seasoned flour. Drop into hot oil or lard and fry 2–3 minutes or until golden brown. The oil should be about 350°.

Favorite Recipes

Creamed Onions

2–3 cups small, whole onions ½ cup buttered crumbs
1½ cups medium White Sauce

Peel onions. Place in a large amount of boiling salted water. Pierce each onion with sharp knife or ice pick in center. This keeps them from coming apart. Boil uncovered about 20 minutes, or until tender. Overcooking develops strong flavor and odor. In a greased casserole arrange onions and medium White Sauce in layers. Top with buttered crumbs; sprinkle with paprika. Bake in moderate oven (375°) about 25 minutes or until browned. Makes 4 to 6 servings.

WHITE SAUCE:
4 tablespoons butter ¼ teaspoon pepper
4 tablespoons flour 2 cups milk
1 teaspoon salt

Melt butter over low heat; add flour, salt and pepper. Stir until well blended. Remove from heat. Gradually stir in milk; return to heat. Cook, stirring constantly, until thick and smooth. Makes 2 cups.

Stephensburg Homecoming Recipes

Glazed Onions

2 pounds small onions or 1 stick oleo
   canned onions 3 tablespoons sugar
1 can beef consommé 4 teaspoons lemon juice
1 cup water Salt and pepper to taste

In large pan cook onions in consommé and water. Drain and pat dry. In large skillet cook oleo and sugar, stirring constantly, until caramel color. Stir in lemon juice. (Be careful; it splatters.) Add onions and coat thoroughly. Simmer until copper color, about 30 minutes.

Campbellsville College Women's Club Cookbook

Baked Curry Onion

1 pound onions, sliced
3 tablespoons butter
2 tablespoons flour
½ cup soup stock (type of your choice)
½ cup milk

¼ teaspoon cayenne
¼ teaspoon curry
¼ teaspoon paprika
1 ounce grated cheese (type of your choice)
Salt and pepper

Boil onions for 15 minutes. Drain well and put in greased baking dish. Melt butter in saucepan. Add flour, making a roux. Add soup stock and milk all at once, stirring until thick. Add cayenne, curry and paprika. Add cheese, stirring until melted. Add salt and pepper to taste, if desired. Pour sauce over onions. Bake at 350° for 45 minutes. Preparation Time: 15 minutes + baking. Yield: 4–6 servings.

Great side dish with beef at a summer cookout.

CordonBluegrass

Fried Corn

Fresh corn on cob (8 to 10 ears)   1½ tablespoons sugar
3 tablespoons butter   ¼ cup water
Salt to taste

Shuck and clean corn. With a sharp knife, cut the top of the corn kernel into a bowl. With corn tilted into bowl, scrape pulp from cob. In a heavy skillet, melt butter and add corn. Add salt, sugar and water. Cook until thickened, stirring often. Add more water if needed.

Mountain Recipe Collection

Corn Soufflé
A light and fluffy vegetable dish.

2 cups fresh corn or 1 package   ½ teaspoon salt
  (10-ounces) frozen corn,   ⅛ teaspoon pepper
  thawed   1 cup milk
2 tablespoons flour   2 eggs, separated
2 tablespoons sugar   Butter

Mix together corn, flour, sugar, salt, pepper, and milk. Add egg yolks to mixture.

Beat egg whites until stiff and fold into corn mixture. Pour into a 1-quart casserole and dot with butter. Bake. Temperature: 350°. Time: 45 to 50 minutes. Yield: 6 servings.

To Market, To Market

The world's largest gold depository is at Fort Knox military reservation.

Robin's Nest Vegetable Pie

One (9-inch) unbaked pie shell	1 cup cooked broccoli
3 eggs	½ cup sautéed onions and
⅔ cup milk	mushrooms, combined
½ teaspoon salt	1 tomato, sliced

Place pie shell on oven rack. Beat eggs, milk and salt together; add vegetables, and pour into pie shell.

Bake at 400° for 35 minutes. Before removing from oven, place tomato slices on top, and bake an additional five minutes. Serves 4.

Dining in Historic Kentucky

Fettuccine with Three Cheeses

1 pound fetuccine	½ cup grated Romano cheese
4 egg yolks	¼ teaspoon basil
1 cup whipping cream	¼ teaspoon cracked pepper
½ cup shredded Swiss cheese	4 ounces goat cheese, crumbled

Cook fettuccine according to package directions. Rinse and drain. Let cool. Beat egg yolks with cream in saucepan. Add next 4 ingredients, fettucini and salt to taste. Cook over low heat until cheeses are melted, stirring constantly. Spoon onto serving plates. Sprinkle with goat cheese. Yields: 6 servings.

Note: Nutritional information does not include goat cheese.

Approx Per Serv: Cal 532, Prot 18.3 gr, Fat 24.5 gr, Chol 239.4 mg, Carbo 58.7 gr, Sod 159.7 mg, Potas 220.1 mg.

Capital Eating in Kentucky

Country Wild Rice

5 slices bacon, finely chopped
1 (6-ounce) yellow onion, finely
  chopped

1 cup wild rice
2½ cups chicken stock
1 bunch scallions, chopped

Cook bacon in skillet until crisp. Stir in onion. Cook until transparent. Add rice. Cook for 1 minute, stirring constantly. Add chicken stock; mix well. Simmer for 45 minutes or until rice is tender. Sprinkle with scallions. Yield: 6 servings.

Approx per serv: Cal 232, Prot 1.6 gr, Fat 13.3 gr, Chol 11.0 mg, Carbo 23.7 gr, Sod 432.6 mg, Potas 195.0 mg.

Capital Eating in Kentucky

Vegetarian Spaghetti Sauce

¼–½ cup olive oil
1 large eggplant, cubed
2 onions, chopped
1 bell pepper, chopped
4 cloves garlic, minced
1 (12-ounce) can tomato paste
1 quart whole tomatoes or
  about 4–5 fresh tomatoes,
  chopped

2 tablespoons oregano
1 tablespoon basil
3 bay leaves
1 tablespoon parsley
Salt and pepper
½ cup wine

Sauté the eggplant, onions and pepper in the olive oil until soft. Add the remaining ingredients, except the wine and mix well. Let simmer 30–40 minutes until thick and rich. Add wine about 10 minutes before serving and heat through. This sauce is delicious served over any type pasta, topped with grated Parmesan cheese. I especially like it over spinach fettucini, with fresh feta or bleu cheese crumbled on top.

The Monterey Cookbook

Hot (Curried) Fruit Compote
Serve with lamb, game, duckling, veal roast.

1 large can pears
2 large cans freestone peaches
1 large can pineapple chunks
1 box dried apricots

1 cup light-brown sugar
½ stick butter
2 tablespoons curry powder
(optional)

Drain fruits very thoroughly in a colander for an hour or more. Arrange fruit attractively in a shallow casserole and pour off any juice. Add sugar. Mix curry powder with sugar, if this is to be a curried compote. Dot with butter and bake uncovered in 350° oven for 1 hour. Just before serving, ½ cup of salted almonds may be sprinkled over the fruit. Serves 12–16.

The Farmington Cookbook

Pan-Fried June Apples

Mother seldom canned or dried June apples. The winter had been long and we yearned for fresh fruit. She fried the June apples and served them with hot biscuits, freshly churned butter, and milk. Sometimes she made applesauce.

2 tablespoons bacon drippings
4 cups peeled (or unpeeled)
   sliced apples

1½ cups sugar
½ teaspoon cinnamon
½ teaspoon salt

Heat bacon drippings in skillet and add apples. Stir in sugar, cinnamon, and salt, then cover and cook for about five minutes, or until the sugar liquefies. Remove lid and fry, stirring occasionally, until apples are tender, and the liquid is cooked away. Good served with fresh butter and hot biscuits. Serves 4 to 6.

*More Than Moonshine: Appalachian Recipes and
Recollections*

Russellville Hot Pickled Okra Or Green Beans

Aunt Eva's favorite.

Fresh okra or green beans
1 quart white vinegar

½ cup water
¼ cup pickling salt

ADD TO EACH PINT JAR:
1 teaspoon dill seed
1 hot red pepper

1 hot green pepper
2 cloves garlic

Place a half teaspoon of dill seed in bottom of each sterilized jar. Wash okra and pack tightly as possible in jars, being careful not to bruise. Add a half teaspoon dill seed, the red and green pepper, and garlic. Bring vinegar, water and salt to a boil and pour this hot mixture over the okra. Seal. Adjust caps and process in water bath canner at simmering temperature for 15 minutes. Cool. Test for seal. Store for 6 weeks before serving. Serve cold. Yield: 4 pints.

A Taste from Back Home

Crispy Pickles

4 quarts sliced cucumbers
1½ cups sliced white onions
2 large cloves garlic
½ cup salt
2 trays ice, crushed

4 cups sugar
1½ teaspoons turmeric
1½ teaspoons mustard seed
3 cups white vinegar

Wash, drain, and slice cucumbers; add onion, garlic, and salt, and mix thoroughly. Cover with ice and allow to stand 3 hours in a crock. Drain, and remove garlic. Combine remaining ingredients and heat to boiling; add cucumber and onion to this mixture. Return to boil, lower heat, and simmer 5 minutes. Fill sterilized jars to within ½ inch of the top and seal. Makes 5 to 6 pints.

More Than Moonshine: Appalachian Recipes and Recollections

Bread and Butter Pickles
(Bernice's)

This recipe originally came from a neighbor "Miss Alice" and is always referred to as Miss Alice's pickle recipe. Mother rarely served a Sunday or "company" dinner without serving some of "Miss Alice's" pickles and some of her own pickled beets. "Miss Alice" was not really a single lady, but lived with her husband, "Mr. George," and their parrot, "Polly," in the house across Main Street from Bernice and her family. Polly was an interesting bird and would call each of us by name. She could sing several bars of the "Old Time Religion," and professed to be both a Republican and a Cambellite.

1 gallon cucumbers	**2 green peppers**
8 small onions	**½ cup salt**

Slice cucumbers, onions, and green peppers thin, sprinkle with salt, then soak in ice water for three hours (keep adding ice to water, if necessary.) Drain and pat dry with clean towels.

SYRUP:

5 cups sugar	**2 tablespoons mustard seed**
1½ teaspoons turmeric	**1 teaspoon celery seed**
½ teaspoon ground cloves	**5 cups vinegar**

When this mixture boils thoroughly, pour pickles in. Scald but do not let boil. (The cucumbers and onions will begin to look transparent just before boiling.) Pack sterilized jars with the pickles, then seal. Do not use the pickles for two weeks, as this time is required for completing the pickling process.

The Wyman Sisters Cookbook

Corn Relish

8 large cucumbers, peeled and
   seeded
20 cobs large sweet corn
3 large onions
8–10 ripe tomatoes
1 red hot pepper
1 red sweet pepper
1 green sweet pepper
3 stalks celery
1 tablespoon celery seed
1 teaspoon mustard seed
5 tablespoons flour
1 tablespoon turmeric
Salt
5 cups white sugar
1½ pints vinegar

Let chopped cucumber, tomatoes, onions, pepper, celery stand with salt for ½ hour. Drain, add vinegar, spices, sugar etc. Boil for 1 hour. Place in jars and seal.

Larue County Kitchens

Home Canned Tomato Sauce

18 tomatoes
2 green peppers
2 medium onions
2 teaspoons salt
1 teaspoon ground cinnamon
½ teaspoon ground cloves
1 teaspoon allspice
2 cups vinegar

Peel, core, and chop tomatoes. Chop peppers and onions. Combine all ingredients and boil slowly 4 hours or until thick. Fill hot jars and process 10 minutes in boiling water bath.

Favorite Recipes

Dill-Cheese Sauce

1 (11-ounce) can Cheddar
   cheese soup, undiluted
2 teaspoons dried dill weed
¼ teaspoon aromatic bitters
½ cup plain yogurt

Combine all ingredients in saucepan. Cook and stir over medium heat until heated through but not boiling. Yields 2 cups. Serve over broccoli, asparagus, cauliflower, or baked potato.

Holy Chow

Cakes

Chief Paduke, for whom General William Clark named Paducah.

Buttermilk Pound Cake

1 cup butter
2 cups sugar
4 eggs
2 teaspoons lemon flavoring

1 cup buttermilk
3 cups flour
⅛ teaspoon salt
½ teaspoon soda

Cream butter. Add sugar gradually and cream well. Add eggs one at a time beating well after each addition. Add flavoring and mix well. Add flour, salt and soda alternately with buttermilk. Bake at 300° for 1 hour.

GLAZE:
¼ cup butter
⅓ cup lemon juice

⅔ cup sugar

Beat ingredients until sugar is dissolved. Allow cake to thoroughly cool before glazing.

Mountain Recipe Collection

Apricot Brandy Pound Cake

1 cup butter or margarine
3 cups sugar
6 eggs
3 cups all-purpose flour
¼ teaspoon baking soda
¼ teaspoon salt
1 (8-ounce) carton sour cream

½ cup apricot brandy
1 teaspoon orange extract
1 teaspoon vanilla extract
½ teaspoon lemon extract
½ teaspoon rum extract
¼ teaspoon almond extract

Cream softened butter; gradually add sugar, beating until mixture is light and fluffy. Add eggs, one at a time, beating well after each addition. Combine flour, soda and salt; mix and set aside. Combine sour cream, brandy and flavorings. Add to creamed mixture alternately with flour mixture; beginning and ending with flour mixture. Pour batter into a greased and floured 10-inch tube pan. Bake 325° for 1 hour and 20 minutes, or until wooden toothpick inserted in center comes out clean. Cool in pan 10 to 15 minutes. Remove from pan and cool completely.

Mountain Laurel Encore

Delectable Sour Cream Pound Cake

This is a soft, velvety pound cake that keeps better than any pound cake I know. It has a delicious crunchy top that comes from being baked in low heat—not from an overload of sugar. This cake is just as delicious when the sugar is cut to 2¾ cups, which makes it especially delightful for breakfast or tea with a dish of strawberries. Bake it both ways. You will love this cake.

3 cups sifted all-purpose flour
¼ teaspoon baking soda
¼ teaspoon salt
1 cup (2 sticks) butter, cut into pieces
3 cups sugar (2¾ cups for cakes to be served with fruit)

6 large eggs, separated
1 cup sour cream
1½ teaspoons vanilla extract or cognac vanilla or ⅔ teaspoon ground mace

Preheat the oven to 325°. Combine the sifted flour with the baking soda and salt, and sift again. Set aside. Cream the butter and sugar thoroughly with an electric mixer. Add the egg yolks, and beat hard until you have a fairly smooth mixture. This will not "ribbon" with just the yolks.

Add the flour mixture in batches, alternating with the sour cream, blending by hand with a rubber spatula or a whisk. Blend in the vanilla or mace.

Beat the egg whites until they hold a stiff peak but are not dry and grainy. Gently fold them into the cake batter. Spoon the batter into a greased and lightly floured heavy 9- or 10-inch tube pan, or two 8 × 4 × 3-inch loaf pans, filling the pans not more than three-quarters full. Bake until the cake springs back at once when lightly touched, about 1 hour and 15 to 20 minutes (this will vary with the pans used). A cake tester or skewer inserted into the cake should come out clean. Remove the cake from the oven and allow it to rest 5 minutes. Run a thin knife around the edges of the pan to loosen the cake, and unmold it onto a rack. Turn the cake right side up to cool. Store in a tightly closed plastic or tin box. Serves 10 to 15.

The Heritage of Southern Cooking

Praline Cheesecake

1½ pounds cream cheese
2 cups brown sugar
3 eggs

2 tablespoons flour
2 teaspoons vanilla
½ cup pecans

CRUST:
1 cup graham cracker crumbs
3 tablespoons sugar

3 tablespoons butter

Combine cream cheese and brown sugar in mixer; when thoroughly mixed, add everything else. Pour into crust that is in 10-inch springform pan. Bake at 350° 35 minutes. Serves 12.

Sample West Kentucky

Cherry Cheesecake

1 box Deluxe II Duncan Hines
  yellow cake mix
2 tablespoons oil
2 (8-ounce) packages cream
  cheese
½ cup sugar

4 eggs
1½ cups milk
3 tablespoons lemon juice
3 teaspoons vanilla
1 (1-pound 5-ounce) can cherry
  pie filling

Preheat oven to 300°. Reserve 1 cup of dry cake mix. In large mixing bowl, combine remaining cake mix, 1 egg and oil. Mix well until crumbly. Press crust mixture evenly into bottom of greased 13 × 9 × 2-inch pan and ¾ way up on sides. In same bowl, blend cream cheese and sugar. Add 3 eggs and reserved cake mix. Beat 1 minute at medium speed. At low speed, slowly add milk and flavorings. Mix until smooth. Pour into crust. Bake at 300° for 45–55 minutes until center is firm. When cool, top with pie filling. Store in refrigerator. To freeze, cover with foil.

Somethin's Cookin' at LG&E

Butter Pecan Cheesecake

1½ cups graham cracker crumbs
⅓ cup sugar
⅓ cup butter or margarine, melted
½ cup finely chopped pecans
3 (8-ounce) packages cream cheese, softened
1½ cups sugar

3 eggs
2 (8-ounce) cartons commercial sour cream
1 teaspoon vanilla extract
½ teaspoon butter flavoring
1 cup finely chopped pecans, toasted

Combine first 4 ingredients, mixing well. Reserve ⅓ cup mixture; firmly press remaining mixture on bottom of a 9-inch springform pan.

Beat cream cheese with an electric mixer until light and fluffy; gradually add 1½ cups sugar, mixing well. Add eggs, one at a time, beating well after each addition. Add sour cream and flavorings; mix well. Stir in 1 cup pecans.

Spoon into prepared pan; sprinkle with reserved crumb mixture. Bake at 475° for 10 minutes; reduce temperature to 300° and bake an additional 50 minutes. Let cool to room temperature on a wire rack; chill. Before serving, spoon Praline Sauce over each piece.

PRALINE SAUCE:
1 cup light corn syrup
½ cup sugar
⅓ cup butter or margarine

1 egg, beaten
1 tablespoon vanilla extract
1 cup coarsely chopped pecans

Combine first four ingredients in a heavy saucepan; mix well. Bring to a boil over medium heat, stirring constantly; boil 2 minutes without stirring. Remove from heat; stir in vanilla and pecans.

A Tasting Tour Through Washington County

Eden Shale's Cheesecake

6 tablespoons butter
8 double graham crackers,
  crushed
3 tablespoons sugar
1 cup butter
3 ounces unsweetened
  chocolate
2 cups light brown sugar
1 cup granulated sugar
2 tablespoons flour
4 eggs

4 teaspoons milk
2 teaspoons vanilla
3 (8-ounce) packages cream
  cheese
1¼ cups granulated sugar
⅛ teaspoon salt
3 eggs
1 teaspoon vanilla
2 cups sour cream
¼ cup granulated sugar
1 teaspoon vanilla

Melt 6 tablespoons of butter. Add crushed graham crackers and 3 tablespoons sugar. Press into bottom and sides of a 10-inch springform pan. Set aside. Melt 1 cup butter with chocolate. Remove from heat. Add 2 cups brown sugar, 1 cup granulated sugar and flour. Beat in 4 eggs, one at a time. Add milk and 2 teaspoons vanilla. Pour into prepared crust.

Cream 3 packages of cream cheese with 1¼ cups granulated sugar and ⅛ teaspoon salt until fluffy. Add 3 eggs separately. Add 1 teaspoon vanilla. Layer over chocolate mixture, do not stir or mix layers. Bake at 350° for 1 hour. Check every 5 minutes thereafter until center is soft set. Allow to rest for 15 minutes.

Combine 2 cups sour cream, ¼ cup granulated sugar and 1 teaspoon vanilla. Spread over top of cake. Return to oven for 10 minutes. Allow to cool for 1 hour, then refrigerate for at least 4 hours. Freezes well. Simply divine! A well-guarded secret until now! Serves 16–20.

Fillies Flavours

Cream Cheese Cupcakes

1 box vanilla wafers
2 (8-ounce) packages cream
  cheese
¾ cup sugar

2 eggs
1 teaspoon vanilla
1 can cherry pie filling

Mix cream cheese and sugar until creamy. Add eggs and vanilla. Put 1 vanilla wafer in each cupcake liner. Put 2 tablespoons of mix on top. Bake at 370° for 15 to 20 minutes. Let cool; put 1 tablespoon pie filling on top. Yields 24.

Best Made Better Recipes, Volume II

Fresh Peach Cake

1 package yellow or white cake
  mix
1½ cups sugar
4 tablespoons flour
4 cups fresh chopped peaches

½ cup water
1 (8-ounce) carton sour cream
2 cartons whipping cream
3 tablespoons powdered sugar

Bake cake and split into layers. Combine sugar, flour, peaches and water. Cook over slow heat until thick; remove from heat and cool completely. Assemble cake by placing first layer on a platter, top with peach mixture, then sour cream and continue to do this until you finish.

Whip the cream and add the powdered sugar. Frost the cake and refrigerate.

The Junior Welfare League 50th Anniversary Cookbook

Harrodsburg was the first permanent settlement west of the Alleghenies. "The Legend of Daniel Boone" and "Lincoln" are two exciting outdoor dramas, performed there each year from mid-June through August.

Almond Cake with Raspberry Sauce
. . . has the consistency of cheese cake

¾ cup sugar
½ cup unsalted butter, at room
   temperature
8 ounces almond paste
3 eggs
¼ teaspoon almond extract

1 tablespoon Kirsch or Triple
   Sec
¼ cup all-purpose flour
⅓ teaspoon baking powder
Confectioners' sugar

Combine sugar, butter and almond paste, blending well; beat in eggs, almond extract and liqueur. Gently blend in flour and baking powder just until mixed. Do not overbeat! Pour batter into a buttered and floured 8-inch round pan. Bake at 350° for 40 to 50 minutes or until tester comes out clean. Invert on a cake plate and sprinkle with confectioners' sugar.

SAUCE:

1 pint fresh, or 1 (12-ounce)
   package frozen, red
   raspberries

2 tablespoons sugar (or less) to
   taste

Combine ingredients in a blender container and purée. Press through a sieve to remove seeds. Serve over thin slices of cake. Serves 10 to 12.

Bluegrass Winners

Pineapple Whipped Cream Cake

1 (8-inch) angel food cake
½ pint whipping cream,
  whipped
1 (8¼ ounce) can crushed
  pineapple

1 (3¾-ounce) package vanilla
  pudding
1 cup milk

Whip cream and fold in pineapple. Prepare instant pudding, using cup of milk instead of amount called for on package. Fold into cream-pineapple mixture. Slice cake crosswise twice, making 3 layers. Spread pineapple filling between layers; cover top and sides of cake. Refrigerate for several hours, then serve.

Kentucky Kitchens

Coconut-Sour Cream Layer Cake

1 (18½-ounce) box butter
  flavored cake mix
2 cups sugar
1 (16-ounce) carton sour cream

1 (12-ounce) package frozen
  coconut, thawed
1½ cups frozen non-dairy
  whipped topping, thawed

Prepare cake mix according to package directions, making 2 (8-inch) layers. When completely cool, split both layers. Combine sugar, sour cream and coconut; blending well. Chill. Reserve 1 cup sour cream mixture for frosting and spread remainder between layers of cake. Combine reserved sour cream mixture with whipped topping; blend until smooth. Spread on top and sides of cake. Seal cake in an airtight container and refrigerate for 3 days before serving. This cake can also be prepared in 9 × 13-inch sheet cake pan. Stores well.

Mountain Laurel Encore

Applesauce Fruitcake

1½ cups sugar	1 cup oats
1 cup margarine	2 eggs (beaten)
2 teaspoons cinnamon	1 cup dark seedless raisins
1 teaspoon cloves	½ cup chopped nuts
1 teaspoon allspice	½ cup chopped candied cherries
1½ cups sifted flour	1 cup chopped dates
½ teaspoon salt	2 cups sweetened applesauce
1½ teaspoons soda	

Cream sugar, butter, spices until light and fluffy. Sift together flour, soda, salt; reserve 1 cup flour mixture. Stir in oats, Add flour-oat mixture to creamed mixture alternately with eggs. Toss fruits and nuts with reserved 1 cup flour mixture. Add to batter. Add applesauce. Pour into greased 10-inch tube pan. Bake in preheated slow oven (325°) about 1½ hours. Cool in pan on wire rack. Remove from pan and wrap in aluminum foil for 2 or 3 days, before slicing. Makes 1 fruitcake.

Note: I make 4 or 5 of these cakes for Christmas gifts each year.

Mountain Recipe Collection

Fresh Apple Cake

CAKE:

1¼ cups cooking oil	1 teaspoon soda
2 cups sugar	3 cups raw, sliced apples
3 eggs	1½ cups chopped pecans or
3 cups flour	walnuts
1 teaspoon salt	1 teaspoon vanilla

Mix oil, sugar and eggs thoroughly with mixer. Stir in dry ingredients, sifted together. Then fold in apples, nuts, and vanilla. Bake in 9 × 13-inch greased baking dish for 1 hour at 325°. Leave cake in pan and cover with the following glaze.

GLAZE:

1 cup light brown sugar	¼ cup cream
1 stick margarine	1 teaspoon vanilla

CONTINUED

CONTINUED

Combine ingredients in small saucepan and cook for 2½ minutes, stirring constantly. Spoon over cake while both cake and sauce are warm. This cake will stay moist for days.

The Junior Welfare League 50th Anniversary Cookbook

Moravian Sugar Cake

CAKE:

1 stick margarine
4 tablespoons shortening
1 cup sugar
2 eggs
1 package dry yeast, softened in
  ¼ cup warm water
2 teaspoons salt
1 cup mashed potatoes, nothing
  added
1 cup potato water
6–8 cups flour

Cream margarine, shortening, and sugar. Beat in eggs. Add yeast, salt, potatoes, and potato water; mix well. Add flour to make soft dough. Let rise 2–3 hours. Pat out in 3 well-greased 12 × 18-inch pans and allow to rise 2 more hours.

FILLING:

1 stick margarine
Cinnamon
1 pound brown sugar
1 small can evaporated milk

After second rising, make holes in top of cake and fill with bits of margarine. Cover heavily with cinnamon, then with brown sugar. Drizzle evaporated milk over top. Bake at 400° for 20 minutes. Preparation Time: 30 minutes + rising + baking. Yield: three 12 × 18-inch cakes.

You can use any size pans. It reheats very well at 300°.

CordonBluegrass

 Ashland was the estate of Henry Clay, "the Great Compromiser," a major national political figure in the first half of the 19th century.

Exquisite Coconut Cake

2¾ cups sifted cake flour
4½ teaspoons baking powder
1¾ cups sugar
1 teaspoon salt
⅔ cup soft shortening

2 teaspoons flavoring
¾ cup milk
½ cup milk
5 egg whites, unbeaten

Sift together dry ingredients. Add shortening, ¾ cup milk, and flavoring. Beat 2 minutes. Add ½ cup milk and egg whites, and beat 2 more minutes. Pour into 2 (9-inch) layer pans that have been greased and floured. Bake in 350° oven for 30 to 35 minutes.

PINEAPPLE FILLING:
¾ cup sugar
¼ teaspoon salt
3 tablespoons cornstarch

1 tablespoon butter
1 small can crushed pineapple
  (reserve juice)

Add enough water to reserved juice to make ¾ cup. Gradually stir into sugar, salt and cornstarch mixture. Bring to boil over direct heat, stirring constantly. Boil 1 minute. Remove from heat and stir in butter and crushed pineapple. Cool. Put layers together with this. Frost with Butter Icing.

BUTTER ICING:
⅓ cup soft butter
3 cups sifted confectioners'
  sugar

3 tablespoons cream
1½ teaspoons flavoring
Coconut

Blend butter and sugar, stir in cream and flavoring until smooth. Frost cake and cover with coconut.

Larue County Kitchens

French Walnut Torte

CAKE:

1½ cups whipping cream
1½ cups sugar
3 eggs

3 teaspoons vanilla
1¾ cups self-rising flour
1 cup ground walnuts

Heat oven to 350°. Grease and flour three 8-inch cake pans. In medium bowl, whip cream until stiff peaks form; refrigerate. In a large bowl, beat sugar, eggs and vanilla 5 minutes at high speed. Lightly spoon flour into measuring cup; level off. Combine flour and one cup ground walnuts. Add flour mixture and whipped cream alternately to sugar mixture, beginning and ending with flour mixture. Pour evenly into pans. Bake at 350° for 25 to 35 minutes. Cool 15 minutes. Remove from pans.

GLAZE:

1 cup apricot or peach preserves   2 tablespoons sugar

In small saucepan, heat preserves and sugar just until warm, and sugar dissolves. Reserve ½ cup glaze for sides of cake. Spread remaining glaze on top of warm layers. Chill layers and reserve glaze (for 30 minutes).

FROSTING:

4 cups powdered sugar
½ cup softened margarine
1 teaspoon vanilla

1 (8-ounce) package softened
    cream cheese
½ to 1 cup ground walnuts

In medium bowl, beat all frosting ingredients, except walnuts, for 2 minutes at medium speed. Use one-third of frosting; frost top of first glazed layer. Place second glazed layer over frosting; spread with one-third of frosting. Top with third glazed layer; spread top with remaining frosting. Do not frost sides. Sprinkle ½ cup walnuts over top. Chill 30 minutes and spread reserved ½ cup glaze on sides of cake. Refrigerate at least one hour or until served.

Country Cookbook

Christmas Jam Cake

1 cup butter or shortening	1 cup buttermilk
3 cups sugar	3 cups flour
6 eggs	1 teaspoon allspice
1 cup blackberry jam	1 teaspoon nutmeg
2 cups strawberry jam	1 teaspoon cinnamon
1½ teaspoons soda	1 cup chopped pecans

Cream butter and sugar. Add eggs, one at a time. Blend well. Do not use mixer for balance of the cake or it will be crumbly. Stir in jam. Stir soda into buttermilk. Sift dry ingredients together two times. Add dry ingredients alternately with buttermilk mixture. Begin and end with flour mixture. Fold in pecans. Pour into three layer cake pans lined with foil and then greased and floured. (The foil prevents a heavy crust from forming.) Bake in 300° oven for approximately 1 hour and 15 minutes. Test for doneness with toothpick. Frost between layers and on sides with carmel or other favorite icing.

What's Cooking for the Holidays

Raspberry Jam Cake

1½ cups sugar	1 teaspoon cloves
1 cup butter	1½ teaspoons soda
2 eggs	A little sour milk or buttermilk
1 teaspoon cinnamon	1 cup raspberry jam
1 teaspoon allspice	2 cups cake flour

Preheat oven to 350°. Cream together sugar and butter. Add well-beaten eggs, cinnamon, allspice and cloves. Dissolve soda in a little sour milk or buttermilk and add to above mixture. Last of all add jam and cake flour. If two cups flour are not enough, add a little more to make proper dough consistency. Bake in a loaf tin or tube pan until cake tests done.

More Than Moonshine: Appalachian Recipes and Recollections

Holiday Chocolate Cake
(Absolutely delicious)

2 cups sugar
1¾ cups unsifted all-purpose
  flour
¾ cup cocoa
2 teaspoons baking soda
1 teaspoon baking powder

1 teaspoon salt
2 eggs
1 cup buttermilk
1 cup strong black coffee
½ cup vegetable oil
2 teaspoons vanilla

Combine sugar, flour, cocoa, baking soda, baking powder, and salt in large bowl. Add eggs, buttermilk, coffee, oil, and vanilla. Beat at medium speed for 2 minutes (batter will be thin). Pour into 2 greased and floured 9-inch round cake pans. Bake at 350° for 30 to 35 minutes. Cool 10 minutes. Remove from pans. Cool completely.

Slice cake layers in halves horizontally. Place bottom slice on serving plate; top with ⅓ of Ricotta Cheese Filling. Alternate cake layers and filling, ending with cake on top. Frost with Chocolate Whipped Cream.

RICOTTA CHEESE FILLING:
1¾ cups (15-ounces) ricotta
  cheese
¼ cup granulated sugar
3 tablespoons Grand Marnier or
  orange flavored liqueur or
  orange juice concentrate

¼ cup candied red or green
  cherries, coarsely chopped
⅓ cup semi-sweet chocolate
  mini-chips

Combine ricotta cheese, sugar, and liqueur in small bowl. Beat until smooth. Fold in candied fruit and mini-chips. (If ricotta cheese is unavailable, use 1 cup heavy cream. Whip with sugar and liqueur until stiff.)

CHOCOLATE WHIPPED CREAM:
⅓ cup confectioners' sugar
2 tablespoons cocoa

1 cup heavy cream
1 teaspoon vanilla

Combine sugar and cocoa in small bowl. Add cream and vanilla; beat until stiff. Cover top of cake.

A Tasting Tour Through Washington County

Luscious Chocolate Cake

There could be only one name for this cake and that is luscious. It is a lovely chocolate sponge cake, and one of the best of its genre. The texture is so soft and moist, one would think it was made with butter. I wish I had a recording of the many telephone calls I have received about this cake. One letter writer said, "I ate all I could, but I did not want to leave it, so I just sat down beside it."

Although this cake has always been wonderful, it was made truly luscious the day I added a thin layer of apricot preserves under the frosting.

4 ounces unsweetened chocolate	1 teaspoon baking powder
1 cup milk	Tiny pinch of salt
5 large eggs, separated	1½ teaspoons cognac vanilla
2 cups sugar	⅓ cup apricot preserves
1 cup all-purpose flour, sifted	Rich Chocolate Frosting (recipe follows)

Preheat the oven to 350°. Grease and dust with flour or line with foil two 9-inch round cake pans.

Combine the chocolate and the milk in the top of a double boiler, and heat over hot water until the chocolate has melted. Beat until smooth. Remove from the heat and allow to cool down just a bit. While the chocolate mixture is cooling, beat the egg yolks and sugar thoroughly with an electric mixer. (The sugar will remain granular.) Add the chocolate mixture and beat very hard until the sugar is no longer granular. Fold the flour, baking powder, salt, and vanilla into the chocolate mixture by hand.

Beat the egg whites until they are stiff but not dry and grainy. Fold them into the chocolate batter. Spoon the batter into the prepared pans. The pans should be no more than three quarters full. Bake until the cake springs back at once when lightly touched, about 35 minutes.

Invert the cakes onto racks or onto a wooden board covered with wax paper. Allow the cakes to cool completely before frosting. Spread 1 cake layer with the apricot preserves. Cover the preserves with a coating of the chocolate frosting. Center the second layer on top of the first. Frost the top and sides of

CONTINUED

CONTINUED

the cake lavishly with the remaining frosting. The frosting must be thick. Serves 16.

Variations: This makes 2 cakes from 1 recipe of Luscious Chocolate Cake: Bake the cake in two 8-inch springform pans. Make a double batch of Rich Chocolate Frosting. When the cakes have cooled, place them on large sheets of wax paper or foil on a flat surface. Slice the cakes in half horizontally with a long, sharp knife. Spread half of the apricot preserves on the bottom layer of each cake. Cover each cake with the second layer and frost them heavily in a swirl design. Place the cakes on platters, and garnish with glazed apricots. Each cake serves 8.

Luscious Chocolate Rum Cake: Bake the cake layers. Make the Rich Chocolate Frosting, adding ¼ cup Jamaican rum. Blend it in thoroughly, then add boiling water a scant tablespoon at a time until the frosting is of good spreading consistency. Spread one cake layer with the apricot preserves. Spread some of the frosting over the preserves. Put the second layer on top, and frost the sides and top of the cake. Garnish the top of the cake with thin slivers of glazed apricots if they are available. Very attractive, indeed, and apricots are delicious with chocolate and rum. You'll see.

RICH CHOCOLATE FROSTING:

4 ounces unsweetened chocolate	1 teaspoon vanilla extract or cognac vanilla (see Index), or more to taste
8 tablespoons (1 stick) butter	
2¾ cups confectioners' sugar	5 tablespoons boiling water, or as needed
Tiny pinch of salt	

Melt the chocolate and the butter in a double boiler over hot water. Sift the powdered sugar with the salt into a large mixing bowl. Blend in the chocolate mixture and the vanilla. Add boiling water a tablespoon at a time, beating constantly, until the frosting is smooth, pliable, but still very thick. Cool a bit before frosting the cake.

If necessary, thin the frosting a bit with boiling water. If the frosting becomes dull looking, a little boiling water will restore its sheen. If the frosting is too thin, beat it extremely hard with an electric mixer—it will thicken up.

The Heritage of Southern Cooking

Bourbon Fudge Cake

½ cup butter, softened
2 cups sugar
4 ounces unsweetened
  chocolate, melted and cooled
2 eggs, at room temperature
1 teaspoon vanilla
2 tablespoons Bourbon

2 cups sifted cake flour
2 teaspoons baking powder
½ teaspoon salt
½ cup – 2 tablespoons milk
1 cup finely chopped pecans or
  walnuts
Bourbon Fudge Frosting

Cream butter; gradually add sugar and beat until fluffy. Blend in chocolate; beat in eggs, one at a time. Add vanilla and Bourbon. Sift dry ingredients together and add alternately with milk in three additions, beginning and ending with flour. Fold in nuts. Bake in two greased and floured 9-inch cake pans at 350° for 35 minutes. Cool and frost with Bourbon Fudge Frosting.

BOURBON FUDGE FROSTING:

½ cup unsalted butter
2 ounces unsweetened
  chocolate
1 egg, at room temperature
About 3 cups sifted
  confectioners' sugar

1 teaspoon vanilla
1 teaspoon lemon juice
3 tablespoons Bourbon
1 cup finely chopped pecans or
  walnuts

Combine butter and chocolate and melt over low heat. Stir to blend; cool slightly. In a mixing bowl, beat the egg and add one cup of the sugar. Gradually add chocolate mixture, beating constantly. Stir in vanilla, lemon juice, and Bourbon. Gradually add remaining 2 cups of sugar. Continue beating, adding sugar as necessary until frosting is smooth and of spreading consistency. Stir in nuts.

Favorite Fare II

Hilbert's Turtle Cake

1 box German chocolate cake
  mix
1 (14-ounce) package caramels
½ cup evaporated milk

1 (6-ounce) package chocolate
  chips
1 cup chopped nuts
Butter

Prepare cake mix according to directions using butter instead of oil. Bake ½ of batter in 9 × 13-inch pan for 15 minutes. In a pan melt caramels and evaporated milk. Pour over cake, add chocolate chips and nuts. Cover with remaining cake batter. Bake 350° for 20–25 minutes.

Entertaining the Louisville Way, Volume II

Kentucky Sauce

1 cup brown sugar
1 cup granulated sugar
1 cup water
1 cup strawberry preserves

1 cup pecans, broken
1 orange
1 lemon
1 cup bourbon

Combine sugars with water and cook until syrup reaches 240° on thermometer, or until it almost spins a thread. Remove from heat and stir in preserves and pecans. Remove rind from orange and lemon with potato parer and chop real fine. Cut off and discard white membrane from fruit and remove sections. Cut sections into small pieces. Add cut-up rind, fruit and bourbon to first mixture; set in refrigerator to ripen. Keeps indefinitely. Must do ahead. Yield: 1 quart plus. Serve over ice cream, gingerbread, plain cake or anything that calls for a topping.

Mountain Laurel Encore

Gingerbread

1½ cups sugar
2 eggs
1 stick butter
1 cup molasses
1 tablespoon vanilla
4 cups plain flour

1 tablespoon baking powder
1 tablespoon soda
1 teaspoon each cinnamon,
    cloves, ginger, nutmeg
1 cup lukewarm water

Cream sugar, eggs and butter. Add molasses and vanilla. Sift flour, baking powder, soda and spices together. Add to sugar mixture alternately with lukewarm water. Mix well until no lumps appear. Pour into muffin tins and bake at 350° until done.

Note: This recipe was handed down to Mrs. Panky by her grandmother who came to Harveyton, Ky in 1920 from Tennessee. Mrs. Panky has been making this gingerbread since she was eight years old and her husband has sold it on the streets of Hazard for twenty years. Everyone calls him "The Gingerbread Man."

Mountain Recipe Collection

Old-Fashioned Lemon Sauce

1 cup sugar
½ cup butter or margarine
¼ cup water

1 egg, well beaten
¾ teaspoon grated lemon peel
3 tablespoons lemon juice

In medium saucepan combine all ingredients. Heat to boiling over medium heat, stirring constantly. Makes about one cup. Delicious over gingerbread.

Campbellsville College Women's Club Cookbook

Cookies
and Candies

The annual High Hope Steeplechase is contested over Kentucky Horse Park's one-mile, 600-foot course. Lexington.

Panned Shortbread

So quick and easy to make, this celebrated delicacy comes from the Highlands of Scotland. It is thick, rich, and buttery with a tempting flavor which makes it an all-time favorite the world over.

¾ cup sugar
1½ cups butter, at room
   temperature

4 cups flour

Cream butter and sugar thoroughly. Add flour, one cup at a time, mixing well after each addition. Mixture will be stiff and crumbly. Knead gently until well blended. Evenly press dough into ungreased 10 × 14-inch jellyroll pan. Using spatula, level top. Imprint in rows with 2-inch cookie stamp, or form designs by pricking with fork all over top.

Bake in preheated 325° oven, 30–35 minutes. Remove from oven, and immediately, while still hot, cut into squares. Remove from pan, and cool on rack to room temperature. Store in tightly covered container. Yield: 35 two-inch squares.

The Cookie Connection

Ginger Snaps

A quick cookie, good hot or cold.

2 cups sifted flour
1 tablespoon baking powder
2 teaspoons baking soda
1 teaspoon cinnamon
½ teaspoon salt
1 tablespoon ginger

¾ cup shortening
1 cup sugar
1 egg
¼ cup molasses
Extra white sugar

Heat oven to 350°. Mix first 5 ingredients. Sift twice. Beat shortening until creamy. Add the cup of sugar gradually, still beating. Beat in egg and molasses. Sift about half of flour into mixture; stir to blend. Repeat until flour is used. Form cookie. Mix into balls by rolling between hands. Roll in sugar. Place 2 inches apart on ungreased sheet. Bake 12 minutes or until tops are slightly rounded or cracking. Cool. Makes 48 cookies.

The Monterey Cookbook

Mother's Old-Fashioned Sugar Cookies

1 cup butter, at room
   temperature
2 cups, scant, sugar
3 eggs, at room temperature
1 teaspoon vanilla
3 cups flour

2 teaspoons, scant, baking
   powder
¼ teaspoon salt
Granulated sugar (for
   sprinkling)

Cream butter and sugar. Add eggs, one at a time, and mix well. Add vanilla. Sift together dry ingredients. Gradually add to creamed mixture, mixing well after each addition. Cover, and refrigerate 1 to 2 hours. On floured board, and using floured rolling pin, roll to ⅛-inch thickness. At all times, keep rolling pin free from pieces of sticking dough. Using floured cutters, cut into desired shapes. With spatula, carefully transfer to well-greased baking sheet, spacing 2-inches apart.

Bake in preheated 375° oven, 8–10 minutes. Immediately, on removing from oven, sprinkle with sugar. Remove to rack, and cool to room temperature. Store in tightly covered container, or freezer. Yield: 6–8 dozen.

Shape Variation: These cookies may also be formed into walnut-size balls, placed on well-greased baking sheet 2 inches apart, and baked at 375°, 12–14 minutes.

The Cookie Connection

Kletskoppen
Holland-Dutch Almond Cookies

This early Dutch recipe is said to have originated on the Havendyck in Holland over 300 years ago. It was brought to America in the mid 1600s by Dutch immigrants aboard the ship Oaktree. The texture is different from the norm of present-day cookies, and the flavor of ground almonds is superb.

1½ cups dark brown sugar
2 tablespoons lukewarm water
¼ cup butter, at room
   temperature
1½ teaspoons cinnamon

1 cup almonds, finely ground
1 cup flour, unsifted
¼ teaspoon almond extract
Dash of salt

In wooden bowl, mix sugar with water to make thick paste. Add remaining ingredients. Using hands, work dough until well blended and leaves sides of bowl. Dough will be stiff. Cover and let rest 5 minutes. Form into marble-size balls and flatten in palms of hands. Place on greased baking sheet, spacing 2-inches apart. Between bakings, keep dough covered.

   Bake in preheated 325° oven, 8–10 minutes. Remove to rack, and cool to room temperature. Store in tightly covered container. Yield: 3–4 dozen.

The Cookie Connection

Buttercup Cookies

1 (12-ounce) package of small
   Reese's Peanut Butter Cups
   (foil wrappings removed)

1 package refrigerated peanut
   butter cookie dough

Slice dough according to package directions, about 1-inch slices, cut in quarters. Place each slice in ungreased miniature muffin tins. Bake according to package directions for cookie dough. Remove from oven and immediately press a peanut butter cup in the center of each cookie so that cookie dough is around sides of peanut butter cup. Let cool. Use a spoon to remove cookies from muffin tins.

Somethin's Cookin' at LG&E

Old-Fashioned Oatmeal Cookies

1 cup seedless raisins	½ teaspoon baking powder
1 cup water	1 teaspoon soda
¾ cup soft shortening	1 teaspoon salt
1½ cups sugar	1 teaspoon cinnamon
2 eggs	½ teaspoon cloves
1 teaspoon vanilla	2 cups rolled oats
2½ cups flour	½ cup chopped nuts

Simmer raisins and water in saucepan over low heat until raisins are plump, 20 to 30 minutes. Drain raisin liquid into measuring cup. Add water to make ½ cup. Heat oven to 400°. Cream shortening, sugar, eggs and vanilla. Stir in raisin liquid. Blend flour, baking powder, soda, salt and spices; Stir in. Add rolled oats, nuts and raisins. Drop rounded teaspoonfuls 2-inches apart onto ungreased baking sheet. Bake 8 to 10 minutes. Makes 6 to 7 dozen cookies.

Note: These were the first cookies I ever baked. They are good.

Mountain Recipe Collection

Bell-Ringer Molasses Cookies

2 cups brown sugar	1 teaspoon cinnamon
1 egg	1 teaspoon vanilla
1 cup shortening	2 teaspoons soda
1 cup molasses	½ teaspoon ginger
4 cups flour	½ teaspoon cloves
1 teaspoon lemon flavoring	

Cream together first four ingredients. Add remaining ingredients. Mix well. Roll dough into balls the size of walnuts. Place on lightly greased cookie sheet. Bake in 350° oven 10–12 minutes. Remove from oven. Sprinkle immediately with granulated sugar. Let stand on cookie sheet 2 to 3 minutes before removing. Cookies will crack on top. Makes 5 to 6 dozen cookies.

What's Cooking for the Holidays

Mexican Wedding Fingers

The panaderos of Mexico are well-known for their outstanding cookies. These tender, decorative little fingers, sometimes known as Holiday Cookies, are usually made for wedding celebrations, anniversaries, and many other holiday occasions.

1 cup butter, at room
  temperature
½ cup confectioners' sugar,
  unsifted
2 cups flour, unsifted
⅛ teaspoon salt
1½ teaspoons almond extract
Confectioners' sugar, sifted (for
  rolling)

OR:
Food coloring (for tinting dough)
Semi-sweet chocolate morsels,
  melted (for dipping)
Chocolate decorating sprinkles
  (for dipping)

Cream butter. Gradually add sugar, and mix until light and fluffy. Add flour, salt, and flavoring. Mix until well blended. With food coloring of choice, lightly tint all or part of dough, if desired. Mix, and knead gently to blend color. Cover and refrigerate 30 minutes. Pinch off small pieces of dough, and on slightly floured board, roll with hands into small finger shapes. Cut into 2½-inch strips. Place 1-inch apart on ungreased baking sheet. Bake in preheated 375° oven, 8–10 minutes. Remove, and while still hot, gently roll in sifted confectioners' sugar.

OR . . . dip ends into melted chocolate, and then into chocolate decorating sprinkles. Refrigerate until chocolate is firm. Layer between waxed paper, and store in tightly covered container, or freezer. Yield: 6½–7 dozen.

The Cookie Connection

Mint Dollies

1 cup Lorna Doone Shortbread
  Cookies, crushed very fine
¼ cup butter, melted
1 cup flaked coconut
1 cup semi-sweet chocolate
  morsels

1 cup pecans, chopped semifine
4 drops oil of peppermint, or to
  taste
1 (14-ounce) can sweetened
  condensed milk

Mix crumbs with melted butter, and evenly press into bottom of 7×11-inch baking pan. Add one layer each of coconut, chocolate morsels, and pecans, in order listed. Add 2-drops oil of peppermint to condensed milk, and mix well. Evenly spoon over dry mixture. Bake in preheated 350° oven, 25 to 30 minutes. Do not overly bake. Remove to rack, and cool in pan to room temperature.

ICING:
2 (1-ounce) squares semi-sweet
  chocolate
2 tablespoons butter

OR:
2 ounces green summer
  coating*
2 tablespoons butter

In double boiler, over very low heat, melt chocolate or: green summer coating, with butter. Add 2 drops oil of peppermint, and mix well. Drizzle over top, tilting pan to spread evenly. Refrigerate until firm, and cut with sharp knife. Store in tightly covered container. Yield: 32 squares.

*Summer Coating can be purchased at candy stores and cake decorating outlets.

The Cookie Connection

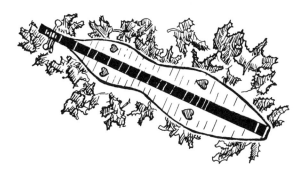

Chocolate Mint Squares

½ cup (1 stick) butter, softened	½ teaspoon salt
1 cup sugar	1 (16-ounce) can chocolate
4 eggs	syrup
1 cup all-purpose flour	1 teaspoon vanilla extract

Cream butter; gradually add sugar, beating until light and fluffy. Add eggs, one at a time, beating well after each addition. Combine flour and salt; add to the creamed mixture alternately with chocolate syrup, beginning and ending with flour mixture. Pour batter into greased and floured 13 × 9 × 2-inch baking pan; bake at 350° for 25 to 28 minutes. Cool completely. (Cake will shrink from sides of pan).

FROSTING:

¼ cup butter, softened	2 tablespoons crème de menthe
2 cups sifted confectioners' sugar	

Cream butter; gradually add sugar and crème de menthe, mixing well. Spread evenly over cake; chill about 1 hour.

CHOCOLATE GLAZE:

1 (6-ounce) package semi-sweet chocolate bits	¼ cup butter

Combine chocolate bits and butter in the top of a double boiler; bring water to a boil. Reduce heat to low; stir until chocolate melts. Spread over frosted cake; chill for at least 1 hour before cutting.

Bluegrass Winners

Cherry-Walnut Bars

1 cup margarine, softened
2¼ cups sifted flour
½ cup sugar
1 cup brown sugar, firmly
  packed
½ teaspoon baking powder
½ teaspoon vanilla
¼ teaspoon salt
2 eggs
1 (2-ounce) jar maraschino
  cherries, chopped
½ cup walnuts, chopped
½ cup coconut

Mix margarine, flour and sugar until crumbly. Press into greased 9 × 13-inch pan. Bake in 350° oven until lightly browned.

Combine brown sugar, baking powder, salt, vanilla, and eggs. Blend well. Add cherries, (reserve juice) and walnuts. Spread over baked crust. Bake another 25 minutes. Cool. Spread thinly with Icing (below). Sprinkle with coconut.

ICING:
1 tablespoon margarine,
  softened
1 cup powdered sugar

Add enough maraschino cherry juice to make of spreading consistency.

What's Cooking for the Holidays

Apricot Bars

12 ounces dried apricots
½ pound butter, softened
½ cup sugar
2⅔ cups all-purpose flour
1 teaspoon baking powder
½ teaspoon salt
2 cups brown sugar, firmly
  packed
4 eggs, well beaten
1 teaspoon almond extract
1 cup almonds, slivered
Confectioners' sugar

Rinse apricots. Cover with water and boil 10 minutes. Drain, chill and chop. Mix butter, sugar and 2 cups flour until crumbly. Press evenly into a greased 13 × 9 × 2-inch pan. Bake 25 minutes at 350°. Sift ⅔ cup flour, baking powder and salt. Gradually beat brown sugar into eggs. Mix in flour, extract, nuts and apricots. Spread over crust and bake 35 minutes or until done. Loosen edges of bars and let cool in pan. Sprinkle with confectioners' sugar. Makes 48 bars.

The Cooking Book

Gooey Bars

1 (18½-ounce) box yellow cake
   mix
½ cup melted butter
1 egg

1 (16-ounce) box powdered sugar
1 (8-ounce) package cream
   cheese, softened
2 eggs

Combine cake mix, melted butter and egg; press into 9 × 12-inch pan. Mix sugar, cream cheese and 2 eggs; beat for 5 minutes with electric mixer. Pour cheese mixture over cake mixture; bake 325° for 35 to 40 minutes. Sprinkle with additional powdered sugar after removing from oven. Allow to cool several hours before cutting. You may add chopped nuts or coconut, if desired.

Mountain Laurel Encore

Chewy Coconut Bars

½ cup firmly packed brown
   sugar
½ cup shortening (half butter)
½ cup flour, sifted
2 eggs, well beaten
½ cup brown sugar firmly
   packed
1 teaspoon vanilla

½ cup Karo syrup (Blue or Red
   Label)
2 tablespoons flour
1 teaspoon baking powder
½ teaspoon salt
1 cup shredded coconut
1 cup chopped nuts

Blend sugar and shortening. Stir in flour. Pat out mixture onto bottom of an ungreased pan. Bake at 350° for 10 minutes. Meanwhile, blend eggs, brown sugar, vanilla and Karo syrup. Add flour, baking powder and salt. Mix well and stir in coconut and nuts. Spread over bottom layer. Return to oven and bake 25 minutes or longer until top is golden brown. Cool and cut into finger-length bars. Makes 24 bars.

Mountain Recipe Collection

Date-Nut Bars

1 (8-ounce) package pitted dates, cut up
1 cup water
1 cup sugar, sifted
1 teaspoon vanilla
1½ cups flour
½ teaspoon soda
¼ teaspoon salt
1 cup brown sugar, firmly packed
1½ cups oats
1¼ cups pecans, chopped fine
1 cup butter, melted

Combine dates, water, and sugar. Cook over medium heat, stirring frequently until thick. Remove; add vanilla and stir well. Set aside to cool.

In large bowl, mix together dry ingredients. Blend in melted butter, and mix well. Mixture makes about 4 cups. Divide evenly and pat half of mixture into bottom of lightly greased and floured 13 × 9 × 2-inch baking pan. Level with spatula. Spoon cooled filling on top, and spread evenly. Crumble remaining half of mixture on top of filling and pat lightly.

Bake in preheated 350°* oven 35 minutes. Remove to rack and cut while still warm. Cool to room temperature. Layer between waxed paper, and store in tightly covered container, or freeze. Yield: 48 bars.

*If glass baking pan is used, bake at 325°.

The Cookie Connection

Apple Squares

2 eggs
1½ cups sugar
1 cup oil
3 fresh apples, peeled and sliced thin
1 teaspoon salt
1 teaspoon soda
2 teaspoons dry yeast granules
3 teaspoons cinnamon
1 teaspoon nutmeg
2½ cups flour
1 cup chopped pecans or walnuts
1 (6-ounce) package butterscotch morsels

Combine eggs, sugar and oil; beat well. Add apples, salt, soda, yeast, cinnamon, nutmeg, flour and nuts. Mix well. Place in greased 9 × 13 × 2-inch pan. Cover with butterscotch morsels.

Bake in 325° oven for 45 minutes.

Cut into squares and serve with ice cream.

The Crowning Recipes of Kentucky

Double-Frosted Bourbon Brownies

BROWNIES:
¾ cup sifted flour
¼ teaspoon soda
¼ teaspoon salt
½ cup sugar
⅓ cup shortening
2 tablespoons water
1 teaspoon vanilla

1 package (6-ounce) semi-sweet
  chocolate chips
2 eggs
1½ cups chopped walnuts
4 tablespoons Kentucky
  bourbon

Sift together flour, soda, and salt. Set aside.

Combine sugar, shortening, and water in saucepan. Bring just to boil, stirring constantly. Remove from heat. Stir in vanilla and chocolate chips, stirring until smooth. Beat in eggs, one at a time. Add dry ingredients and nuts and mix well.

Bake in 9-inch square greased pan 325° for 30 minutes. Remove from oven and sprinkle with bourbon. Cool. Yield: 30 brownies.

WHITE ICING:
½ cup butter, softened
1 teaspoon vanilla

2 cups powdered sugar

Combine butter and vanilla, beating until creamy. Gradually add powdered sugar, beating until smooth. Spread over cooled brownies.

CHOCOLATE GLAZE:
1 package (6-ounce) semi-sweet
  chocolate chips

1 tablespoon shortening

Melt together chocolate and shortening in double boiler over hot water. Spread over iced brownies.

To Market, To Market

Bourbon Fudge Brownies
The Aristocrats of Chewy Cookies

½ cup black walnuts, broken*
2 teaspoons bourbon
⅓ cup butter, melted
2 (1-ounce) squares semi-sweet chocolate, melted
2 eggs, at room temperature

¾ cup flour
½ tablespoon baking powder
Pinch of salt
1 cup sugar
2–3 tablespoons bourbon

Soak nuts in 2 teaspoons bourbon. Cover and set aside. Melt over low heat ⅓ cup butter and 2 squares chocolate. Cool. Beat eggs separately. Combine flour, baking powder, salt, and sugar. Add beaten eggs and cooled chocolate mixture. Mix only until ingredients are well blended. *Do not overly mix.* Stir in bourbon-soaked nuts. Spoon mixture into well greased 8 × 8-inch pan, and bake in preheated 350° oven 25 minutes. *Do not overly bake.* Cool in pan on rack to room temperature. Evenly brush top with 2–3 tablespoons of bourbon, and allow to soak in.

3 (1-ounce) squares semi-sweet chocolate, melted

3 tablespoons butter, melted

Melt over low heat 3 squares semi-sweet chocolate and 3 tablespoons butter. Blend well. Drizzle over top, tilting pan to cover evenly. When chocolate topping is firm, cut into squares. Layer between waxed paper, and store in tightly covered container in refrigerator, or freeze. Yield: 25 small squares.

*Make certain walnuts are free of any pieces of shell.

The Cookie Connection

Five Cup Cookies

1 stick butter
1 cup graham cracker crumbs
1 cup chocolate chips
1 cup peanut butter chips

1 cup coconut
1 cup chopped pecans
1 can Eagle Brand milk

Place stick of butter in 8½×11 inch pan. Then put pan in preheated 325° oven until butter is melted. Remove from oven and spread graham cracker crumbs all over bottom of pan. Spread chocolate chips, peanut butter chips, coconut and chopped pecans, in that order, over graham cracker crumbs. Pour whole can of Eagle Brand milk on top of all ingredients. Bake at 325° for 10–15 minutes or until golden brown. Let cool for 30 minutes, then cut into squares. Makes 24–30 cookies.

Somethin's Cookin' at LG&E

Chocolate Stars

½ cup smooth peanut butter
½ cup brown sugar, packed
½ cup shortening
½ cup sugar
1 teaspoon vanilla
2 tablespoons milk

1 egg
1½ cups flour
¼ teaspoon salt
1 teaspoon soda
Chocolate star candy

Cream together first four ingredients. Add vanilla, milk and egg. Sift dry ingredients. Add to creamed mixture. Mix well. Roll into small balls. Roll balls in granulated sugar. Place on ungreased cookie sheet. Bake in 350° oven for 8 minutes. Remove from oven. Press quickly into center of each cookie 1 chocolate star shaped candy. Return to oven for 3 minutes.

What's Cooking for the Holidays

Mint Julep Kisses

2 egg whites, stiffly beaten
¾ cup sugar
½ teaspoon peppermint extract

2 drops green vegetable coloring
6 ounces chocolate bits

Preheat oven to 325°. Beat egg whites until stiff, gradually adding sugar. Add peppermint and green coloring. Stir in chocolate bits. Drop by spoonfuls on cookie sheet. Put in preheated oven and turn off immediately. Leave in oven overnight or for several hours. Store in tin box. Yield: 2 dozen.

The Kentucky Derby Museum Cookbook

Coconut Meringue Cookies

2 egg whites
¼ teaspoon vanilla extract
¼ teaspoon almond extract

½ cup sugar
1 cup coconut, shredded

Beat egg whites with vanilla and almond extracts to soft peaks. Gradually add sugar while beating to soft peaks. Fold in the coconut. Drop on well-greased baking sheet by rounded tablespoons. Bake 20 minutes at 325°. Makes 2 dozen cookies.

A Tasting Tour Through Washington County

Cream Cheese Cookies

1 (8-ounce) package cream
  cheese
1 cup margarine, softened

1 cup sugar
2 cups all-purpose flour

Blend all ingredients. Drop by teaspoonfuls or roll into 1-inch balls; flatten with bottom of glass dipped in sugar and milk or just sugar. Top with small goodies: raisins, dates, cherry pieces, nuts, etc. Bake 350° for 7 to 9 minutes. Yield: 4 dozen cookies. *Note:* A delightful variation is to roll into rectangle; spread with marmalade or pineapple ice cream topping. Roll up like jelly-roll. Chill, slice, bake a little longer than plain cookies.

Mountain Laurel Encore

Pecan Drops

1 cup brown sugar	1 cup pecan halves
½ teaspoon salt	1 stiffly beaten egg white

Combine sugar, salt and pecan halves, fold in egg white. Dip out the pecans with a fork and spoon so that dough adheres to the pecans. Place on buttered baking sheet. Bake 30 minutes in 275° oven, or until dry. If dough remains, continue to add pecan halves until all dough is used.

What's Cooking in Kentucky

Kentucky Colonels

½ pound butter, softened	½ rectangle paraffin
2 pounds confectioners' sugar	12 ounces semi-sweet chocolate
Dash salt	
½ cup crème de menthe or bourbon	

Gradually blend butter with sugar, salt and liquor. Roll into balls the size of marbles. Roll balls in powdered sugar. Refrigerate until firm. Melt paraffin in double boiler. Slowly add chocolate and, if desired, 1 tablespoon liquor. Do not let water under pan boil. Dip balls in chocolate. Place on wax paper and refrigerate. If necessary, thin chocolate with a few drops of salad oil. Makes 120.

The Cooking Book

Tiny Holiday Wreaths

30 marshmallows or 3 cups miniature marshmallows	½ cup butter or margarine
2 teaspoons green food coloring	1 teaspoon vanilla
	3½ cups corn flakes

Combine all but corn flakes in saucepan and cook on low heat, stirring constantly, until melted. Gradually stir in corn flakes. Drop by teaspoonfuls onto waxed paper. Butter hands and shape into wreaths 1½ to 2 inches in diameter. Decorate with red cinnamon drop candies. Makes 33 two-inch wreaths.

What's Cooking for the Holidays

Easy Delicious Peanut Butter Fudge

¾ cup evaporated milk
2 cups sugar
1 cup peanut butter (creamy)

1 teaspoon vanilla
1 cup marshmallow cream

Cook cream and sugar over low heat until when tested in cold water a soft ball forms. Remove from heat. Add peanut butter, vanilla and marshmallow cream. This must be done quickly. Pour into buttered dish. Makes about 2 pounds.

Mountain Recipe Collection

Coconut Bonbons

1 (14-ounce) can sweetened
  condensed milk
2 (16-ounce) boxes
  confectioners' sugar
½ cup butter or margarine,
  melted

1 (3½-ounce) can flaked coconut
3 cups crushed pecans
1 (4-ounce) block of paraffin
1 (6-ounce) package chocolate
  chips

Combine condensed milk, confectioners' sugar, butter, coconut and pecans. Chill thoroughly. Shape into balls and freeze. Melt together paraffin and chocolate chips. Using a toothpick, dip frozen balls into chocolate. Let stand on waxed paper until firm.

Note: These may be frozen for an extended period.

What's Cooking for the Holidays

Turtlette Candies

192 pecan halves
2 cups light cream or evaporated
   milk
2 cups sugar
½ teaspoon salt

1 cup light or dark corn syrup
⅓ cup butter or margarine
1 teaspoon vanilla
1 (12-ounce) package semi-
   sweet chocolate pieces

Arrange pecan halves, in groups of 4, on greased baking sheet. In a large, heavy saucepan, heat 2 cups cream until lukewarm, reserve one cup. Add sugar, salt and corn syrup to milk in saucepan, cook and stir constantly over moderate heat until mixture boils. Very slowly, stir in so that mixture does not stop boiling, the reserved cup of cream. Cook and stir constantly for 5 minutes. Stir in butter or margarine 1 teaspoon at a time. Turn heat low. Boil gently. Stir constantly until 248° is reached on candy thermometer or until small amount dropped in very cold water forms firm ball that does not flatten when taken out of water. Remove from heat. Gently stir in vanilla. Cool slightly. Pour about 1 teaspoon slightly cooled caramel mixture over center of each group of pecan halves, half covering each nut to resemble turtles. Cool 10 minutes. Melt over water, without stirring the chocolate pieces. Spread over each candy turtle.

What's Cooking in Kentucky

Cherry-Date Holiday Balls

2 eggs, well beaten
1 cup sugar
½ teaspoon almond extract
½ teaspoon vanilla extract
½ cup flaked coconut

⅛ teaspoon salt
1 cup chopped nuts
1 cup chopped dates
36 candied cherries
Confectioners' sugar

Combine eggs, sugar, and extracts. Add coconut, salt, nuts and dates. Pour into buttered 8 × 8 × 2-inch pan. Bake in 350° oven 30 minutes. Stir mixture thoroughly every 10 minutes. Remove from oven and stir well. Cool until able to handle. Shape around candied cherries. Make sure ball covers cherry completely. Roll in sifted confectioners' sugar. Makes 36 balls.

What's Cooking for the Holidays

Good Basic Caramel

2 cups sugar
1 cup light corn syrup
2 cups heavy cream

½ teaspoon salt
½ teaspoon vanilla

Mix sugar, syrup, and 1 cup cream in heavy 3-quart saucepan. Cook 10 minutes stirring constantly. Insert thermometer. Then stir only if necessary to prevent scorching. Add other cup of cream very slowly so as not to stop cooking. When thermometer reaches 230°, cook more slowly to 244°. Remove from heat and add salt and vanilla, stirring only to mix. Pour into well-buttered pan and cool. Cut into squares and wrap each piece in waxed paper.

Note: May add nuts with salt and vanilla, if desired. Caramel Marshmallows: make basic caramel recipe. Cool slightly. Dip ½ of large marshmallow in caramel and cool on greased sheet. Wrap in waxed paper.

Favorite Recipes

Bourbon Candy

1 box sifted confectioners' sugar
5 tablespoons margarine

¼–⅓ cup bourbon

Knead and roll into balls. Add a nut to each ball. Cool and then dip into mixture of:

3 cakes bitter chocolate
3 cakes semi-sweet chocolate

5 tablespoons paraffin

Melt the above over hot water, not boiling. Use a fork or toothpick to dip the balls into the chocolate mixture and place on waxed paper to cool.

Best Made Better Recipes, Volume II

Microwave Caramel Corn

1 cup brown sugar
1 stick margarine
¼ cup corn syrup

½ teaspoon salt
½ teaspoon soda
5 quarts popped corn

Combine brown sugar, margarine, syrup and salt in 2-quart dish. Place in microwave and bring to a boil. Cook on HIGH for 2 minutes. Remove from microwave and stir in soda. Mix well. Put popped corn into heavy brown grocery bag. Pour syrup over corn. Close bag and shake to mix and coat the corn. Close bag by turning top down. Cook in microwave on HIGH for 1½ minutes. Shake well and cook another 1½ minutes. Shake again and cook another 1½ minutes. Pour into shallow pan, cookie sheet or tin foil. Cool. Break apart. Store in closed container.

You can add 1 cup peanuts to the popped corn before you pour the syrup over.

Country Cookbook

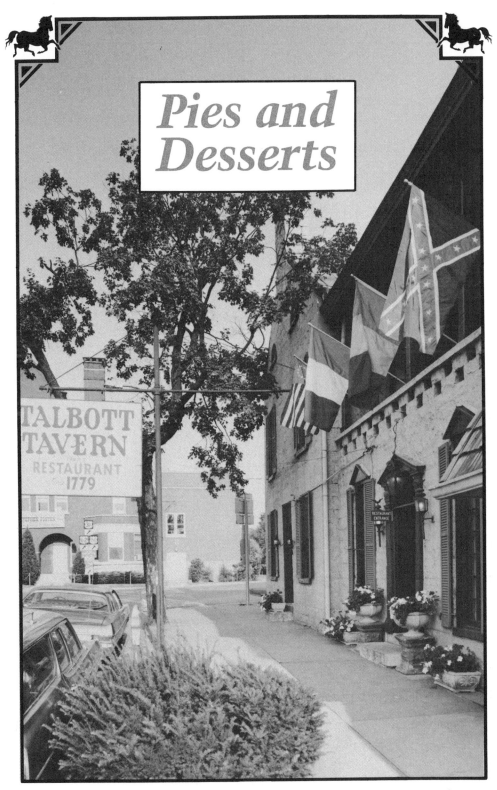

Pies and Desserts

Old Talbott Tavern in Bardstown, founded in 1779, is the oldest continuously operated tavern west of the Alleghenies, and the oldest western stagecoach stop in America.

Janice Williams' Sweet Potato Pie

4 cups grated raw sweet
   potatoes
¾ cup butter
1 cup self-rising flour

2 cups sugar
1 teaspoon cinnamon or vanilla
4 eggs, beaten
1 cup milk

Preheat oven to 350°. Grate sweet potatoes. Melt butter. Mix flour, sugar, and cinnamon or vanilla. Then add eggs and melted butter. Add milk and beat well. Mix in sweet potatoes and again beat well. Pour into 9 × 13-inch pan and bake 35 to 40 minutes. Sweet potatoes will rise to the top and will be crunchy. Filling settles to the bottom.

More Than Moonshine: Appalachian Recipes and
Recollections

Old Fashioned Egg Custard Pie

3 eggs, beaten
¾ cup sugar
¼ teaspoon salt
1 teaspoon vanilla

½ teaspoon ground nutmeg
1½ cups milk, scalded
1 unbaked (9-inch) pie shell
Ground nutmeg

Combine eggs and sugar, beating well. Add salt, vanilla, and nutmeg. Gradually add scalded milk, stirring constantly. Pour mixture into pie shell and sprinkle with additional nutmeg. Bake at 400° for 10 minutes. Reduce heat to 325° and bake an additional 25 minutes or until a knife comes out clean. Cool thoroughly before serving.

Favorite Recipes

Brown Sugar Pie

1 cup brown sugar
4 tablespoons flour
1 cup milk

2 egg yolks
4 tablespoons butter
½ teaspoon vanilla

Place sugar and flour in top of double boiler. Add milk slowly. Cook until thick, stirring all the time. Add egg yolks, slightly beaten and cook 3 minutes. Remove from heat, add butter. When cool, add vanilla. Pour in baked crust. Top with meringue or whipped cream.

Favorite Recipes

Old Talbott Tavern Pie

FILLING:

¾ cup granulated sugar
½ cup flour
¼ teaspoon salt
1¼ cups water

2 egg yolks
½ cup orange juice
1 tablespoon grated orange rind
2 tablespoons lemon juice

Combine sugar, flour, salt in top double boiler. Stir in water, keeping mixture free from lumps. Cook, stir over direct flame 5 minutes. Add egg yolks, slightly beaten, and cook 5 minutes longer over rapidly boiling water, stirring constantly.

Remove from heat, add fruit juice and rind. Chill. Turn into baked pie shell, cover with meringue.

MERINGUE:

2 egg whites
½ cup sugar
Dash salt
2 tablespoons water

1 orange
¾ cup moist sweetened
coconut

Put whites eggs, sugar, salt, water in top double boiler; beat with rotary beater until mixed. Place over rapidly boiling water, beat 1 minute. Remove from fire and continue beating until mixture will stand in peaks about 1 minute longer. Pile lightly on filling. Peel a Valencia or navel orange and separate into sections, removing membrane. Arrange on top of meringue.

Sprinkle with coconut. We like this with graham cracker crust, too.

Cabbage Patch: Famous Kentucky Recipes

The Old Talbott Tavern in Bardstown, founded in 1779, is the oldest continuously operated tavern west of the alleghenies.

Coconut Pie

1 baked pie shell	2½ cups milk
½ cup sugar	1 teaspoon vanilla
¼ cup plain flour	1 tablespoon margarine
Dash of salt	1 can flake coconut
3 eggs (room temperature)	

MERINGUE:

3 egg whites	1 eggshell of water
¼ teaspoon cream of tartar	⅓ cup sugar (or more, to taste)

In a heavy skillet, mix well the sugar, flour and salt. Separate eggs that have been at room temperature for awhile. Place milk in blender; add egg yolks. Turn blender off and on until thoroughly mixed. Pour a small amount into mixture in skillet; blend well. Then pour in remaining; mix. Place on medium hot burner; stir constantly until thick; let bubble for a minute. Add vanilla and margarine; keep on warm burner while meringue is being prepared.

In a large mixer bowl have egg whites, add cream of tartar and 1 eggshell of water. Start beating on high; add sugar gradually as soon as whites are frothy. Beat until stiff; add vanilla. Add about ⅔ can coconut to hot filling; pour into baked pie shell. Spread meringue over hot filling (this prevents weeping); cover with remaining coconut. Lightly brown at 375°; turn oven off leaving pie in oven until oven and pie are completely cool. This also prevents weeping.

Stephensburg Homecoming Recipes

Southern Pecan Pie

¼ cup butter	3 eggs, beaten
1 cup brown sugar	1 teaspoon vanilla
¼ teaspoon salt	1½ cups pecan halves
1 cup dark Karo syrup	1 (9-inch) unbaked pie shell

Cream butter and sugar together until fluffy; add next four ingredients. Sprinkle pecans on bottom of pie shell. Pour the filling over pecans.

Bake 450° for 10 minutes, reduce temperature to 350° and bake 35 minutes longer. Outer edges of filling should be set, slightly soft or until knife inserted in center comes out clean.

The Crowning Recipes of Kentucky

Wayne Lawson's Favorite Shoofly Pie

Granny Brock also made a pie which was my favorite (and later became my oldest son's favorite of all the things I ever cooked for him). Granny called it Shoofly Pie. I suppose it got that name because of its richness and tantalizing aroma which was sure to attract any errant fly.

FILLING FOR 2 UNBAKED (9-INCH) PIE SHELLS:

1 cup sugar	4 teaspoons flour
2 cups water	1 teaspoon vanilla
1 cup light molasses	

TOPPING:

½ cup lard	1 teaspoon soda
2 cups flour	1 teaspoon cream of tartar
1 cup sugar	

Mix sugar, water, molasses, and blend in flour slowly to avoid lumps. Boil together for 5 minutes, then set aside and add vanilla. With fingers work together lard, flour, sugar, soda and cream of tartar for the topping. Pour the filling into pie crusts. Sprinkle topping over top of each pie and bake at 350° until filling is set and crust is nicely browned.

More Than Moonshine: Appalachian Recipes and Recollections

Triple Crown Pie

4 tablespoons butter, softened
3 ounces cream cheese, softened
1 cup flour
2 eggs
¼ pound butter, melted
⅓ cup flour
⅛ teaspoon salt

1 cup semi-sweet chocolate
  chips
1 cup nuts, chopped
1 cup sugar
1 tablespoon bourbon or 1
  teaspoon vanilla

Cream 4 tablespoons butter and cheese. Add 1 cup flour. Roll in wax paper and chill 1 hour. Roll dough out and fit into 9-inch pie pan. Beat eggs until frothy in food processor or blender. Add melted butter and ⅓ cup flour with other ingredients. Process until chocolate is very coarsely chopped. (Do not overprocess.) Pour into pie shell and bake at 325° for 45–60 minutes, or until the center rises and the pastry is tan. Serve topped with whipped cream.

To make miniature tarts, cream ¼ pound butter with 6 ounces cream cheese then blend in 2 cups flour. Chill in wax paper for 1 hour. Press 1-inch balls of dough into tiny muffin tins. Trim excess dough. Using the same filling as you make for the pie, fill the tins ⅔ full. Bake at 325° for 25–35 minutes, or until centers rise and pastry is tan. Yields 48 tarts.

The Cooking Book

Phyllis' Race Day Pie

¼ cup butter
1 cup sugar
3 eggs, beaten
½ cup chocolate chips
¾ cup white corn syrup

¼ teaspoon salt
1 teaspoon vanilla
½ cup chopped nuts (pecans are
  best)
2 tablespoons bourbon

Cream butter and sugar together. Stir in other ingredients. Pour in unbaked pie shell and bake at 375° for 40–50 minutes. Serve topped with whipped cream.

Somethin's Cookin' at LG&E

Chocolate-Nut Pie

½ cup margarine, melted
1 cup sugar
½ cup flour
2 eggs, slightly beaten

1 teaspoon vanilla
¾ cup English walnuts
¾ cup chocolate chips

Mix in order given. Pour into unbaked 9-inch pie shell. Bake at 350° for 30 minutes.

My Old Kentucky Homes Cookbook

Cheeky's Chess Pie

1½ cups sugar
½ cup butter, melted
1 tablespoon plus 1 teaspoon
  cornmeal

1 tablespoon white vinegar
1 teaspoon vanilla
3 eggs, beaten
1 unbaked (8-inch) pastry shell

Combine sugar, butter, cornmeal, white vinegar, and vanilla. Add beaten eggs. Mix thoroughly. Pour into pie shell. Bake at 350° for 50 minutes. Preparation Time: 15 minutes + baking. Yield: 8 servings.

This tried and true classic Southern recipe was selected from 15 chess pies submitted for printing. Enjoy!

CordonBluegrass

Lemon Chess Pie

1½ cups sugar
1 tablespoon flour
2 tablespoons cornmeal
4 eggs

½ cup melted butter
4 teaspoons grated lemon rind
¼ cup milk
¼ cup lemon juice

Combine sugar, flour, cornmeal and eggs. Blend thoroughly. Add butter, lemon rind, milk and lemon juice. Mix well. Pour into 9-inch unbaked pie shell. Bake in 425° oven 10 minutes. Reduce heat to 325° and back 40 to 45 minutes longer.

What's Cooking in Kentucky

Bourbon Apple Pie

½ cup raisins
4 tablespoons bourbon, divided
6–7 cups peeled, cored apples, sliced
¾–1 cup sugar (to taste)
2 tablespoons flour

1 teaspoon cinnamon
⅛ teaspoon nutmeg
½ cup walnuts or pecans, chopped
Dough for 9-inch 2-crust pie

Preheat oven to 425°. Plump raisins in 2 tablespoons bourbon. Sprinkle remaining 2 tablespoons bourbon over sliced apples.

Combine sugar, flour, cinnamon, and nutmeg. Add sugar mixture, raisins, and nuts to apples and mix thoroughly. Put in crust. Bake in lower third of oven for 50–60 minutes. Preparation Time: 30 minutes + baking. Yield: 1 pie.

Leave it to a Kentuckian to improve on this traditional American pie!

CordonBluegrass

Pecan Pumpkin Pie

My favorite pumpkin pie recipe.

2 baked (9-inch) pie shells
4 tablespoons butter
⅔ cup brown sugar
⅔ cup chopped pecans
1 cup evaporated milk
½ cup water
3 eggs

1½ cups pumpkin
½ cup granulated sugar
½ cup brown sugar
1½ teaspoons pumpkin pie spice
½ teaspoon salt
½ cup heavy cream, whipped

Prepare pie shells and put in 9-inch pie pans. Cream butter with the ⅔ cup brown sugar in small bowl; stir in pecans. Press over bottom of prepared shells in an even layer. Bake in 450° oven for 10 minutes, remove and cool. Turn heat down to 350°.

Combine milk and water in a 2-cup measure. Beat eggs slightly in large bowl; stir in pumpkin, granulated sugar, the ½ cup brown sugar, pumpkin pie spice and salt; beat in milk mixture. Pour into cooled shells. Bake in 350° oven for 50 minutes. Do not overbake. Custard will set as it cools. Cool completely and serve with whipped cream.

A Taste from Back Home

Black Bottom Pie with Bourbon
Delicious! Different! Dazzle your guests!

1 (9-inch) baked pie shell
1 envelope unflavored gelatin
¼ cup cold water
1 cup sugar, divided
3 tablespoons cornstarch
2 cups milk
4 large eggs, separated

3 tablespoons Kentucky
  bourbon
1½ ounces unsweetened
  chocolate, melted
1 teaspoon vanilla
¼ teaspoon cream of tartar

Sprinkle gelatin into cold water. In saucepan, stir together ½ cup sugar and cornstarch. Gradually stir in milk. Add egg yolks. Cook over medium heat, stirring constantly until mixture becomes as thick as mayonnaise. Remove from heat. Reserve one cup of mixture. Into remaining hot mixture, stir gelatin and bourbon. Refrigerate until cooled thoroughly (about 30 minutes).

Stir chocolate and vanilla into reserved one cup of mixture. Spread over bottom of pie shell. Refrigerate. When refrigerated mixture is cooled, beat egg whites with cream of tartar; gradually add remaining ½ cup sugar, beating until soft peaks form. Fold into chilled gelatin mixture. Spoon over chocolate layer in pie shell. Refrigerate at least 3 hours before serving. Yield: 1 pie (9-inch).

To Market, To Market

Heavenly Pie
(Lemon Ice Box Meringue)

1 cup granulated sugar
¼ teaspoon cream of
   tartar

4 egg whites at room
   temperature
3 tablespoons shredded coconut

SHELL:
Sift 1 cup sugar and cream of tartar together; separate eggs. Beat whites in stiff peaks but not dry. Slowly add sugar, beating constantly. Spread meringue over bottom and sides of well-greased pie pan; make bottom about ¼-inch thick, sides thicker. Sprinkle 2 tablespoons coconut on top. Bake in 275° oven for 1 hour. Cool.

FILLING:
4 egg yolks
½ cup sugar
3 tablespoons lemon juice
1 tablespoon grated lemon rind

⅛ teaspoon salt
1 pint heavy cream (use for top
   and filling)

Beat 4 egg yolks slightly in double boiler, stir in ½ cup sugar, lemon juice, rind and salt. Cook, stirring over boiling water until thick (about 8 minutes). Cool, add 1 cup whipped cream to custard. Pour into cooked shell. Spread on rest of whipped cream (unsweetened); sprinkle on 1 tablespoon toasted coconut. Chill at least 12 hours.

Cabbage Patch: Famous Kentucky Recipes

Japanese Pie

1 stick margarine (melted)
1 cup sugar
1 teaspoon flour
2 eggs beaten

1 tablespoon vinegar
½ cup flaked coconut
¼ cup pecans (chopped)
½ cup raisins

Mix and bake in pastry crust at 350° for 45 minutes.

Larue County Kitchens

Parfait Pie

BUTTER CRUST:

½ cup butter   1 cup flour
2 tablespoons sugar

Combine butter and sugar; don't cream. Add flour. Mix until dough will form. Place ½–⅓ cup mixture in a small pan. With well-greased fingers press remaining mixture into a large pan. Bake both the crust and the crumbs at 375° for 12–15 minutes. Stir the crumbs while they are baking to avoid burning. Cool.

FILLING:

18 caramels   1 unbeaten egg white
⅓ cup milk   1½ teaspoons vanilla
⅔ cup sugar   1 teaspoon lemon juice
¼ cup water   1 cup cream

Melt caramels in milk over hot water. Cool slightly. Combine sugar, water, egg white, vanilla, and lemon juice in small bowl. Beat at high speed for 3–5 minutes.

Beat 1 cup cream. Fold into the egg white mixture. Put ½ of this filling over crust and dribble ½ syrup over filling. Repeat. Cut through with a knife. Sprinkle with crumbs, and freeze until firm—at least 4–6 hours.

Larue County Kitchens

Strawberry Pie
(Bernice's)

(Better than Jerry's.)

1 cup sugar   4 tablespoons strawberry Jello
3 tablespoons cornstarch   Pinch salt
1 cup water   2 cups fresh, sliced strawberries

Mix cornstarch and sugar, add water, bring to boil. Add the dry Jello and the salt. Cook until partly set. Add strawberries, pour into pie shell, and decorate with whipped cream. Refrigerate until ready to serve.

The Wyman Sisters Cookbook

Little Chess Tarts

1 stick butter, softened
1½ cups sugar
2 whole eggs
2 tablespoons cornmeal
2 tablespoons flour
1 cup light cream

2 tablespoons lemon juice
½ teaspoon vanilla
Pinch of salt
1 recipe Cream Cheese Pastry
Damson preserves

Cream butter and sugar, beat in eggs. Mix cornmeal with flour and add other ingredients except pastry and preserves. Beat well.

Pinch off small pieces of pastry and form into balls about 1¼ inches in diameter. Put in 1½-inch muffin pans and press dough evenly to line the bottom and sides. Fill half full and bake at 350° 15–20 minutes until the filling is brown around the edge. Remove from pans and place on a rack to cool. Top each tart with a tiny bit of damson preserves. These freeze well. Makes 48.

CREAM CHEESE PASTRY:

2 sticks butter, softened
2 small packages cream cheese,
   softened

2 cups flour

Mix butter and cheese, add flour ½ cupful at a time, blending thoroughly. Use your fingers to mix it well. Refrigerate for half an hour or more. Makes 2 pie shells (9-inch).

The Farmington Cookbook

Lemon Tarts

PASTRY LAYER:

⅓ cup butter, at room
  temperature

¼ cup granulated sugar
¾ cup flour

Cream butter and sugar. Add flour, and mix well. Evenly sprinkle crumbs over bottom of 8 × 8-inch baking pan. Press down and level with spatula. Bake in preheated 350° oven 8–12 minutes.

FILLING:

1 egg, at room temperature
½ cup granulated sugar
Pinch of salt

¼ teaspoon baking powder
½ cup flaked coconut
⅔ cup English walnuts, chopped

Combine egg, sugar, salt, and baking powder. Mix well. Stir in coconut and nuts, and mix until well blended. Spread evenly over partially baked layer. Return to preheated 350° oven and bake 18–20 minutes longer. Remove from oven and cool in pan on rack to room temperature.

LEMON ICING:

1 cup confectioners' sugar
1 tablespoon soft butter
1 tablespoon lemon rind, finely
  grated

2 tablespoons lemon juice
Chocolate decorating sprinkles,
  optional

Sift sugar. Combine with butter, rind, and juice. Mix until smooth and of spreading consistency. Ice top of tart, and garnish with decorating sprinkles if desired. When icing has set, cut into squares*. Layer between waxed paper, and store in tightly covered container or freeze. Yield: 25 squares.

*Shape Variation: Cut with sharp round biscuit cutter. Allow leftover pieces to dry out, and serve over vanilla ice cream, if desired.

The Cookie Connection

I Can Not Tell A Lie Peach Cobbler Pie

1 package pie crust mix (Jiffy will do)
2 cans of sliced peaches in heavy syrup
1 cup of sugar
1 cup cold water
Dash of nutmeg
Butter

Prepare 2-crust pie as directed on package (Use ½ package of crust for a small pie.)

Stir peaches, sugar and water together. Add a dash of nutmeg. Pour filling in a medium-size Corning Ware pie container or Pyrex. Cover with strips of pie dough vertically and horizontally (similar to lattice.) Dot with butter. Bake in oven 350° for 30 minutes or until crust is brown. Cool, serve, and eat. Yum-yummy.

Momma was a school teacher. Daddy worked at the aluminum plant. He got off from work at 2 o'clock. She got off from work at 3 o'clock. Therefore, Daddy would be anxiously waiting for her to come home and cook dinner. Because she was so tired she would open up some canned goods, thaw out some frozen foods and whip up something quick. She would cook her big meals and yummy desserts on Saturdays and Sundays. One day when Momma came home, Daddy gave her a sack of peaches and demanded that she bake him a peach pie with "fresh peaches and lots of juice." He also said, "And I don't want to wait until Saturday to eat it."

Momma didn't protest. She just replied, "If you want lots of juice you want a cobbler, not a pie."

After dinner Momma served us the best tasting homemade peach cobbler. Daddy really loved it.

Later that evening as we sat in the living room, peaches began to roll across the floor one by one.

"Those are my peaches," shouted Daddy.

Amazed by what she saw, momma confessed, "I cannot tell a lie; I used a can of peaches."

Momma had hidden the fresh peaches, but my little brother, Barry, had found them in the kitchen and was using them for baseballs.

The Corn Island Cookbook

Super Blackberry Cobbler

4 cups blackberries
1 cup sugar
¼ cup quick tapioca
1⅓ cups water
2 tablespoons butter
2 cups flour

2 teaspoons sugar
5 teaspoons baking powder
¼ teaspoon salt
6 tablespoons shortening
⅔ cup milk
¼ teaspoon lemon extract

Combine berries, sugar, tapioca, water, and butter and let stand while making crust. Sift flour, the 2 teaspoons sugar, baking powder and salt together. Cut in shortening. Add milk all at once. Stir to dampen. Roll out. Cut into eight 2½-inch rounds. Sprinkle with sugar. Add lemon extract to berries and pour into buttered baking dish. Place rounds over berries and bake at 425° for 30 minutes.

A Taste from Back Home

Apple Cobbler

7 full cups sliced apples
1/8 teaspoon salt
1/4 teaspoon cinnamon
3/4 cup sugar

1 tablespoon lemon juice
2 tablespoons butter
1/4 teaspoon nutmeg
1/2 teaspoon grated lemon rind

Place apples in pan. Sprinkle them with all ingredients and dot with butter. Top with pie crust and bake at 350° for one hour.

Historic Kentucky Recipes

Apple Dumplings

6 cups apples, chopped

DOUGH:
1 teaspoon salt
¾ cup shortening
2 cups flour

2 teaspoons baking powder
½ cup milk

Mix as for pie dough and roll out. Cut into 6 or 8 squares. Put some apples in center of each square. Press dough together. Bake in 350° oven until done.

SAUCE:
1½–2 cups sugar
½ teaspoon cinnamon
¼ cup butter

2 cups water
¼ teaspoon nutmeg

Cook ingredients together 5 minutes. Pour over dumplings when done while they are hot.

Lake Reflections

Gateau au Chocolat à La Garniture

8 ounces sweet chocolate
1 (8-ounce) milk chocolate bar
1 teaspoon water
1 tablespoon flour
1 tablespoon sugar
⅔ cup butter, softened
4 eggs, separated

Confectioners' sugar
4 portions seedless grapes (red
    or green), halved
1½ teaspoons rum
1½ teaspoons brown sugar
½ cup or more sour cream

Melt chocolate and water over hot water (not boiling). Remove from heat and stir in next 3 ingredients. Beat egg yolks vigorously; stir into the chocolate mixture. Beat egg whites until stiff and fold into the batter. Pour into a round, greased, and lined 8-inch cake pan. Bake at 425° for 15 minutes, *no longer.* Cool. Marinate grapes in mixed rum and sugar for several hours, stirring occasionally. To serve, mix grapes with sour cream and garnish each serving. Very rich. Serves 10.

Favorite Fare II

Judy's Chocolate Angel Dessert

2 egg whites
Pinch of salt
⅛ teaspoon cream of tartar
½ cup sugar
½ cup finely chopped pecans
½ teaspoon vanilla
4 ounces semi-sweet
   chocolate

3 tablespoons water
1 teaspoon vanilla
1 cup whipping cream
¼ cup chopped pecans
1 teaspoon shaved bitter
   chocolate
¼ cup whipping cream,
   whipped

Combine egg whites, salt and cream of tartar, beat until foamy. Add sugar, 1 tablespoons at a time. Beat after each addition. Continue beating until mixture stands in peaks. Fold in pecans and ½ tablespoon vanilla. Spoon into lightly greased 8-inch pie pan. Make a nest-like shell building up ½-inch edge above pan. Bake 55 to 60 minutes in 300° oven, or until lightly browned. Cool to room temperature.

In top of double boiler, at low heat, stir until melted 4 ounces semi-sweet chocolate in 3 tablespoons water. Set aside to cool. Add 1 teaspoon vanilla. Whip 1 cup whipping cream. Fold into chocolate mixture. Pile into meringue shell. Chill at least 2 hours before serving.

If desired, garnish with whipped cream, pecans or shaved bitter chocolate.

What's Cooking in Kentucky

French Silk Dessert

CRUST:

½ cup brown sugar
1 cup all-purpose flour

½ cup chopped pecans
¼ pound soft butter

Pat above mixture into 13 × 9-inch pan and bake at 400° for 15 minutes or until lightly browned. Mix again after taking from oven. Pat down once again.

FILLING:

½ pound butter, softened
1½ cups sugar
2 teaspoons vanilla
3 squares unsweetened
    chocolate, melted

4 eggs
2 cups whipped topping
Chocolate shavings

Cream sugar and butter together. Add vanilla and melted chocolate. Beat in eggs, beating 5 minutes between each egg (very important). Pour mixture over crust and place in freezer for 20–30 minutes. Remove and spread with whipped topping. Top with chocolate shavings. Store in freezer until ready to serve. Yield: 10–12 servings.

Seasons of Thyme

The Mansion Almond Chocolate Mousse

2 cups whipping cream
3 ounces butter
1 pound Tobler semi-sweet
    chocolate
3 eggs, divided

½ cup powdered sugar
¼ cup hot coffee
¼ cup Amaretto liqueur
Sliced almonds, toasted

Whip cream until stiff; chill. In a double boiler over hot water, melt butter with chocolate. In a small bowl, beat egg yolks with sugar until thick and lemon colored.

Add hot coffee to melted chocolate, beat yolk/sugar mixture and Amaretto into mixture and chill to slightly below room temperature.

Beat egg whites until stiff. Fold whipped cream into chocolate, then fold in beaten egg whites. Chill at least two hours before serving. Garnish with almonds. Serves eight.

Dining in Historic Kentucky

Chocolate Éclairs

CREAM PUFFS:

½ cup (1 stick) butter
½ teaspoon salt
1 cup water

1 cup all-purpose flour
4 eggs, unbeaten

Combine butter, salt and water in a heavy saucepan over medium heat; bring to a boil. When butter is melted, add flour all at once. Stir vigorously over very low heat until dough forms a smooth ball. Remove from heat and add eggs, one at a time, beating after each addition with electric mixer at medium speed. Continue beating until dough is no longer sticky, but quite glossy. Shape by dropping a spoonful onto a greased cookie sheet and elongating it with 2 spoons or by using a pastry tube. Bake cream puffs at 400° for 30 to 40 minutes; place on a wire rack to cool. Slit on one side and fill with Filling; pour Glaze on top. Refrigerate until serving time. Makes about 12.

FILLING:

1 (3¼-ounce) package vanilla
  pudding mix

1½ cups milk
½ cup heavy cream, whipped

Prepare pudding mix according to directions on package, using only 1½ cups milk. Cover pudding with wax paper and refrigerate; when well chilled, beat pudding and then fold in whipped cream.

GLAZE:

1 (6-ounce) package semi-sweet
  chocolate

2 tablespoons butter

Melt chocolate and butter in the top of a double boiler, stirring until well blended and smooth.

Bluegrass Winners

Caramel Delight

GRAHAM CRACKER CRUST:

1 package graham crackers, crushed

1 stick oleo, melted
1 tablespoon sugar

Pour melted butter over crackers and sugar; mix well and press into a 12 × 7¼ × 1¼-inch glass dish. Reserve about 2 tablespoons to sprinkle on top. I spray my dish with Pam, or you could grease it with butter.

1 large package (50) Kraft caramels
⅔ cup water

1 cup (8-ounces) sour cream
1 large container (1 pound) Cool Whip, slightly thawed

Melt caramels with water. I use the microwave and it takes about 7 minutes. You have to stir them until all the caramel is melted. You can also use a double boiler to melt the caramels. Allow the mixture to cool slightly (won't burn your finger when touched). After mixture has cooled, add the sour cream and Cool Whip. Stir until blended, do not beat.

Pour mixture into the dish with the graham cracker crust. Sprinkle reserved mixture on top, cover with Saran Wrap and freeze.

You need to allow the mixture to stand at room temperature about 10 to 15 minutes before cutting into squares. You can refreeze this if all is not eaten at once. (I don't usually have any left.)

This is a great dessert for any occasion, and everytime that I take it to a social function, I am always asked for the recipe. This will feed about 15, depending on how large you cut your squares. This is a very rich dessert, but it is worth every calorie.

The Junior Welfare League 50th Anniversary Cookbook

Kentucky borders seven states: Ohio, Indiana, Virginia, West Virginia, Tennessee, Missouri, and Illinois.

Coffee Chocolate Mold With Flaming Nut Sauce

1 quart chocolate ice cream,
  softened slightly

1 quart coffee ice cream,
  softened slightly

Using a chilled two-quart bowl or mold, quickly spread chocolate ice cream over bottom and sides. Cover with aluminum foil and freeze until firm. Fill center of mold with coffee ice cream. Cover and freeze until firm. Unmold onto chilled serving platter and freeze until serving time.

SAUCE:
¾ cup Brazil nuts,
chopped
¾ cup almonds, chopped

4 tablespoons butter
½ cup brandy, warmed

Sauté nuts in butter until light brown. Add brandy and carefully flame at the serving table. Pour nut sauce over slices of ice cream mold. Serves 10.

Let Them Eat Ice Cream

Banana Pudding

1½ cups water
1 box (small) instant French
  vanilla pudding
1 box (small) instant regular
  vanilla pudding
1 can Eagle Brand milk
½ teaspoon banana flavoring

1 large container Cool Whip
1 box vanilla wafers, crumbled
  or broken
4 bananas
4 tablespoons graham cracker
  crumbs

Combine first 3 ingredients with mixer. Add milk and flavoring. Stir in Cool Whip. Layer in serving dish in following order: crushed or broken wafers, bananas, pudding—repeat. Top with additional crumbs (vanilla wafer or graham cracker). This is a rich and delicious dessert! It is loved by anyone who has tried it.

Campbellsville College Women's Club Cookbook

Easy Boiled Custard

This dessert tastes like you may have spent a long time stirring it over a hot stove. We add apricot brandy to it for flavoring.

1 (3¾-ounce) package French
   vanilla instant pudding mix
4 cups milk
½ cup sugar

1 teaspoon vanilla
1 (8-ounce) carton Cool Whip
   whipped topping

Add pudding mix, sugar and vanilla to milk. Stir until smooth. Fold in whipped topping. Chill until very, very cold.

Cooking With Curtis Grace

Kentucky Tombstone Pudding

6 egg yolks
1 cup sugar
1 teaspoon flour
1 cup dessert sherry
2 dozen almond macaroons

2 egg whites
Pinch of salt
Pinch of cream of tartar
2 tablespoons sugar
½ cup whole almonds

Beat yolks until thick and lemon colored. Mix sugar and flour and beat into yolks. Add sherry and cook over low heat, stirring constantly until thickened. Pour over macaroons which have been arranged in a shallow, oven-proof baking dish.

Add cream of tartar and salt to whites. Beat until stiff, gradually adding sugar. Beat until the sugar is dissolved. Spread over the custard, covering it completely. Stud with almonds (tombstones!) and bake at 300° for 15 minutes until lightly browned. Serve hot. Serves 8.

The Farmington Cookbook

Cheese Pudding

1 cup soda cracker crumbs	4 hard-cooked eggs, grated
2 cups medium white sauce	1 (7-ounce) can pimento, grated
½ pound grated American cheese	Buttered crumbs

Grease the casserole; place a layer of crumbs well moistened with sauce, stir with fork to see that all crumbs are moistened. A layer of grated cheese, a layer of grated eggs, a layer of grated pimento. Repeat layers; again stir with fork until all crumbs are moistened (the pudding will be dry unless crumbs are moistened). You may have to add milk to be sure crumbs are moistened. Top with buttered crumbs. Bake at 350° for about 30 minutes.

In the 30s when the Wimsetts were proprietors of the Lynn Hotel, this dish was served every Sunday. In 1954, when President Eisenhower was served cheese pudding at the Hodgenville Women's Club, he asked for a second helping and the recipe.

Larue County Kitchens

Hot Brownie Pudding

1 cup flour	1½ teaspoons cocoa
¼ teaspoon salt	½ cup milk
¾ cup sugar	½ cup nuts
2 teaspoons baking powder	2 tablespoons melted butter

Sift dry ingredients and add milk, nuts and butter. Pour into greased casserole. Mix together:

½ cup brown sugar	3 tablespoons cocoa
½ cup white sugar	1 cup water

Pour over other mixture and bake 1 hour in moderate (350°) oven. Serve warm with ice cream or whipped cream.

Best Made Better Recipes, Volume II

Fruit Pizza
(This is a cool, refreshing summertime dessert; it is also pretty.)

1 box Duncan Hines golden
  sugar cookie mix
1 egg
1 (3-ounce) package
  Philadelphia Cream Cheese
½ stick margarine or butter

1 cup powdered sugar
1 banana
1 peach
A few strawberries
Watermelon
Seedless grapes

Mix cookie mix according to package directions, without water. Pat out out on a pizza pan and bake about 4 to 5 minutes at temperature on package, until lightly browned at edges. Cool. Whip egg and cream cheese together with butter and powdered sugar. Spread on cooled cookie. Cut up fruit onto pizza. Chill and serve.

I use the preceding combination, but feel free to use the fruits of your choice. I always toss my bananas in lemon juice to keep them from turning brown or put them on at serving time.

Kentucky Kitchens

Aunt Blanche's Strawberry Pizza

CRUST:
1 stick butter
1 cup flour

¼ cup powdered sugar

TOPPING:
1 pint fresh or frozen
  strawberries
4 tablespoons cornstarch
Red food coloring

1 (8-ounce) package cream
  cheese at room temperature
1 can Eagle Brand milk
¼ cup lemon juice

Melt butter, add sugar and flour, mix well. Put crust in pizza pan or 8-inch pie pan. Bake at 325° until brown. Cool.

Place strawberries and cornstarch in heavy saucepan and cook until thick, stirring constantly. Add red food coloring until desired shade of red. Set aside and cool. Combine cream cheese, Eagle Brand milk and lemon juice; beat well. Spread over crust. Top with cooled berries and chill. Serves 6 to 8.

Cooking with Curtis Grace

Pineapple Cream Loaf

This is an easy dessert to prepare in advance. Just remove from refrigerator, slice and serve.

½ cup butter
1½ cups sifted powdered sugar
2 egg yolks
½ teaspoon lemon extract
18¾ ounce can crushed
  pineapple, drained

1 cup dairy sour cream
2 egg whites, stiffly beaten
8 lady fingers, split

Cream butter and sugar until fluffy. Add egg yolks, one at a time, beating well after each one. Stir in lemon extract and drained pineapple. Fold in sour cream and egg whites. Line bottom of $9 \times 5 \times 3$-inch loaf pan with half of the lady fingers. Top with half of the pineapple mixture. Repeat layers. Place in refrigerator and chill overnight. Slice and serve. Serves 8 to 10.

Cooking With Curtis Grace

Martha Wadlington's Scalloped Pineapple

4 cups bread crumbs (French or sour dough is good)
1 (20-ounce) can pineapple chunks, drained

3 eggs, beaten
2 cups sugar
1 cup butter, melted

Put pineapple and crumbs into baking dish. Mix beaten eggs, sugar and butter together. Pour over pineapple and bake at 350° for 30 minutes.

Sample West Kentucky

Fruit Flambé

1 (No. 2½) can peach halves, drained (reserve liquid)
1 large banana

1 cup flaked coconut
¼ teaspoon nutmeg
¼ cup brandy or rum

Arrange peaches in a 1-quart shallow baking dish. Slice banana over peaches. Sprinkle coconut over fruit. Combine peach liquid and nutmeg. Pour over fruit. Bake at 350° for 15 minutes. Heat brandy over low flame. Pour brandy over fruit and ignite. Serve immediately. Yield: 6 servings.

Seasons of Thyme

Meringue Shells
(Never Fail)

Whites of 4 large eggs
¼ teaspoon salt
1 teaspoon cream of tartar
1 cup granulated sugar

1 cup and 2 tablespoons powdered sugar, sifted and measured in cup lightly.

Beat eggs until foamy, beat in salt and cream of tartar. Then add sugar a tablespoon at a time, beating gradually; then add powdered sugar in same manner. Beat until won't drop from beaters. Shape on a lightly greased wax paper. Bake 275° for 20 minutes. Turn off heat and leave in oven 15 minutes. Cool and remove from pan.

Larue County Kitchens

Macaroon-Sherbet Dessert
(Flossie's)

12 macaroons (packaged kind), crushed
⅓ cup cashew nuts, chopped

2 packages whipped topping mix, whipped
½ gallon raspberry sherbet

Combine ingredients and spread ½ of the mixture in a 9×9-inch Tupperware container. Cover with ½ gallon of softened raspberry sherbet. Put in freezer until firm. Cover with the other ½ mixture of macaroon crumbs, nuts, and cream. Keep frozen until ready to serve.

The Wyman Sisters Cookbook

Fudge Sundae Pie

¼ cup corn syrup
2 tablespoons firmly packed
  brown sugar
3 tablespoons margarine or
  butter

2½ cups Rice Krispies cereal
¼ cup peanut butter
¼ cup fudge sauce
3 tablespoons corn syrup
1 quart vanilla ice cream

Combine ¼ cup corn syrup, brown sugar, and margarine. Cook over low heat until mixture begins to boil. Add Rice Krispies, stirring until well coated. Press into 9-inch pie pan to form crust. Mix peanut butter, fudge sauce and 3 tablespoons corn syrup; spread ½ over crust. Freeze. Spoon softened ice cream into frozen pie crust. Pour remaining fudge mixture over top, drizzling it. Freeze until firm.

Stephensburg Homecoming Recipes

Frozen Coffee Soufflé

1 quart coffee ice cream
¼ cup cookie crumbs
  (chocolate, macaroon, or
  vanilla wafers)

1 cup whipping cream
4 tablespoons Kahlua
¼ cup almonds, toasted and
  chopped

COFFEE WHIPPED CREAM:
1 cup whipping cream
1 tablespoon confectioners'
  sugar

1 tablespoon instant coffee
  powder
1 teaspoon vanilla

Soften ice cream slightly and fold in crumbs. Whip cream until stiff and fold into ice cream mixture with Kahlua and almonds. Spoon into a 1½-quart mold or soufflé dish and freeze until firm. Whip additional cream until stiff and fold in sugar, coffee powder, and vanilla. To serve, unmold soufflé onto chilled serving place and decorate with or surround with coffee whipped cream. Serves 8.

Let Them Eat Ice Cream

Deep Fried Ice Cream

1 pint vanilla ice cream	1 cup toasted almonds, chopped
1 egg white, lightly beaten	3 cups oil

Using an ice cream scoop, shape 10 (1½-inch) balls and freeze until firm. A muffin tin works well for this. Quickly roll balls in egg white, then almonds, egg white again, and almonds again. Replace in freezer until ready to deep fry. Heat at least 3 inches of oil to 375°. Lower 4 fritters only into the oil and fry for 15 seconds. Drain quickly and serve 2 in an individual dessert dish. Top with favorite sauce. Serves 5.

Let Them Eat Ice Cream

Peach Ice Cream Mousse

1 cup sugar	1 cup cream
¼ cup water	1 cup crushed peaches
4 egg yolks	1 teaspoon vanilla

Mix sugar with water and boil for one minute. Pour slowly over egg yolks; place in double boiler, stirring constantly until mixture thickens. Beat well and cool. Add cream. Chill for 30 minutes. Add peaches, vanilla and freeze.

The Junior Welfare League 50th Anniversary Cookbook

Blackberry Sauce

¾ cup water	2 tablespoons lemon juice
⅓ cup sugar	¼ cup blackberry brandy
2 cups blackberries	

In a heavy saucepan, boil water and sugar together for five minutes. Add blackberries and lemon juice and simmer until berries are very soft. Pureé in a blender or food processor and add brandy. Pureé may be pressed through a sieve to remove seeds. Makes 1½ cups.

Let Them Eat Ice Cream

Spicy Chocolate Ice Cream

2 ounces unsweetened
   chocolate, melted
2 cups milk, scalded
1 teaspoon cinnamon
½ teaspoon ginger
2 tablespoons flour
2 tablespoons cold water

¾ cups sugar
2 egg yolks, slightly beaten
¼ teaspoon salt
1 teaspoon vanilla
¼ teaspoon almond extract
1 cup whipping cream

Melt chocolate in a heavy saucepan; add milk slowly, stirring constantly. Add cinnamon and ginger. Mix flour and water to a smooth paste and add to the chocolate mixture. Cook, stirring constantly, over low heat until mixture is thick enough to coat a metal spoon.

Mix sugar and egg yolks and beat a small amount of the hot mixture into egg mixture and then combine both mixtures, stirring well. Cook 2 more minutes, stirring constantly. Chill thoroughly and beat with egg beater or in food processor, if necessary, to make the mixture smooth. Add salt, vanilla, and almond extract.

Beat whipping cream to a custard consistency and add to chocolate mixture. Chill thoroughly and freeze in machine until firm. Serve immediately or ripen in freezer. Serves 8.

Let Them Eat Ice Cream

Index

Frozen Niagara, a 75-foot cascading formation in Mammoth Cave, a 52,000-acre national park. South Central Kentucky.

INDEX

INDEX

INDEX

INDEX

INDEX

INDEX

INDEX

INDEX

Catalog of Contributing Cookbooks

Cumberland Gap National Historical Park. South of Middlesboro.

CATALOG
of
CONTRIBUTING COOKBOOKS

All recipes in this book have been submitted from the Kentucky cookbooks shown on the following pages. Individuals who wish to obtain a copy of a particular book can do so by sending a check or money order to the address listed. Prices are subject to change. Please note the postage and handling charges that may be required. Kentucky residents add tax only when requested. Retailers are invited to call or write to same address for wholesale information. Some of these contributing cookbooks may have gone out of print since the original publication of this book. Quail Ridge Press is proud to preserve America's food heritage by keeping many of their recipes in print.

BELL RINGING RECIPES
Bowling Green Municipal Utilities
Bowling Green, KY

Bell Ringing Recipes: The Kitchen is the Heart of the Home contains 80 pages of tested recipes that are suitable for entertaining and everyday use in serving food to family and friends. Currently out of print.

BEST MADE BETTER RECIPES, VOLUME II
Lincoln County 4-H Council
P. O. Box 326
Stanford, KY 40484   606/365-2447

To you who like to cook, we offer 499 recipes. Some are new, and many are treasured old ones, but they all reflect the love of good cooking. A perfect gift for the cook and the collector.

$6.00 Retail price
$ .30 Tax for Kentucky residents
$1.50 Postage and handling
Make check payable to Lincoln County 4-H Council

BLUEGRASS WINNERS

The Garden Club of Lexington, Inc.
P. O. Box 22091
Lexington, KY 40522   606/255-8095

There is an intimate relationship between horse farms and entertainment that has made the hospitality of central Kentucky famous throughout the world. Forty full-color photographs of horse farms, their history, and their menu celebrations make the book as beautiful as it is interesting. . . and ultimately delicious to use. Hardcover. 368 pages.

$ 17.95   Retail price
$ 1.08   Tax for Kentucky residents
$ 4.00   Postage and handling
Make check payable to The Garden Club of Lexington, Inc.
ISBN 0-9614442-0-7

CABBAGE PATCH: FAMOUS KENTUCKY RECIPES

Cabbage Patch Circle
1196 Innis Court
Louisville, KY 40204   502/584-5557

This book was compiled by members of the Cabbage Patch Circle with all proceeds to benefit the Cabbage Patch Settlement House—an inter city support facility.   Recipes are from members and various famous establishments which feature gourmet cuisine in Kentucky.

$ 10.00   Retail price
$ 3.00   Postage and handling
Make check payable to Cabbage Patch Circle

CAMPBELLSVILLE COLLEGE WOMEN'S CLUB COOKBOOK

Campbellsville College Women's Club
111 Hunter's Trace
Campbellsville, KY 42718   502/465-2470

Campbellsville College is a senior, liberal arts, Christian College located in the geographical center of Kentucky. Proceeds from the sale of this book will be used for student scholarships and service projects on campus. Drawings were provided by art students.

$ 10.00   Retail price
$ 1.00   Postage and handling
Make check payable to Campbellsville College Women's Club

CAPITAL EATING IN KENTUCKY
American Cancer Society, Kentucky Division
Louisville, KY

Capital Eating in Kentucky is a 208-page cookbook that contains: Appetizers, Soups & Salads, Meats, Poultry and Seafood, Delicious Vegetables, Homemade Breads, Tempting Desserts. . . PLUS beautiful color photographs of Kentucky. It contains over 400 dishes from the Bluegrass State. Currently out of print.

THE COOKIE CONNECTION
by Lottye Gray Van Ness
Louisville, KY

In the 10th printing, this unique all-cookie cookbook proves to be an outstanding selection in the art of cookie making. 315 pages of "Terms and Meanings"; "Guide to Cookie Making"; and 117 triple-tested, mouth-watering recipes, both antique and modern, of America and 14 foreign countries. In spiral binding, with 4-color laminated cover. Currently out of print.

THE COOKING BOOK
The Junior League of Louisville, Inc.
Louisville, KY

With approximately 500 recipes in 300 pages, *The Cooking Book* has a washable cover, spiral ring binding, and convenient section tabs. It has a Derby Menu Planning Section and a Special Children's Section. Over 35,000 copies have been sold. Currently out of print.

COOKING WITH CURTIS GRACE
by Curtis Grace
McClanahan Publishing House, Inc.
P. O. Box 100
Kuttawa, KY 42055   502/388-9388

A cookbook featuring "easy to use" recipes from owner/chef Curtis Grace of the popular Ninth Street House restaurant in Paducah, Kentucky. Everyday ingredients combined in unusual ways make up delicious dishes for luncheons, parties and elegant entertaining. Anecdotes and line illustrations add interest. 192 pages. softback with comb binding.

$ 21.95 Retail price
$ 4.00 Postage and handling
Make check payable to McClanahan Publishing House
ISBN 0-913383-05-8

CORDON BLUEGRASS
The Junior League of Louisville, Inc.
627 West Main Street
Louisville, KY 40202   502/584-7271

CordonBluegrass: Blue Ribbon Recipes from Kentucky offers 300 recipes tested for accuracy and excellency from individuals, professional chefs and inns from throughout the state. Colorful and whimsical original artwork makes this book a stunning print piece. *CordonBluegrass* contains a special Derby entertaining section.

$ 17.95 Retail price (Visa/MC accepted)
$ 1.08 Tax for Kentucky residents
$ 3.20 Postage and handling

Make check payable to The Junior League of Louisville, Inc.
ISBN 0-961333-0-6

THE CORN ISLAND COOKBOOK
International Order of E.A.R.S., Inc.
11905 Lilac Way
Middletown, KY 40243
502/245-0643

In 132 pages of recipes, this is not only a cookbook, but a storybook, too. Many recipes have historical stories behind them. The recipes are kinda "down home cooking" with a yarn. E.A.R.S. (non-profit) sponsors the annual Storytelling Festival, the largest festival of its kind in the world, the third weekend in September.

$ 8.75 Retail price
$ 2.00 Postage and handling
Make check payable to E.A.R.S. Inc.

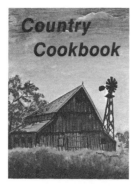

**WDFB Christian Radio Station
AM-1170**

COUNTRY COOKBOOK

WDFB Christian Radio Station
P. O. Box 106
Danville, KY 40423 606/236-9333

The Country Cookbook contains nearly 300 recipes and has 154 pages of recipes. The variety of recipes is good and there are many helpful hints for all your cooking needs.

$ 6.50 Retail price
$ 1.50 Postage and handling
Make check payable to WDFB Christian Radio

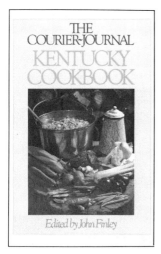

THE COURIER-JOURNAL KENTUCKY COOKBOOK

The Courier Journal
Louisville, KY

The collection of 600 recipes in this cookbook spans five decades of *Courier-Journal* food editors—from 1936, when Marie Gibson's byline first appeared, to the ever-popular Cissy Gregg, to Elaine Corn. There's a lot of good eating and good reading. The recipes are reprinted very much the way they originally appeared in *The Courier-Journal.* Currently out of print.

THE CROWNING RECIPES OF KENTUCKY

By Madonna Smith Echols
Marathon International Book Company
P. O. Box 40
Madison, IN 47250-0040 812/273-4672

The Crowning Recipes of Kentucky is a 348-page cookbook of favorite recipes of Kentucky celebrities. Bringing together past contest title holders was a dream of Madonna Smith Echols, Miss Kentucky of 1946. The project of compiling a book of tried-and-tested recipes resulted from the initial Miss Kentucky reunion.

$ 12.95 Retail price
$ 2.00 Postage and handling
Make check payable to Marathon International Book Company
ISBN 0-915216-93-0

DINING IN HISTORIC KENTUCKY

By Marty Godbey
McClanahan Publishing House
Kuttawa, KY

Brief histories of 48 restaurants housed in historic buildings—some dating from 1779! Exciting recipes join stories from Kentucky's past with all the information needed for cooking, armchair travel, or planning a Kentucky trip. The "original" Hot Brown from the famous Brown Hotel and Shakertown's Popcorn Soup are included. 209 pages. Hardback. Currently out of print.

ENTERTAINING THE LOUISVILLE WAY

The Queens Daughters Inc.
Louisville, KY

Published in 1983 by members of the Queens Daughters, a benevolent organization of Louisville, the book has in addition to its members recipes, specialities from the White House, Kentucky Governors Mansion and chefs of local restaurants. Each category is preceded by a sketch of a Louisville scene as sketched by two local member artists, 331 recipes, spiral-bound. Currently out of print.

THE FARMINGTON COOKBOOK

Farmington Historic House Museum
3033 Bardstown Road
Louisville, KY 40205   502/452-9920

This well-indexed, spiral-bound book was created by six of Louisville's most gracious hostesses. Together they've served up more than 800 good ideas for everyone and organized them into two sections—Freewheeling in the Kitchen and Distinction in the Kitchen. Includes ideas and methods that make even the novice feel confident.

$10.95 Retail price
$ .55 Tax for Kentucky residents
$ 1.75 Postage and handling
Make check payable to *Farmington Cookbook*
ISBN 0-9602646-0-4

FAVORITE FARE II

The Woman's Club of Louisville, Inc.
Louisville, KY

Favorite Fare II, 236 pages, plastic bound, with durable varnished cover, contains over 560 favorite recipes of members of the Woman's Club of Louisville. Directions are clear, concise, and complete, and the index superb. Proceeds provide needed financial assistance to the Louisville Deaf Oral School and other selected charities. Currently out of print.

FAVORITE RECIPES

Nelson County Extension Homemakers
317 South 3rd Street
Bardstown, KY 40004   502/348-9204

This treasury of family recipes has been contributed by friends and members of the Nelson County Homemakers Association. These taste-tempting recipes have not been tested by the committee, but by each donor in their own kitchen, and at their own table. 248 pages.

$ 8.00   Retail price
$ 2.00   Postage and handling
Make check payable to Nelson County Homemakers

FILLIES FLAVOURS

The Fillies, Inc.
Louisville, KY

Fillies Flavours was created and compiled by The Fillies, Inc. A fantastic collection (over 300 pages) of the sumptuous flavors surrounding the Kentucky Derby Festival. Add this Official Kentucky Derby Festival cookbook to your collection. Not a Genuine Risk*. You will not Regret*. Book is done in Winning Colors.* Currently out of print.

*The only Fillies to win the Kentucky Derby.

THE HERITAGE OF SOUTHERN COOKING

by Camille Glenn
Workman Publishing Co.
Consumer Orders
708 Broadway
New York, NY 10003   212/254-5900

Camille Glenn, raised in the kitchen of her parents Kentucky country inn, has run her own cooking school and catering business, and writes a food column for the Louisville Courier-Journal. Her heirloom favorites, regional specialties, and original dishes paint a gastronomic portrait of the South. 550 recipes.

$ 16.95   Retail price paperback
$ 3.00   Postage and handling (each additional: $.50)
Make check payable to Workman Publishing Co.

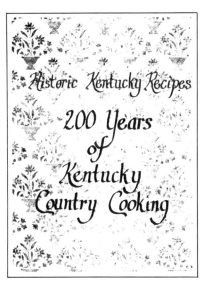

HISTORIC KENTUCKY RECIPES

Mercer County Humane Society
Harrodsburg, KY

Historic Kentucky Recipes consist of 180 pages containing more than 500 very popular recipes from local and historic statewide inns and restaurants. In 1976 it was designated the official cookbook to be sold at all Kentucky State Parks. Proceeds go to Mercer County Humane Society. Currently out of print.

HOLY CHOW

Episcopal Churchwomen
Church of the Ascension
Frankfort, KY

Holy Chow emerged as a combined love of some really great cooks and the sharing of ideas. Scattered throughout the book are poems of Ascension's own "poet laureate" Agnes O'Rear, combined with the artistic illustrations of another famed member, Rosalee Anderson. The book features recipes that range from simple to more challenging. 153 pages. Currently out of print.

THE JUNIOR WELFARE LEAGUE 50TH ANNIVERSARY COOKBOOK

The
Junior
Welfare
League

50th
Anniversary
Cookbook

1936 *JWL* 1986

Mayfield-Graves County Junior Welfare League
Annie Gardner Foundation
East College Street
Mayfield, KY 42066   270/251-2731

This is a cookbook of recipes that dates back for 50 years. The first Junior Welfare League cookbook was published in 1936. Approximately 100 current recipes was added to the original cookbook when we reprinted it. None of the old recipes were changed (and they may sound a little unusual). 184 pages; 552 recipes.

$ 10.00   Retail price (includes postage and handling)
$ .60   Tax for Kentucky residents

Make check payable to Mayfield-Graves County Junior Welfare League

KENTUCKY DERBY MUSEUM COOKBOOK

Kentucky Derby Museum
P. O. Box 3515
Louisville, KY 40201   502/637-1111

In this beautiful 257-page, 9¾ x 11⁵⁄₁₆-inch hardback book with hidden wlre-o binding, there are 500 recipes (everyone tested) and 32 full color pictures. The top of each recipe page features "track talk" or food trivia. Some features include small stories on Derby activities, Derby Menus for a week, wine suggestions, and Derby party and decorating suggestions.

$ 22.00   Retail price
$ 1.32   Tax for Kentucky residents
$ 6.50   Postage and handling

Make check payable to Kentucky Derby Museum
ISBN 0-9617103-0-6

KENTUCKY KITCHENS

Kentucky Chapter #32
Telephone Pioneers of America
601 W. Chestnut Street, 4W
Louisville, KY 40203   812/949-7001

Kentucky Kitchens cookbook is a 646-page collection of approximately 1600 mouth-watering recipes. These recipes were contributed by Telephone Pioneers and friends. The recipes are not necessarily originals but are favorites of the contributors and represent a warm cross-section of kitchens throughout the eastern United States.

$ 9.50   Retail price
$ 2.00   Postage and handling

Make check payable to TPA-Kentucky Chapter #32

LAKE REFLECTIONS
Wayne County Extension Homemakers
Monticello, KY

Visit the Lake Cumberland, Green River, Dale Hollow and Big South Fork areas of Kentucky through recipes and scenic photos. The twelve-section cookbook features 601 "tried and true" recipes of some of the best cooks in South Central Kentucky—Extension Homemaker Club members. Currently out of print.

LARUE COUNTY KITCHENS
Hodgenville Woman's Club
65 Ronnie Drive
Hodgenville, KY 42748

270/358-4749

Larue County Kitchens was a Bicentennial project for the Hodgenville Woman's Club, LaRue County, the National Historic Site of the birthplace of Abraham Lincoln. The 1636 recipes are from persons who have lived or been a part of the life of this county. This book is an ambassador for this historical area of Kentucky. 405 pages.

$ 12.95 Retail price
$ .78 Tax for Kentucky residents
$ 3.50 Postage and handling
Make check payable to *Larue County Kitchens*

LET THEM EAT ICE CREAM
Karen Rafuse and Margaret Minster
Amity Unlimited, Inc.
P. O. Box 15697
Cincinnati, OH 45215   **606/431-6130**

This 108-page book by Kentucky authors Karen Rafuse and Margaret Minster is chock full of over 300 recipes for making home-made ice creams and sorbets and creating delicious and glamorous bombes, parfaits, pies, cakes, coupes, and trifles from your own or "bought" ice cream and sauces. Some ingredients as mint and blackberries have a special Kentucky emphisis.

$7.95 Retail price
$1.25 Postage and handling
Make check payable to Amity Unlimited, Inc.

THE MONTEREY COOKBOOK

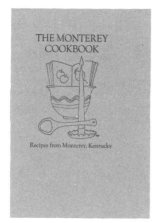

Larkspur Press
340 Sawridge Creek West
Monterey, KY 40359   502/484-5390

The Monterey Cookbook celebrates different kinds of cookery from a rural community in northern Kentucky. It includes traditional recipes, canning secrets, vegetarian dishes, game recipes and kids favorites. The cookbook has 29 original illustrations by local artists. The cover was printed with hand-set type by Gray Zeitz, resident printer of Monterey.

$ 8.00   Retail price
$ .48   Tax for Kentucky residents
$ 4.00   Postage and handling

Make check payable to Larkspur Press

MORE THAN MOONSHINE:
Appalachian Recipes and Recollections

University of Pittsburgh Press
127 N. Bellefleld Avenue
Pittsburgh, PA 15260   412/624-4141

More Than Moonshine is both a cookbook and a narrative that recounts the way of life of southern Appalachia from the 1940s to 1983. Survival skills are recounted, with instructions for making moonshine whiskey, for fixing baked groundhog with sweet potatoes, for making turnip kraut, cracklin bread, egg pie, apple stackcake, and other traditional dishes.   230 pages.

$ 29.95   Retail price hardcover ($15.95 paperback)
$ 3.50   Postage and handling (each additional: $.75)

Make check payable to University of Pittsburgh Press
ISBN 0-8229-5347-1

MOUNTAIN LAUREL ENCORE

Bell County Extension Homemakers
Pineville, KY

The Bell County Extension Homemakers Association goal in publishing *Mountain Laurel Encore* cookbook was to provide college scholarships to boys or girls who were planning to major in some field of Home Economics. The book contains 306 pages and 598 favorite recipes of Bell County Homemakers. Currently out of print.

MOUNTAIN RECIPE COLLECTION

by Valeria S. Ison
285 Peachtree Street
Hazard, KY 41701   606/439-5026

Mountain Recipe Collection contains over 550 Kentucky mountain recipes, eight pen-and-ink sketches, and stories depicting true mountain customs. 318 pages with fine quality binding, hardcover, printed "antique style" in brown ink on cream stock. An excellent representation of traditional Kentucky mountain cooking.

$ 18.00 Retail price includes postage and handling

Make check payable to Ison Collectibles, Inc.
ISBN 0-9617605-0-8

MY OLD KENTUCKY HOMES COOKBOOK

A Taste of Kentucky
Louisville, KY

This book has wonderful recipes that represent the true nature of Kentucky cooking. It also has beautiful color pictures of old homes throughout the state, with bits of history interwoven throughout. Currently out of print.

SAMPLE WEST KENTUCKY

Edited by Paula Cunningham
Kuttawa, KY

A cookbook and guidebook to restaurants in West Kentucky. A book with tourists in mind, it features menus with prices, dining information and reservation hints, maps, and recipes from the chefs. From catfish to cordon bleu this recipe guidebook leads to some of Kentucky's best dining. Currently out of print.

SEASONS OF THYME
Charity League of Paducah
Paducah, KY

Proceeds from the cookbook go to fund special projects and requests from the West Kentucky Easter Seal Center. "Party Thyme" section has suggestions and menus for each month. There are camping recipes and recipes for (and by) children, including "Worm Pie" which received national attention from Johnny Carson on The Tonight Show. 358 pages. Currently out of print.

SOMETHIN'S COOKIN' AT LG&E
Louisville Gas & Electric Co. Employees Association
Louisville, KY

A variety of recipes for appetizers, beverages, desserts, candy, meat and seafood, soups, vegetables, and casseroles. Over 300 recipes and cooking and household tips submitted by LG&E Company Employees Association members and friends. Ringbound. 210 pages. Currently out of print.

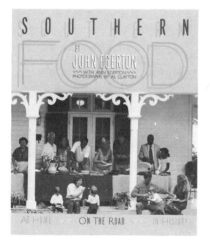

SOUTHERN FOOD: At Home, On the Road, In History
by John Egerton with Ann Egerton

A kitchen-stove and dinner-table history of the South, this 400-page narrative includes a long historical essay, a travel and dining section featuring approximately 160 old-favorite Southern recipes and their origins, a 300-book bibliography, quotes from other writers on Southern food, and over 100 photos by Al Clayton. Currently out of print.

STEPHENSBURG HOMECOMING RECIPES
Stephensburg Homemakers Club
Cecilia, KY

Fifth edition, 115 pages and 399 recipes gathered from our members, their families and friends. Each divider is hand drawn by Linda Owsley. our club president, with the history of our club on the back of each. Many recipes are from club lessons, dinners or functions we have served. Currently out of print.

A TASTE FROM BACK HOME
by Barbara Wortham
Marathon International Book Company
P. O. Box 40
Madison, IN 47250   812/273-4672

The phrase "Back Home" brings to mind fresh garden vegetables, homemade pickles, and country biscuits with jam. *A Taste from Back Home* is a collection of passed-down recipes by a Kentuckian from Russell-ville. Barbara Wortham, the author, gathered over 800 tested, tried, and true recipes from her relatives and friends. 328 pages.

$ 12.95 Retail price
$ .78 Tax for Kentucky residents
$ 2.00 Postage and handling
Make check payable to Marathon International Book Company
ISBN 0-915216-79-5

A TASTING TOUR THROUGH WASHINGTON COUNTY KENTUCKY
The Springfield Woman's Club
201 Lincoln Park Road
Springfield, KY 40069   606/336-9947

The Springfield Woman's Club presents an historical cookbook from Kentucky's oldest county. Over 750 different tested recipes from our county's best cooks, combine with 22 photographs of historic homes to capture a taste of the past and present Washington County. Special entertaining section with selected menus and recipes is included.

$ 8.00 Retail price
$ .65 Tax for Kentucky residents
$ 2.00 Postage and handling

TO MARKET, TO MARKET

The Junior League of Owensboro, Kentucky, Inc.
P. O. Box 723
Owensboro, KY 42302   502/683-1430

Fast becoming a classic, *To Market, To Market* features an outstanding array of regional cookery, reflecting the warmth of the South and the bounty of the Mid-West. Illustrated in a jaunty pink pig motif, its 344 pages offer taste-tempting selections for casual barbecues to elegant dinner parties. A true collectors item—unparalleled in quality-tested recipes and artistic design.

$ 18.00   Retail price
$ 1.08   Tax for Kentucky residents
$ 2.00   Postage and handling
Make check payable to *To Market, To Market*
ISBN 0-9611770-0-4

WHAT'S COOKING IN KENTUCKY

WHAT'S COOKING FOR THE HOLIDAYS

by Irene Hayes
T. I. Hayes Publishing Co., Inc.
P. O. Box 17352
Ft. Mitchell, KY 41017
                              606/341-3201

A book "of unusual merit and practical value," says *The Cook's Catalogue*. Called the "Bible" of Kentucky cooking by a Lexington Food Editor. Both books are sold on a money-back guarantee if returned within 10 days. Each book has heavy, laminated covers, 400 pages and over 850 recipes. Rated "one of the best" by both food writers and individuals, these outstanding cookbooks are sure to become your favorites, also.

$ 19.95   Retail price each book (Visa/MC accepted)
$ 1.20   Tax for Kentucky residents
$ 3.00   Postage and handling
Make check payable to *What's Cooking in Kentucky*
ISBN 0-938402-01-3 *What's Cooking in Kentucky*
ISBN 0938402-05-06 *What's Cooking for the Holidays*

THE WYMAN SISTERS COOKBOOK

Edited by Laura F. Tesseneer
Crescent Springs, KY

Recipes and life stories of eight sisters born in a small western Kentucky village during the late 19th century. "All of the Wyman sisters were good cooks," according to my father and many others. Currently out of print.

286

Preserving America's Food Heritage

"BEST of the BEST" Cookbook Series

Best of the Best from **ALABAMA** 288 pages, $16.95	Best of the Best from **INDIANA** 288 pages, $16.95	Best of the Best from **MISSISSIPPI** 288 pages, $16.95	Best of the Best from **PENNSYLVANIA** 320 pages, $16.95
Best of the Best from **ARKANSAS** 288 pages, $16.95	Best of the Best from **IOWA** 288 pages, $16.95	Best of the Best from **MISSOURI** 304 pages, $16.95	Best of the Best from **SOUTH CAROLINA** 288 pages, $16.95
Best of the Best from **COLORADO** 288 pages, $16.95	Best of the Best from **KENTUCKY** 288 pages, $16.95	Best of the Best from **NEW ENGLAND** 368 pages, $16.95	Best of the Best from **TENNESSEE** 288 pages, $16.95
Best of the Best from **FLORIDA** 288 pages, $16.95	Best of the Best from **LOUISIANA** 288 pages, $16.95	Best of the Best from **NEW MEXICO** 288 pages, $16.95	Best of the Best from **TEXAS** 352 pages, $16.95
Best of the Best from **GEORGIA** 336 pages, $16.95	Best of the Best from **LOUISIANA II** 288 pages, $16.95	Best of the Best from **NORTH CAROLINA** 288 pages, $16.95	Best of the Best from **TEXAS II** 352 pages, $16.95
Best of the Best from the **GREAT PLAINS** 288 pages, $16.95	Best of the Best from **MICHIGAN** 288 pages, $16.95	Best of the Best from **OHIO** 352 pages, $16.95	Best of the Best from **VIRGINIA** 320 pages, $16.95
Best of the Best from **ILLINOIS** 288 pages, $16.95	Best of the Best from **MINNESOTA** 288 pages, $16.95	Best of the Best from **OKLAHOMA** 288 pages, $16.95	Best of the Best from **WISCONSIN** 288 pages, $16.95

Cookbooks listed above have been completed as of January 1, 2000.

Special discount offers available!

(See previous page for details.)

To order by credit card, call toll-free **1-800-343-1583** or send check or money order to:
QUAIL RIDGE PRESS • P. O. Box 123 • Brandon, MS 39043
Visit our website at **www.quailridge.com** to order online!

☒ Order form

Send completed form and payment to:
QUAIL RIDGE PRESS • P. O. Box 123 • Brandon, MS 39043

❏ Check enclosed
Charge to: ❏ Visa ❏ MasterCard
❏ Discover ❏ American Express
Card # _____
Expiration Date _____
Signature _____
Name _____
Address _____
City/State/Zip _____
Phone # _____

Qty.	Title of Book (State)	Total

SubTotal	_____
7% Tax for MS residents	_____
Postage ($3.00 any number of books)	+ 3.00
Total	_____